AF600609

CHALLENGING ADDICTION IN CANADIAN LITERATURE AND CLASSROOMS

CARA FABRE

Challenging Addiction in Canadian Literature and Classrooms

UNIVERSITY OF TORONTO PRESS
Toronto Buffalo London

Toronto Buffalo London
www.utppublishing.com

ISBN978-1-4426-3196-0

Library and Archives Canada Cataloguing in Publication

Fabre, Cara, 1978–, author
Challenging addiction in Canadian literature and classrooms / Cara Fabre.

Includes bibliographical references and index.
ISBN 978-1-4426-3196-0 (cloth)

1. Alcoholism in literature. 2. Alcoholism – Social aspects. 3. Drug addiction in literature. 4. Drug addiction – Social aspects. 5. Eating disorders in literature. 6. Eating disorders – Social aspects. 7. Self-destructive behavior in literature. 8. Self-destructive behavior – Social aspects. 9. Psychology, Pathological, in literature. 10. Canadian fiction (English) – 20th century – History and criticism. 11. Canadian fiction (English) – 21st century – History and criticism. I. Title.

PS8191.P93F33 2016 C813.0093561 C2016-903643-X

This book has been published with the help of a grant from the Federation for the Humanities and Social Sciences, through the Awards to Scholarly Publications Program, using funds provided by the Social Sciences and Humanities Research Council of Canada.

University of Toronto Press acknowledges the financial assistance to its publishing program of the Canada Council for the Arts and the Ontario Arts Council, an agency of the Government of Ontario.

Canada Council for the Arts Conseil des Arts du Canada

Funded by the Government of Canada Financé par le gouvernement du Canada

Contents

Acknowledgments

To Dr Sam McKegney, thank you for your incisive feedback and your unflagging support. I am also grateful to Dr Laura Murray; your critical insights on the early draft were pivotal in giving the project theoretical clarity. To Drs Jennifer Andrews, Elizabeth Comack, Margaret Little, Elaine Power, Roxanne Rimstead, Ella Soper, Dale Tracy, and Glenn Willmott, as well as Siobhan McMenemy, thank you for providing analysis of my work at various stages of its development and offering your expertise and guidance to move the project forward.

To Ma and Keith, you've supported the writing of this book in every way possible from start to finish. Our lively debates, celebrations, and games nights have deeply influenced my beliefs in justice, compassion, and healing. To Papa, I am grateful for your enduring moral support and instilling in me a work ethic I wouldn't trade, even if it meant more sleep. To Emmy, the strength of your convictions and your creativity have deeply inspired me.

To my friends, comrades, and colleagues who have spent countless hours wrestling with me the questions that animate this book – Mollie, Jess, Joanna, Emmy A., Krystle, Dave, Greg, Joan, Sarah, Giselle, Lokchi, Kate, Tanya, Karen, Jaime, Meg, and the incredible folks at WoodGreen and St. Stephen's – thank you for also believing with me that stories are so powerful in their potential to set us free.

To Robyn "Hawk Eyes" Hartley, my extraordinary partner and incisive proofreader, thank you for knowing when to coax me back to my desk and when to run away with me to play.

Finally, I cannot forget Doodle, Mo, Rupert, and Tabby – because they never let me forget that snuggles and naps are a crucial part of the writing process.

Indexing by Clive Pyne Book Indexing: http://www.cpynebookindexing.com.

CHALLENGING ADDICTION IN CANADIAN LITERATURE AND CLASSROOMS

Introduction

Reading and Teaching Addiction as Social Suffering

"'You've got to take better care of yourself. It's our responsibility as drunks to look after ourselves, make sure we eat right and get regular exercise and all that, because the bastards are just looking for any excuse to tell you how irresponsible you are, how you're ruining your health, how you're a drain on society.'"

– Lynn Coady[1]

Addicts are cheeky lately. Emerging within contemporary Canadian literature are figures who profoundly trouble cultural stereotypes and dominant explanatory models of addiction: unapologetic young women who resist external and internalized forces that would isolate, pathologize, and ostensibly 'cure' them of their habits. Through a reworking of Michel Foucault's assertion about madness – that "curing the [addict] is not the only possible reaction to the phenomenon of [addiction]" – this book examines the ways in which several Canadian novelists rewrite addiction as a form of social suffering, rather than individual pathology.[2] Dominant representations of and discourses for understanding addiction persistently essentialize behaviours labelled "addictive" as signifying individual dysfunction and aberrance. Such narratives are not only misleading, but are also instrumental in obscuring social determinants of health and stigmatizing social suffering as addiction. Recent Canadian novelists revisit such pervasive cultural and institutionalized scripts about addiction in ways that forge structural, thematic, and linguistic links among presumably addictive behaviours and capitalism, patriarchy, and settler colonialism.[3] Consequently, recurrent or habitual acts are refigured as adaptive or survivalist in relation to the ideological, social, and structural forces that characterize these "interlocking systems of domination."[4] In order to appropriately attend to the sociocultural significance of these texts, this book will pursue four lines of analysis. The first chapter will map dominant discourses of addiction, and argue that they must be recognized as hegemonic reinforcements of systems of privilege and oppression. Each subsequent chapter will examine different ways in which select Canadian fiction works to challenge hegemonic depictions of addiction; the main body chapters will also consider how principles and practices of transformative pedagogy can help students develop the critical consciousness necessary to perceive the novels' subversive elements, and propose ways in which educators can socially mobilize the systemic critiques produced by these narratives. The Conclusion will reflect on how writers, critics, and teachers can engage with literature as a means of social change, which is the question that fuels this study.

Challenging Addiction examines in detail six novels that exemplify an emergent trend in Canadian literature: *Heave* (2002) by Christy Ann Conlin, *lullabies for little criminals* (2006) by Heather O'Neill, *Skinny* (2005) by Ibi Kaslik, *Consumption* (2007) by Kevin Patterson, *In Search of April Raintree* (1983) by Beatrice Culleton Mosionier, and *Monkey Beach* (2000) by Eden Robinson. These novels refigure the development of addiction and its treatment as social suffering, which Kleinman et al. define as that which "results from what political, economic, and institutional power does to people, and reciprocally, from how these forms of power themselves influence responses to social problems."[5] Predominantly employed to analyse the social consequences of global conflict, colonialism, and class struggle, the concept of social suffering also assists in tracing the psychic and material consequences of inequality and injustice for marginalized peoples, as well as analysing how such suffering is often essentialized as an intrinsic dysfunction of the sufferer – whether morally, constitutionally, or a combination of both.[6] Such reciprocal socialization characterizes the trajectory of the narratives of addiction included in this study. This trajectory is traced by investigating how capitalism, patriarchy, and settler colonialism intersect in each of the novels to shape the protagonists' relationships to substances, their bodies, and their social realities. Chapter 1 will outline in detail the theory and application of my intersectional approach to reading addiction narratives.

By suggesting that such systemic conditions shape the protagonists' actions in complex yet contextually logical ways, the novels explore "what political, economic, and institutional power does to people" through its enforcement of normative ideologies.[7] Even as Serrie (in *Heave*) rails that, "there is nothing rational about trying to be a good girl," she still uses alcohol to manage the emotional strain of coping with class- and gender-based confinements and violence.[8] Baby (in *lullabies for little criminals*), "enraptured and furious with the world,"[9] negotiates the stigmatization and criminalization of her poverty through imaginative withdrawal, "doing heroin … because no one was prepared to give [her] a good enough reason not to do it."[10] Similarly, Marie (in *Consumption*) cannot tolerate an existence characterized by familial, cultural, and social alienation; "just her, in the world" becomes scant reason for her to eat, or ultimately, reject suicide.[11] Conversely, Giselle (in *Skinny*) anxiously strives to *meet* her parents' expectations of perfection – scholastic, moral, and physical – by "learn[ing] to control [her] desire for people, for food … discover[ing] a new intimacy which required no one."[12] Cheryl (in *In Search of April Raintree*) becomes increasingly flooded with shame because she is Métis and resolves the struggle to "describe the feeling" by "swallow[ing] more beer."[13] And Lisamarie (in *Monkey Beach*) faces the unremitting degradation of her Haisla community, using alcohol to "blur" and "smudge" her pervasive feelings of cultural alienation.[14]

In all the novels examined, addiction and self-harm are represented as adaptive strategies of social reproduction.[15] Through each narrative's focus on contextualized functions of inebriation and self-harm, the novels destabilize the attribution of addiction to identity; instead they facilitate an interpretation of drug use similar to the one Eve Kosofsky Sedgwick describes in a pre-capitalist "old country," in which "opium use was functional as a form of control: it brought into realistic conformity with the material exactions of their lives their levels of concentration, their temporality, or their alertness to such stimuli as pain."[16] This psychic movement towards emotional and temporal equilibrium is the strongest shared quality of addiction across all the novels studied. I read this quality as producing counter-hegemonic depictions of addiction, which destabilize pervasive portrayals of addicts as diseased or dysfunctional individuals requiring reformation. Moreover, the novels also expose the formative role of individualism, consumption, and assimilation in shaping treatments of addiction in ways that conceal or naturalize their causal power. Because "the term 'social suffering' is used in part to expand understandings of the consequences of inequality, injustice, and oppression within social and political norms and institutions,"[17] it is a crucial conceptual framework within which to examine the normalized consequences of systemic inequalities. The self-harming behaviours of these fictional young women, then, cannot be understood outside the sociopolitical dynamics of their settings. I want to be clear, however, that I do not read "addictive" behaviours as inevitable consequences or markers of settler colonialism, capitalism, and/or patriarchy. The interlocking conditions of these systems inform such behaviours and their treatment and must be recognized as such. But to mistake contextualization for causality erases the complexities of how broader structures of power, privilege, and oppression play out in individual lives – and how individual and collective attempts to resist and subvert those systems can be fostered. It is the reciprocity of this dynamic among individuals and social structures that is of particular interest to this study.

It is also this reciprocity that leads me to include anorexia narratives under the broader rubric of addiction narratives. The logic of anorexic behaviours in *Skinny* and *Consumption* is constructed as similarly adaptive to familial, social, and institutional regimes of normalization. Specifically, Giselle's and Marie's somatic symptoms are portrayed as direct negotiations of individualistic and consumer expectations. Moreover, their anorexia is interpreted within a similar framework of personal pathology as substance addiction. The behaviours associated with the protagonists' pathologization are marked in both novels as maladaptive, rhetorically yoking addiction to anorexia via disease. *Consumption* links them together under the label of "Diseases of Affluence,"[18] while *Skinny* suggests that alcoholics and anorexics are both "toxic, addicted to the speed of [their] own destruction."[19] Examining habitual substance use and anorexia as forms of addiction is also necessary methodologically because it acknowledges the historical development of what Sedgwick calls the "addiction attribution."[20] Sedgwick traces the progression of addiction in the nineteenth century (as signifying dependence on substances for particular psychophysiological effects) to addiction in the latter half of the twentieth century (as describing willful acts, like food consumption, food refusal, habitual food purging, and excessive exercise, work, and dependence on relationships).[21] She then argues that

> activities newly pathologized under the searching rays of this new addiction attribution are the very ones that late capitalism presents *as* the ultimate emblems of control, personal discretion, freedom itself ... As each assertion of *will* has made voluntarity itself appear problematical in a new area, the assertion of will itself has come to appear addictive.[22]

Sedgwick contends that the label 'addiction' is attributed to behaviours based on the degree of intensity expressed through the habitual act rather than the specific type of behaviour. Habits can be valourized if they signify an individual's productive autonomy, but those same acts become pathologized when they come to signify an individual's preoccupation. This analysis frames the target of pathologizing addiction discourse as the exertion of will to a degree that seems to compromise personal freedom and choice. The suspect behaviours only become a problem when the individual is intent on maintaining the habit to a degree that he or she resists social regulation. The symbolic threat implied by this pathologization of "the assertion of *will*" is its perceived irrational and anti-social tendencies.

Skinny and *Consumption* each subvert this view of anorexia/addiction by refiguring food refusal as directly and inversely related, respectively, to the desire to belong socially, thereby inviting analysis of the circuitry between the social constitution of desires and habitual behaviours. Anorexia is also included in this study of fictional depictions of addiction because of the characteristic representations of treatment as discipline. There are striking methodological similarities in the identification, interpretation, and treatment of anorexia and addiction in both novels that are expressive of biomedical and cognitive behavioural explanations for addiction and anorexia, and these are examined in chapter 1.

By reading addiction – the category and the identity – as social suffering, this study is necessarily attentive to the politics of representation, an approach which is distinctive in both focus and methodology from the two extant works on literary addiction published in Canada. Both *Writing Addiction: Towards a Poetics of Desire and Its Others* (2004) and *Addicted: Notes From the Belly of the Beast* (2001) survey the metaphorical and literal connections between writing and addiction. Bela Szabados and Kenneth G. Probert's *Writing Addiction* is particularly concerned with letting "the light of the depiction of the experiences of addicts illuminate our lives as writers/authors."[23] Immediately troubling is the imbalanced comparison between the writing life and addictive behaviours. To privilege an analysis of the compulsions, pleasures, and pains of writing over those of substance-based and often harmful habits certainly denies the significant physiological differences between the two acts. It also dangerously elides recognition of the vulnerable sociopolitical contexts in which those labeled addicts are frequently embedded. For example, Szabados and Probert identify themes of self-division, desire and emotion, self-destruction and self-creation, transgression, modernity and post-modernity, the recovery of particularity, and the expression of all of these themes through the embodied act of writing as constituent features of the writing process, as well as of the psycho-physiological experience of addicts.[24] An underlying problem here is the definition upon which they base their analysis of writing as a form of addiction. After pointing out that "[in] Roman law, 'addiction' was a technical term" for a court sentence that rendered an addict "bound to a master"[25] in servitude, Szabados and Probert reclaim the term as accurately capturing the physiological state of addiction, while further asserting that "its metaphorical and extended uses are best understood by way of comparing a variety of cases in light of the master-slave relationship."[26] The stated intent, implicit assumptions, and ultimate implications of such comparisons risk producing an aesthetically depoliticized view of addiction, while simultaneously reproducing a profoundly political, hegemonic portrayal of addiction – distilling its meaning down to a constellation of symptoms, burying its mystic cause inside the individual addict-artist, and tacitly accepting its inevitable (re)occurrence.

Conversely, Lorna Crozier and Patrick Lane's *Addicted* presents the personal stories of prominent authors' experiences with various kinds of addiction – alcohol, drug, food, sex, gambling, cutting – as courageous acts of disclosure in a public forum that misunderstands the constituent elements of the addict's struggle with self, stigma, shame, and desire. Unlike Szabados and Probert, Crozier and Lane situate their literary notes on addiction within a realm of competing social narratives. The stories are offered as reality-checks against two "simplistic attitudes"[27] towards addiction that Crozier identifies as incomplete and erroneous: first, the shaming public voice that says, "why don't the drunks, the junkies, the smokers, the bulimics just smarten up? Pull themselves up by the bootstraps. Get some willpower. Stop;"[28] and second, the romantic vision of the "wild, self-destructive painter or poet who shatters complacency and taboos."[29] And yet, while Crozier and Lane name confrontations between liberal humanist demands for individual autonomy and the diversity of addiction experiences, the socio-economic circuitry between these imperatives and addiction remains oblique. The collection leaves vital questions unanswered. What are the social determinants of addiction? How are popular attitudes towards addiction produced, replicated, and institutionalized, and with what consequences? And how can literature intervene in the cacophony of stigmatizing addiction narratives in ways that might incite consideration of Jeff Shantz's argument that "peoples' vices and follies often give real satisfaction. They are not the expressions of the fallen";[30] indeed, they are often acts of survival.[31]

This book responds to such demanding questions by identifying three shared qualities of the novels studied. First, the narratives foreground the historical, material, and gendered contexts in which acts defined as addictive arise; second, they reveal the influences of individualism, consumption, and assimilation underlying both causal explanations for and institutional treatments of addiction; and third, they begin to clarify the processes by which these ideologies are naturalized and enforced, and in service to what interests. The examined texts demand critical attention to these three factors – attention that is surprisingly absent from literary as well as scientific and sociological discourse on the politics of addiction and its treatment.

I point to a particular kind of critical silence, however. Addiction studies is an immense field in which literary criticism participates prominently. Yet literary critical interventions proceed largely along aesthetic, historical, or biographical lines of inquiry. Literary criticism has failed to explore the links between systemic ideologies and addiction, as well as to expand its myopic – and masculinist – focus on William S. Burroughs (and the Beat Generation in general), Thomas de Quincey, Edgar Allen Poe, Hunter S. Thompson, and David Foster Wallace. This inattention emphasizes the urgency to develop resistant reading strategies that lay bare the capitalist, patriarchal, and settler colonial economies of both narrative representations of addiction *and* literary critical practices that are instrumental in the social and pedagogical dissemination of these stories. The stakes of literary criticism's failure to deploy and extend existing systemic analyses to representations of addiction should not be underestimated: interpretation that does not attend to institutional power is both symptomatic of and complicit in the naturalization and perpetuation of oppressive ideologies that depend on reducing systemic injustices to individual pathologies.

In order to situate my literary analysis, chapter 1 defines and analyses the ideological tropes of current trends in addiction discourses as they are produced within several cultural and political domains. The objective is to contextualize the significance of the ideological conflicts and symbolic subversions at the centre of the novels studied in each subsequent chapter, as well as to provide critical context and resources for teachers interested in critically interrogating depictions of addiction in the classroom. The intersectional approach elaborated therein constitutes the methodology of this study. I identify five particular domains of addiction narratives – popular culture, biomedical discourse, cultural studies, systemic analyses, and literature and literary criticism – in order to highlight the specific and shared constructions of the Addict as an essentialized identity across cultural locations, while also mobilizing an underrepresented branch of addiction studies that contests hegemonic explanatory models. Such analyses will be discussed in all chapters in relation to other cultural and political narratives. This initial survey is necessary because the novels examined evoke and contest the legitimacy of pervasive dominant narratives of addiction, and they do so in ways that illuminate the implications of their underlying pathologizing assumptions. My intention in chapter 1 is to distinguish the most persistently reproduced ideological tropes infusing addiction discourses, as well as identify an emerging category of counter-hegemonic depictions of addiction.

Chapter 2 examines the ways in which two contemporary poverty narratives – Christy Ann Conlin's *Heave* and Heather O'Neill's *lullabies for little criminals* – refigure addiction as social suffering by reframing habitual alcohol and drug use as emotionally adaptive behaviours in relation to individualizing logics of stigma. By employing Marx's theory of estranged labour and Pierre Bourdieu's concept of habitus, I argue that such individualism creates dramatic tension between the limits of each protagonist's agency and external pressures that demand from her full self-determination and control – imperatives that are reinforced both interpersonally and institutionally. Serrie's grandmother insists that Serrie just "get used to it"[32] or adapt to external realities, and Baby's father tells her that personal reinvention, or reformation, is the key to social mobility, even if he cannot achieve such appropriate transformations himself. These pressures are associated with the alcohol and drug use of both protagonists, especially as they come to understand the socioeconomic obstacles to personal empowerment. Inebriation then becomes a vehicle of imaginative freedom. For Serrie, the release is total – she blacks out – while Baby's illusory freedom comes from creatively transforming her world. In an intriguing reformulation of her father's encouragement to reform herself, Baby instead reforms her perceptions of the world around her. Each novel refigures addiction through unique structural and rhetorical strategies: *Heave* rehearses the Alcoholics Anonymous script of addiction but problematizes its central claims of individual disease and responsibility through the use of retrospect and social synecdoche; similarly, *lullabies for little criminals* evokes and contests stigmatizing views of poor people and addicts through plotting strategic confrontations between contextualized characterization and decontextualized diagnosis, thereby foregrounding the adaptive, but disciplined, logics of the protagonist's drug use.

Responding to Roxanne Rimstead's axiom that "poverty exists in relation to affluence,"[33] Chapter 3 explores the circuitry between the relative socioeconomic privileges of middle-class life and social suffering in Ibi Kaslik's *Skinny* and Kevin Patterson's *Consumption*. Sue Saltmarsh's notion of economically oriented subjects helps to interrogate the ideological circuitries among individualism, consumption, and practices of self-formation. This fundamentally disrupts dominant and pathologizing narratives about disordered eating that proliferate in medical, cultural, political, and literary discourses. Using feminist and gender studies analyses of the causes and treatment of eating disorders, the chapter troubles and expands ongoing cultural criticism that implies eating disorders can be prevented when what Susan Bordo calls "the empire of images" begins to represent more diverse and positive images of women's and men's bodies.[34] The novels demonstrate that the heteronormative, impossibly thin figures represented in the media also represent socioeconomic values that operate on an everyday experiential level of social interaction. As in *Heave* and *lullabies for little criminals*, the protagonists' families in *Skinny* and *Consumption* inadvertently discipline Giselle and Marie to conform to pressures to adapt, succeed, and reform themselves, underscoring their own negotiation and perpetuation of such pressures. By tracing such intimate circuitries of capitalist and patriarchal norms, chapter 3 explores examples of how compulsive behaviours marked as addictive are treated socially and institutionally as moral and/or physical pathology, rather than symptoms of systemic strain.

Chapter 4 argues that Eden Robinson's *Monkey Beach* and Beatrice Culleton Mosionier's *In Search of April Raintree* refigure addictive behaviours among Indigenous peoples as negotiations of estrangement within capitalist colonialism, as well as estrangement from everyday cultural practices that are becoming increasingly threatened by settler colonial policies of acquisition and assimilation. Robinson's novel frames drinking as a response to alienation from traditional practices of subsistence and familial belonging, as well as a practice of (attempted) social belonging. Moreover, the chapter explores the political purchase of reproducing pathologized views of addiction among Indigenous peoples. Indeed, it is incendiary terrain to plot, as *In Search of April Raintree* demonstrates. The novel exposes and contests neocolonial and capitalist re/productions of the myth of the "Drunken Indian" by foregrounding the ways in which drinking is essentialized as an intrinsic characteristic of Métis people. In this way, the narrative provokes a denaturalization of the myth through foregrounding how the image differently affects April's and Cheryl's willingness to claim Métis identity and affiliation. The reproduction of the stereotype not only masks the roots of real addiction crises among Indigenous peoples, but it also has a regulatory power in the novel. As both sisters come to differently assess their place in the mainstream Canadian economy, they feel their survival threatened by the existence of and possible association with "gutter-creature[s]."[35] In these ways, the assimilative aspects of capitalism are revealed as insidiously embroiled in experiences of addiction in these two canonical novels by Indigenous writers.

My discourse analysis of fictional accounts of addiction seeks to enable more nuanced understandings of the ways in which ideologies of individualism, consumption, and assimilation are transmitted intergenerationally, and with what consequences. The texts plot these ideologies as antagonistic to the protagonists' development, which demonstrates how state responses to addiction are not only practiced institutionally – by social services, police, and medical and psychiatric personnel – but interpersonally as well. Redefined and treated as individual pathologies, the systemic determinants of addiction and self-harm are largely ignored by available treatment models in the novels considered, and consequently become conveyed as ultimately enforcing the very imperatives that give rise to addiction in each instance. Significantly, as the narratives trace the ways capitalism, patriarchy, and settler colonialism are reproduced, they also dramatize confrontations between competing ideologies of what constitutes kinship, survival, social responsibility, and success, and how institutionalized ideologies are policed and reinforced. These confrontations denaturalize the socioeconomic circuitry of capitalism, in particular, which is unbearable for many of the protagonists and betrays the inadequacy of individualizing models for understanding the addictive behaviours of the protagonists.

A dramatic tension driving the plots of all the examined novels is that, under conditions of inequality – regardless of class – protagonists must still socially reproduce themselves, and they must do so while maintaining particular codes of conduct. By reading social reproduction and moral regulation[36] as interconnected processes animating the narratives, I contend that the affective re/actions of the protagonists to their respective socioeconomic realities, as well as the oppressively corrective methods of their families, become contextually intelligible as performative behaviours. As Judith Butler describes gender, so too do I perceive addictive or habitual behaviours as "improvisation[s] within scene[s] of constraint."[37] In representing trajectories of addiction as social suffering, Conlin, O'Neill, Kaslik, Patterson, Mosionier, and Robinson replot ostensibly self-harming behaviours as adaptive responses to systemic (and often unattainable) demands. As chapter 1 explores, dominant narratives represent addiction in ways that figure the Addict as a dysfunctional identity. Because dominant views elide the causal role of sociopolitical factors, as Stephanie Irlbacher-Fox argues about social suffering among Dene peoples, dysfunction comes to imply that individuals "can change the circumstances they are in, in order to become 'functional.'"[38] Conversely, then, "the term 'social suffering' understands unwellness as symptoms of ongoing injustice, circumstances created and imposed by external agents."[39] In reading addiction as being produced performatively, I contemplate as a crucial object of study the dialectic between the behaviours (or utterances) of so-called "addiction" and the social, literary, and political fields in which these behaviours emerge.

This dialectic invites three levels of analysis. First, examining representations of addiction as performative assists in discerning the reiterative echoes of dominant discourses in the performance, identification, and treatment of addiction. Second, rather than linear or predictable, causality becomes circuitous, internally logical, and contextual. Third, addressing the Addict as a performative identity acknowledges the corporeal, affective, and linguistic elements of his or her performative utterances, which in the examined narratives, refer to specific narrations of substance use, self-harming acts, and psychic trips, as well as declarative social admissions or denials of addiction. By tracing circulations of capitalist, heteronormative, and settler colonial power relations, I attend to how addiction emerges within such relations as responses to forces that would refigure bodies into products or producers – commodities to be regulated by self and others to perform particular functions. Thus, a methodology of reading addiction that recognizes its performative qualities challenges the individualistic and pathologizing theories of addiction discussed in chapter 1. Moreover, such contextualizing reading strategies are required by the literature under examination. To take what Félix Guattari calls the "chemotherapeutic"[40] approach of carving protagonists out of the scenes of constraint from which they emerge in order to dissect their symptoms would render their acts unintelligible and leave unexamined and intact the circuitries of power and subversion along which the narratives unfold.

As the narratives examined in the following chapters proceed to trace affective and material circuitries between individual acts and systemic conditions, they each take an ironic turn: the protagonists' actions are read and treated by those around them as symptoms of physical and moral disease rather than (perhaps unhealthy) mediations of social forces. The dramatic tension arises from this dissonance. Testing an enduring cultural notion that an addict's greatest struggle is against herself,[41] these stories reframe the struggle as negotiating ongoing forms of systemic power that simultaneously define and treat behaviours as maladaptive and aberrant identity traits. The ostensibly self-destructive young women of recent Canadian fiction call attention to legacies of colonization, as well as economic and gender inequalities. Often, their addictions are depicted as symptoms rather than causes of social suffering. In fact, the conflict in these works stems from the protagonists' confrontations with economic, psychiatric, and legal institutions that firmly place the responsibility of sobriety, adaptation, and recovery on the individual, while ignoring the ways in which forms of oppression provoke and perpetuate self-destructive behaviour. The meanings produced from this dissonance not only challenge public and private stereotypes about addiction, but also suggest that the reproduction of such stereotypes shores up the values and interests of settler colonial state capitalism and heteropatriarchy.

Undoing Addiction in Classrooms

This book offers a series of pedagogical approaches that provide educators with the critical tools necessary to question in the classroom stereotypes of addiction that circulate unchallenged in mainstream culture. But it does so in agreement with Sherene Razack's view that "education for social change is not so much about new information as it is about disrupting the hegemonic ways of seeing through which subjects make themselves dominant."[42] Addiction is tied to poverty, racism, colonialism, patriarchy, and other forces of power and oppression, while critical pedagogy offers tools to foster awareness, discontent, and vigilant, critical engagement with these systems. Such tools do not assign responsibility to a single text or genre to incite social action, but instead approach addiction studies as a process of developing critical consciousness – a process that is incremental, interdisciplinary, multigenerational, and ideally, transformative. Critical pedagogies also grapple with the fact that classrooms are neither exempt from the power dynamics teachers and learners are themselves subject to and seek to contest, nor are they safe havens from the relentless advance of neoliberal policies and ideologies. Learners are not viewed as separate from the subject of investigation, but rather ongoing participants in the creation of meaning. As such, critical pedagogical practices offer ways to break down stereotypes of addiction and to contest its social determinants.

Several additional, pressing reasons inform my choice to consider how the tools of critical pedagogies can be applied to this study of addiction narratives: to address limitations of text and context; to foster interdisciplinary approaches to literary criticism and teaching; and to ground theory in teaching and social practice. When examined in relation to the dominant stories of addiction outlined in this introduction, *Heave*, *lullabies for little criminals*, *Skinny*, *Consumption*, *In Search of April Raintree*, and *Monkey Beach* are clearly antagonistic to the pathologizing premises of such discourses by provoking a wider and multidimensional view of addiction and its treatment. For this reason alone, it is a matter of some urgency to initiate dialogue among social justice-oriented educators about how to most effectively pursue textual analysis according to principles of critical pedagogy. The fact that the conclusions of these novels are troublingly limited in their subversive potential only amplifies the need to consider their pedagogical effectiveness. Each text examined variously erects a common central conflict between the protagonists' improvisational (or survivalist) behaviours within scenes of economic, class, gendered, and colonial constraints, and external forces that seek to label those behaviours as willfully and/or morally pathological. However, the dramatic resolutions of these tensions operate according to a kind of sacrificial logic: at the end of novel, the protagonist either dies or is cast out of her or his respective community. Read together, such endings are vexing; not only do the shared narrative resolutions potentially reinscribe the dominant views of addiction that were destabilized throughout each text, but they also depict the very questioning of logics of capitalism, patriarchy, and settler colonialism as mortally dangerous. In other words, while their challenges to institutionalized and socially pervasive explanations for addictions express their revolutionary nature, the narratives also rehearse an unsettling pattern of narrative closure that seems to affirm the sacrificial logic of dominant addiction discourses. Therefore, the texts become limited in their transformative potential and even run the risk of serving as cautionary tales, especially if read in isolation from other cultural products.

It is precisely because of their shared contradictions that the texts must be taught according to Paulo Freire's model of "problem-posing education,"[43] which invites students to "recognize the interaction of the various components" within "a total vision of the context."[44] Decontextualized and individually pathologizing depictions of addiction flourish culturally; by asking students to grapple with how and why certain writers portray addiction as inextricably linked to social circumstance, teachers both destabilize the truth claims that pervade hegemonic depictions of addiction, and involve students in fleshing out the variable stories of addiction. The subversive elements of the novels need not be cancelled out by their hegemonic endings – rather, they may even provoke a critical response in students to reevaluate social and institutional treatment of addicts, which operate according to a "conform or be cast out"[45] mentality.

And yet, while they can be reframed pedagogically as subversive, a second limitation which requires attention is how or if these texts can inspire or mobilize social transformation. If one novel could change Canada, as the 2014 CBC Canada Reads competition contends,[46] how can one or even several texts do so outside the realms of the imaginary or theoretical? Because their elevated cultural and educational status rests not only on their aesthetic merit, but also on their social relevance, the examined novels raise vital questions about how and whether audiences can be provoked to change their beliefs about addiction and their treatment of addicts. Kimberly Nance argues that literary critics often conflate "writing with concrete action," and yet "to speak the truth" while systems of power are still intact is "merely to join in the contest to shape world opinion, not to win it, and much less to guarantee social action."[47] Tools of critical pedagogy seek to go beyond literary interpretation that "teach[es] the conflict"[48] when we analyse such representations of addiction. Critical pedagogy does not "neutrally present the debates over canons, cultural value, multiculturalism, identity-thinking, and so on for students";[49] rather, as Simon During argues, "it aims to produce knowledge from perspectives lost to and in dominant public culture, and to listen to far-off or marginalized voices."[50] The distinction here is between a teaching that presents debate as an objective process of analysis by removed practitioners of intellectual research (which firmly situates narrative as object), to a teaching that explicitly calls into question the socially constructed, politicized lenses through which students and teachers read the world around them (which firmly situates readers in dialectical, power-inflected relationships among one another and with texts). These fraught dynamics of text and social context can and must be meaningfully engaged in the classroom in order to motivate the urgency for social change often expressed through addiction narratives.

Employing critical pedagogies of addition narratives also answers recent calls to ground pedagogical theory in practice. Rebecca Tarlau notes that critical pedagogy is focused on both "deepening social theory by analyzing public schooling as an 'ideological state apparatus,'"[51] and suggesting pedagogical tools to help students perceive systems of inequality "through concepts such as the teacher-intellectual, banking versus problem-solving education, collective learning, and constructing a language of resistance."[52] Tarlau argues, however, that the first line of analysis is most prevalent, while the latter approach "often fail[s] to make the connection between radical educational practices and concrete examples of social change."[53] This observation certainly seems to bear out in a North American context. Crucial book-length interrogations of how neoliberalism is shaping, or some would say dismantling, universities abound,[54] while articles proposing ways in which to interrogate privilege, identify oppression, and inspire collective agency in neoliberal classrooms are regularly circulated in critical pedagogy and social movement journals.[55]

These works are not necessarily problematic individually or collectively. Rather, the field of critical pedagogy urgently needs expansion. Analysis is vital, but so too is sharing strategies, reevaluating those strategies, and continually pushing our approaches further. So, critiques of neoliberalism should continue apace of the advance of neoliberalism, as should theorizations of how the problem-solving approach to education can be pushed towards social action. Undoubtedly, paradigm-shifting works on critical pedagogy, such as those of Paulo Freire, bell hooks, Henry Giroux, and Sherene Razack, have built an indomitable framework of guiding principles and practical examples of transformative pedagogy. Kim A. Case and Elizabeth R. Cole point out that such work "most often presents a single instructor's perspective."[56] Yet, the problem of transforming theory into social action raised by Tarlau seems less an issue of authorial focus than of contextual application. Ample resources exist on how to frame discussions about racism, heteronormativity, sexism, settler privilege, and colonialism, but scant examples exist of how we might apply these foundational principles to literary studies in the neoliberal university. Critically thinking educators and learners must communicate in more organized, sustained ways on how they apply the tools of feminist, anti-racist, decolonizing, and anti-capitalist pedagogies across various disciplines, regions, and sociopolitical contexts. The Transformative Pedagogy section of each chapter will contribute to this dialogue by exploring ways to foster critical consciousness through the study of literature in the classroom.

The overarching reasons for including transformative teaching strategies as part this study of subversive literary depictions of addiction are to address the limitations of text and reception, to consider how critical pedagogies work in literature classrooms, and to investigate how transformative pedagogies may mobilize social action. Three principles of critical pedagogies that undergird my interrogation of depictions of addiction in literature classrooms are using the problem-posing approach; anticipating and engaging student resistance to critical thinking; and employing anti-oppression guidelines. Freire's pivotal distinction between the banking model and "the problem-posing method"[57] of education rests on the premise that students are not vessels waiting to be filled by lecture-delivered information; rather, they bring diverse knowledge, experiences, and assumptions to the classroom, which inform the ways in which they recognize, interrogate, and produce knowledge. The task of the "dialogical teacher" is to facilitate discovery, or "*conscientização*," in students of how they are "rooted in temporal-spatial conditions which mark them and which they also mark. They will tend to reflect on their own 'situationality' to the extent that they are challenged by it to act upon it."[58] Similarly, before counter-hegemony can be analysed, hegemony must be discovered by students as an ongoing part of their daily lives. In Gramscian terms, students must first cultivate awareness of how "common sense" is a form of cajoled consent through cultural hegemony.[59] This process is part and parcel of developing a "world perspective,"[60] or what Gramsci calls "a critical and coherent conception of the world" rather than one that is "disjointed and episodic."[61]

Posing stereotypes of addicts and addiction as a problem demands that students and educators consider connections between texts and cultural contexts, and readers and their sociopolitical world. Relying on lecture, or informative pedagogy, fosters a more passive learning environment which too easily allows students to see the problem as external, while their participation – intentional or not – in hegemonic processes of meaning-making is left unexamined. Each chapter will explore strategies for breaking down 'Us/Them' thinking, which is "embedded in narratives designed to maintain the neoliberal status quo."[62] Interrogating such othering, dehumanizing dichotomies not only does the difficult work of challenging essentialism in all its insidious guises, but it also illuminates how stereotypes render oppression invisible. As Razack puts it, "without an understanding of how responses to subordinate groups are socially organized to sustain existing power arrangements, we cannot hope either to communicate across social hierarchies or to work to eliminate them."[63] Each chapter will include possible strategies for encouraging the collective naming of stereotypes, reflection on their utility in power relations, and how they might be contested.

Freire's literacy work stemmed from his work with Brazilian farmers and rural workers who were "directly connected to larger movements struggling for social change."[64] His legacy is a teaching methodology of resistance and empowerment – but the students in the neoliberal classroom are not Freire's students. While diverse in terms of social positionality, power, and privilege – making the stakes of learning considerably different from student to student – learners encountered in contemporary universities are not uniformly invested in social change; indeed, they can be explicitly resistant to it. Moreover, Rimstead cautions that "because Freire's theory of transformative dialogue was grounded on direct contact between intellectuals and the oppressed in small groups … it is both theoretically problematic and ethically suspect for academics to claim to speak for, to, or with oppressed people."[65] Certainly, I share Rimstead's call to interrogate the power relations within which academics are embedded; yet, the way this caution is articulated implies an identity politics that might not be strategically useful. Speaking with the oppressed is an act of solidarity and demands the kind of reflexivity, accountability, and sustainable commitment to dismantling circuitries of power and privilege that is aligned with the foundational principles of critical, transformative pedagogy. Solidarity is a practice imbedded in power relations, and can serve as a productive way to think about how to ethically import transformative pedagogies from South American to North American social, economic, and settler colonial contexts.

The significant differences between these contexts inform a major aspect of critical pedagogy practice in neoliberal universities. Practitioners have identified common forms of student resistance to perceiving and analysing oppression. Drawing on the works of bell hooks, Gayatri

Chakravorty Spivak, Chandra Talpade Mohanty, Sherene Razack, Andrea Smith, and Martin J. Cannon, I focus on six of these seeming barriers to transformative education; that is, claims of absolute choice, authority of experience, minimization of oppression, futility, denial of historical influence, and essentialism. Undergirding these claims is an inattention to how privilege and oppression create blind spots in our analytical lenses. These "increasingly predictable set of responses … inhibit[s] the development of a critical consciousness … [which] can be summed up as a denial of oppression."[66] Such denial underscores the student responses described above. As several theorists have argued, in order for literature to be transformative it must implicate its audience in the call for social justice (see Nance, Episkenew). But if and when readers actively resist implication, it is vital that educators develop strategies to open up dialogue about what it means to be implicated or complicit in ongoing injustices. Part of emergent, interdisciplinary attempts to interrogate privilege is Kim A. Case's edited collection *Deconstructing Privilege: Teaching and Learning as Allies in the Classroom.* This provides compelling resources that partially inform the strategies I offer to engage and ideally transform these pervasive expressions of student resistance, specifically in relation to the study of addiction narratives and their critiques of capitalism, patriarchy, and settler colonialism.

Finally, critical pedagogy practitioners uniformly grapple with how to facilitate classroom dynamics that incite transformative questions and discussions, but remain aware that such an atmosphere can potentially reproduce oppressive racialized, gendered, and classed dynamics. If the classroom "remains the most radical space of possibility in the academy,"[67] it can only be so if learners actively seek to disrupt the relations of inequality that follow us into the classroom. This is complex work. For students to renounce stereotypes, they must first identify, articulate, and interrogate the content and sources of their own assumptions, and reason for themselves how such beliefs work interpersonally, socially, and politically. This initial step towards critical thinking is most effective when taken in collaboration with other students because, as connections and differences between assumptions are made apparent, students can begin to investigate and question how they have come to know what they know. As hooks asserts, "seeing the classroom always as a communal place enhances the likelihood of collective effort in creating and sustaining a learning community."[68] And yet, because self-reflection can often lead students to voice racist, classist, and sexist statements, anti-oppressive[69] guidelines can foster a framework of accountability among everyone in the classroom – both among students and between students and teacher. Given my focus on breaking down stereotypes of addiction through transformative pedagogy, anti-oppression principles have a clear applicability. Such principles also emphasize that the ideas expressed and the process of their interrogation in the classroom are not neutral, nor are the students and teacher participating from an objective, authoritative remove. In my own teaching, forging an atmosphere of collective effort has meant actively and transparently facilitating discussion about anti-oppressive principles, often through building shared values or rules of engagement in the classroom at the beginning of term.

These three central concerns of critical pedagogy – problem-posing teaching, engaging resistance, and anti-oppression – form the structure and content of each of this book's literary analysis chapters. Beginning with a substantial Informative Pedagogy section, which provides an intersectional analysis of depictions of addiction in two novels (summaries above), chapters 2, 3, and 4 then include Transformative Pedagogy sections. I borrow this distinction from Baldev et al., who posit that "informative learning adds to what we already know with minimal alternation to our worldview. Transformative learning invites a transformation of our perspective of the world."[70] I also prefer the term "transformative" rather than "critical" to highlight the action-oriented trajectory of this book. Opening with problem-posing approaches to teaching the novels, these sections are followed by strategies to engage two specific types of student resistance. These sections are intended to be read cumulatively. The discovery and engaging resistance strategies are applicable to all novels examined in the book, but I've chosen to focus on different approaches in each chapter to offer a great number of possible pedagogical techniques to teaching depictions of addiction. Chapter 2 examines the intersections among poverty, patriarchy, and addiction, and examines student resistance based on assertions of choice and authority of experience. Chapter 3 examines the intersections among privilege, patriarchy, settler colonialism, and eating disorders, and offers strategies to engage student resistance based on feelings of futility and minimizing oppression. Chapter 4 examines the intersections among settler colonialism, capitalism, patriarchy, and addiction, and considers ways to transform student resistance rooted in essentialism and the denial of historical influence. Finally, each of the body chapters will engage Tarlau's call for social justice educators to go a step further in theorizing and implementing ways to transform critical consciousness into social action. The concluding section of each chapter ultimately considers how systemic analyses can be mobilized beyond the classroom.

These may seem like lofty goals for a literature classroom, especially considering that engaging with various forms of students' denials of oppression might be perceived as a barrier to such future- and action-oriented thinking. Despite the considerable challenges to fostering critical consciousness in the classroom, grappling with forms of resistance through open dialogue can have transformative effects for students and teachers beyond the formal learning environment. Yet, whether or not students make connections between the politics of representation and their individual participation in cultural hegemony and counter-hegemony in ways that change their personal behaviour and ways of thinking, teachers can maintain the urgency to break down barriers between classroom discussion and real-life discursive relations of power, oppression, and resistance by employing action-oriented pedagogical strategies. These might include cultural interventions (e.g. short film, blog posts); designing policy change proposals; writing letters to public officials; doing research about and/or participating in existing initiatives that do anti-oppressive work; talking to family and friends and reflecting on the difficulties and possibilities of challenging stereotypes through conversation; or designing a science experiment or research project that tests the questions raised by literature.

Such modest approaches to bridging the gap between course content and social interactions are important because the classroom setting and traditional assignments – however much guided by principles of critical thinking pedagogy – often do not challenge students to step outside their comforts zones to apply, reflect on, and modify the concepts learned through course work and class discussion. Michael D. Giardina and Norman K. Denzin argue that academics should take every opportunity to broadly communicate our research beyond just the academic journal;"[71] so too should students be encouraged to voice their critiques of culture by interacting with others outside the formal learning environment. These suggestions towards transformative action take seriously Freire's contention that "there is no true word that is not at the same time a praxis," that words are both "reflection and action."[72] Encouraging students to take their words outside the classroom does not suggest that classroom discussion is not transformative. However, too easily can students (and teachers), through articulating power relations and identifying individual privileges and oppression, "create a climate of hopelessness"[73] in which hegemonic structures colonialism, capitalism, and patriarchy "can appear as fetters or as insurmountable barriers."[74] Seizing the opportunity to show students that critical engagement with their social world is not only possible but necessary might mean, for example, that teachers introduce students to existing critical communities by inviting campus and community group organizers into the classroom. As Andrea Smith argues, while "political projects of transformation necessarily involve a fundamental reconstitution of ourselves ... the undoing of privilege occurs not by individuals confessing their privileges or trying to think themselves into a new subject position, but through the creation of collective structures that dismantle the systems that enable these privileges."[75] A transformative pedagogy provides students with critical tools and expands ideas of resistance beyond individual acts. In doing so, teachers can foster a sense of critical, creative, transformative social action as sustainable because it is necessarily collective and collaborative.

The stakes of this critical and pedagogical work are clear. As the National Treatment Strategy Working Group insists, "a transformation in the way we serve and support Canadians with substance use problems is not possible until *stigma* and *discrimination* are confronted. Stigma (negative attitudes) leads to discrimination (associated negative behaviour), which prevents people from getting the services and supports they need."[76] Such work cannot be relegated solely to public health campaigns. For example, harm reduction is one effective initiative to reduce the personal, social, and spiritual effects of substance use, but the implementation of crucial life-saving programs like safe injection sites[77] has come under attack by Harper's Conservatives, attacks which doggedly rely on stigmatizing and criminalizing portrayals of drug users. We need an informed, critical public that can assess harm reduction from an evidence-based, social justice perspective, and teaching critical literacy around issues of addiction and substance use combats stigma.

Teaching destigmatizing understandings of addiction also challenges punitive responses to substance use. While current statistics on the number of people in prison who use alcohol and drugs are difficult to find, in 2004 the Canadian Centre on Substance Abuse (CCSA) reported that 51 per cent of people in federal prisons had problems with alcohol and 48 per cent reported issues with other drugs.[78] While Correctional Service Canada has a policy of "zero tolerance for drugs or alcohol,"[79] the CCSA report found that the drug prohibition strategies employed to enforce zero tolerance (e.g. search and seizure, drug detection technologies, staff and visitor screening, perimeter security measures) are not supported by evidence-based research. In fact, "the notion of a 'drug-free' prison has been acknowledged by some prison systems as 'unrealistic.'"[80] And yet, despite the fact that the majority of people in prison struggle with substance use issues, as well as return to prison because of substance use ("as many as 70 per cent of offender release suspensions involve alcohol and other drugs"[81]), treatment inside prisons and release conditions rely on an abstinence model. This is the model that undergirds the War on Drugs and relies on the criminalization of drug users – legally, socially, and culturally. As Gabor Maté explains, "a core assumption in the War on Drugs is that the addict is free to make the choice not to be addicted and that harsh social or legal measures will deter him from pursuing his habit. It is not that easy."[82]

Angela Davis describes the prison as "an abstract site into which undesirables are deposited, relieving us of the responsibility of thinking about the real issues afflicting those communities from which prisoners are drawn."[83] So too is treatment conceptually situated in the majority of the novels included in this study. Treatment is depicted as populated with predominantly poor people, "the undesirables" who must learn to fashion themselves in the image of the penitent addict or "should they 'fail,' ... lie as individuals on the bed they have made for themselves."[84] Within a cultural and political framework that divides poor people into two categories – "the undeserving 'poor' as licentious, drunk, and disorderly; and the 'deserving' poor as children and the working poor"[85] – addiction treatment is imposed as a transitional process from the former to the latter. Therefore, by reading addiction treatment as a carceral force in marginalized communities in particular, we can conceptualize more clearly and urgently alternatives to punitive treatment, which must involve reevaluating economic, race, and gender hierarchies. While the novels studied in this book do not imagine such alternatives, they provide vital creative critiques of the pathology paradigm, which call on readers, teachers, and scholars to challenge stereotypes and the social inequalities that depend on them.

Chapter One

Ideological Tropes of Contemporary Addiction Narratives

"Soaked in alcoholism and addiction, this story plumbs the bottomless human genius for self-deception and our singular talent for wandering into hellholes of our own design."

– Alan Cumyn [1]

Addiction narratives emerge from various media besides literature; in fact, they abound in our everyday cultural environments. Consider the multiple encounters you can have in one unremarkable day: drive time DJs report that Lindsay Lohan is back in rehab; your iPod shuffles to Amy Winehouse's song "Rehab"[2]; the cover of *Reader's Digest* at the laundromat asks you, "Addicted or afflicted?: Should your tax dollars buy drugs for abusers?"[3]; your family doctor asks how many drinks per week you consume; an Addictions Awareness Campaign table placard at a CFB Kingston pub reads, "Our Forces Know … I Know … Do You Know? When to say I've had enough – When to step in – When and how to ask for help"; and CBC quotes Stephen Harper's statement that harm reduction is not a "distinct pillar"[4] of the Conservative anti-drug strategy. Radio, music, magazines, TV and film, social networking sites, newspapers, national policy: whether passive or active, our engagement with the stories media tells about addicts and addiction informs our common sense understanding of its meaning.

Dominant representations of addiction are most often expressed in tones of warning about "the terrible consequences of drug and alcohol addiction," such as "crime, loss of earnings and productivity, and social damage,"[5] but they vary in terms of their assumptions, contradictions, objectives, and reception. This chapter analyses the ideological tropes that animate these stories of caution, fascination, disgust, sympathy, and sensationalism that circulate in dominant Western culture. Neither produced nor consumed in a vacuum, these narratives cannot be read independently of the broader discourses with which they intersect, including choice, autonomy, individualism, disease, and free will. Attending to the effects of such interactions among addiction narratives that materialize through different media, as well as institutional policy and academic disciplines, is central to the analytical methodology outlined in this chapter and pedagogical strategies offered in each subsequent chapter. By identifying and analysing five key narrative trends in dominant and emerging addiction discourses, the novels are positioned in each chapter as explicitly and complexly troubling hegemonic addiction narratives. This survey is also necessary pedagogically. In order to guide students towards articulating the problems and possibilities raised by Canadian literary depictions of addiction, educators should be familiar with the broader discourses such fiction evokes and contests.

Alcoholics Anonymous and Popular Culture

Late twentieth-century portrayals, both real and fictional, construct addiction as involuntary and yet subject to control, pending the addict's willingness to choose recovery. The influence and endurance of this sentiment pervades television and film plots. For over ten years the A&E network reality television show *Intervention* has rehearsed the same script: the addict's behaviour is identified by others as destructive; an intervention is staged outlining how such behaviour affects the lives of the addict and their[6] loved ones; the addict ultimately chooses or refuses to pursue rehabilitation. Whether redemption-seeking confessions, triumphant returns from rock bottom, or posthumously mourned tragedies, the subjects of fictional and celebrity addiction narratives in popular culture commonly are depicted as fighting a battle with the self for freedom from compulsion – a struggle which casts them as either as-yet unwitting victims, knowing reformers, or lost causes. Echoing what Peter Ferentzy argues are the Enlightenment beliefs in "free will … [and] the curability of everything,"[7] dominant cultural addiction narratives share the corresponding conviction that people with so-called diseases of the will (e.g. madness, addiction, homosexuality) "[are] not considered responsible for their afflictions, but [are] held responsible for their recovery."[8] By foreclosing any interrogation of causality, this view of addiction seems intrinsically contradictory. There is no cause and effect, only effect and treatment, which inevitably position the addict as morally culpable in the choice to recover. Undergirding this narrative is a naturalized, unquestioned understanding of addiction and its treatment – one in which the fate of the addict is neatly accounted for by appraising her will to choose recovery. This pervasive dominant interpretive lens is shaped by the Alcoholics Anonymous view of addiction.

Alcoholics Anonymous is arguably the most recognizable addiction organization in Western culture. The spiritual foundations of what the official AA website calls "a fellowship like no other"[9] are traced back to the Oxford Group, a religious movement which "practiced a formula of self-improvement by performing self-inventory, admitting wrongs, making amends, using prayer and meditation, and carrying the message to others."[10] These principles structure the Twelve Steps that the original 100 members of AA recorded in the 1930s based on their practical experiences supporting each other in their struggles with drinking and their central belief that "alcoholism is a progressive illness, that it cannot be cured in the ordinary sense of the term, but that it can be arrested through total abstinence from alcohol in any form."[11] The group's initial members went public in 1939 with the release of the 'Blue Book' (officially entitled *Alcoholics Anonymous: The Story of How Many Thousands of Men and Women Have Recovered from Alcoholism*), which is currently in its fourth edition and available online in several languages. The redeployment of the Twelve Steps to the ever-widening category of addiction, as well as within medical, penal, and psychiatric institutions, appear to have made AA the common sense approach to treating alcoholism.

Mariana Valverde argues that this approach to recovery marks a dramatic and enduringly influential shift in Western views of addiction in three ways. First, by redefining addiction as a non-medical, incurable disease[12] that strikes people of any class, race, or gender, AA continues to frame drinking as an intrinsic urge. However, such urges are seen as impervious to the will's efforts to control consumption. In fact, the attempt to control the drive to drink is symptomatic of the disease of alcoholism itself. So within the AA model, the will is diseased not when languishing from use, but when it is compulsively flexed against an insurmountable force. Second, the subsequent process of treatment marks the profound influence of Alcoholics Anonymous over public perception of addiction. In contrast to pre-AA definitions of addiction, which demanded individual heroic acts of victory over self, AA, at least in theory, insists on surrender to a higher power for strength, and non-coercive, cooperative, mutual support in learning to adapt to an irreversible lifelong affliction and struggle to stay sober. As Valverde points out, this ostensibly democratic approach to recovery has been particularly meaningful for blue-collar men, who perceive "their allegiance to AA as a form of resistance against medical power."[13] AA philosophy at its inception does seem to privilege individual assessment of one's own experience over impositions of external judgment. However, as argued in chapter 2, contemporary AA practices have not preserved this principle of non-interference, as medical and juridical powers have come to use AA as a tool of moral regulation. Such evolutions in AA practice occur along a third legacy of the twelve steps. In Valverde's view, extending AA's treatment methods to various other behaviours has become "the common denominator ... for today's broad-ranging recovery movement."[14] Certainly, even a brief survey of addiction narratives in popular culture shows that alcohol and drug dependence are just two of several behaviours that are now called addictions. As "addiction attribution"[15] has extended beyond substance-focused behaviours, so too has the AA-structured treatment format been applied to overeaters (OA), eating disorders (EDA), anorexia and bulimics (ABA), sex addicts (SAA), workaholics (WA), and co-dependents (CoDA).

Such contemporary iterations of AA narratives emerge within political and moral economies that demand self-control and self-containment from people, imperatives that are naturalized within and ideologically vital to neoliberal and neoconservative agendas. Valverde demonstrates that framing addiction as a battle against the self is a circular but politically useful argument. As addiction comes to signify a struggle with the will over self, it refers to a "relation of the soul to itself, not to any objective state of affairs."[16] Evident at the cultural level through such reality television programs as *My Strange Addiction* and *Intervention*[17] are the ways in which, "by directly focusing on volitional impairment, the concept of addiction can render details irrelevant."[18] Crucially, when discourses of addiction are caught within a dialectic of free will and determinism, multiple social issues disappear from view. For example, Jason Kosovski and Douglas Smith posit that the "most glaring misrepresentation" reproduced by *Intervention* is "the degree to which inpatient treatment is framed as available, desirable, and successful."[19] Not only does inpatient treatment form only a small fraction of therapeutic care, but it is also extremely expensive, which makes class, racial, and gender status barriers to access it. The chapters that follow will examine how *Heave, lullabies for little criminals, Skinny, Consumption, Monkey*

Beach, and *In Search of April Raintree* depict social and systemic obstacles to recovery. Such narratives challenge views perpetuated by popular narratives like *Intervention*, which imply the only obstacle to recovery is the uncommitted and unrepentant addict.

Kosovski and Smith also point out that "the narrative presented by the addict is often framed as clouded and distorted by drug and alcohol abuse," while "the narrative presented by friends and family is coded as authoritative and honest."[20] The addict is persistently framed as an unreliable narrator, and when given space to speak, is positioned as compromised, unable to assess or provide a legitimate perspective on his or her own circumstances, and incapable of articulating any substantive truth or critical insight about addiction.[21] Within popular representations of AA, it is typical for addicts to cast themselves and others as liars when they are using.[22] Within literature classes, narrators revealed to be substance users are typically considered to be unreliable as well.[23] In the last five years, two notable attempts to reject this notion of the addict as unreliable narrator vis-à-vis rejection of the AA script have emerged in popular television, however problematically. For example, Charlie Sheen's highly public rejections of AA in 2011 deny the doctrine that accepting powerlessness is empowering, while simultaneously assert the will as the principal site of personal freedom.[24] In addition, as in novels I examine, Showtime's *Nurse Jackie* (at least in the early seasons) simultaneously produces scenarios in which inebriate behaviours and desires appear adaptive,[25] not maladaptive, to socioeconomic conditions, while inviting the audience to interrogate the ability of the Twelve Step process to address the scope of Jackie's problems. The forms of critique expressed by Charlie Sheen and *Nurse Jackie* are also emerging in contemporary Canadian literature. In all cases, attempts are made to fundamentally refigure addiction beyond the framework of free will versus determinism – a limitation that locates the genesis and resolution of addiction in the individual – even if the influence of this dichotomy shapes attempts to refute it.

Despite the contradictions and limitations of Alcoholics Anonymous, it is ubiquitous in popular culture. According to Dr Bernard LeFoll at the Centre for Addiction and Mental Health in Toronto, this ubiquity has meant "it's frequently the first place people try … But if it doesn't click for them, they may give up hope of recovery."[26] It is crucial, then, to foster the production and dissemination of alternative depictions of addiction to arm those struggling with addiction with viable options and autonomy over choosing their preferred course of treatment, "such as in-patient or outpatient individual therapy, as well as group support that offers behavioural strategies, insights into addiction and relapse prevention tools."[27] Facilitating this eclectic view of treatment does not necessarily presuppose one cause of addiction. It also affords people who use drugs or alcohol the recognition that they can make their own decisions regarding their health. Finally, replacing AA in the public imaginary (and institutions, such as Correctional Services Canada) with various alternatives makes space for the development of addiction treatment that takes into consideration the social determinants of health, as well as the physical, emotional, and spiritual.

The Biomedical Disease Model of Addiction

Whether reproduced uncritically or subversively, the Alcoholics Anonymous model of addiction pervades popular culture. Rarely, however, does popular culture engage with the scientific disease model of addiction, a narrative that functions at an institutional level as well as in relation to the Twelve Steps. Like the AA theory of addiction, the biomedical model assumes the presence of an innate dependence on a substance or behaviour. The *Diagnostic and Statistical Manual of Mental Disorders* (Fourth Edition, Text Revision [DSM-IV-TR]) was the standard North American tool for defining, identifying, and treating mental disorders, including addiction, until May 2013.[28] And yet, the DSM-IV-TR does not define addiction. It defines instead "Substance Abuse" and "Substance Dependence" as broad categories, as well as "Abuse" and "Dependence" under multiple categories of specific substances.[29] Stanton Peele explains that the term addiction was replaced with abuse and dependence "in the hope of defining the syndrome more precisely and less emotionally."[30] The semantic move sought a migration from a theoretical or philosophical to an empirical diagnosis. In other words, while addiction had come to signify an assessment of moral intentionality, abuse and dependence is thought to more precisely describe measurable effects of substance use. In effect, the DSM-IV-TR classifies abuse and dependency according to individuals' frequency levels of use and/or when physiological tolerance or dependence has occurred. A crucial tipping point into dysfunction occurs when patients "[fail] to fulfill major role obligations at work, school, or home."[31] In the biomedical formulation, then, addiction is defined as a disorder of regular functioning as a result of behavioural abuse and physiological dependence.

Ostensibly, the DSM-IV's shift in terminology towards objective assessment of individual action and social effects seeks to evacuate moral judgment and assumptions of intentionality from the diagnostic criteria. It also avoids asserting a causal analysis of addiction. Leaving aside questions of whether or not the moral specter of addiction lingers in practice and whether the term "abuse" might also carry "emotional" weight, it is the manual's ahistorical and narrowly focused methodology that is particularly contentious socially and politically. In *The Birth of the Clinic*, Foucault argues that the historical and philosophical roots of clinical practice in the nineteenth century "perceived [disease] fundamentally in a space of projection without depth, of coincidence without development. There is only one plane and one moment."[32] Similarly, the DSM-IV-TR perceives substance abuse and dependence as a set of symptoms of disorder that does not overlap with social experiences like class, race, and gender; that is, the DSM-IV-TR does not recognize the development of that which it interrogates – nor its own legitimacy – as emerging within a complex of regulatory power.

While the depoliticized story of addiction told – and imposed – by the DSM-IV-TR is dangerously inadequate, it remains the standardized account. And crucially, its disease model framework carries with it historical associations between addiction and "deviance,"[33] which Caroline J. Acker argues not only create social stigma but also work to legitimize "increased intrusion into the private lives of clients and great arbitrary power to intervene in those lives."[34]

The novels discussed in chapters 2 and 4 each contend with this latter consequence of biomedical diagnostic procedures. As this study will explore at length, not only does the scientific disease model fail to account for the social determinants of health articulated in both fiction and non-fiction, but it also becomes one of those determinants informing the production and reproduction of social suffering. This is partially due to the fact that, as Valverde argues, the DSM-IV-TR "criteria tend to assume certain norms of social responsibility."[35] It may not advance a causal analysis of addiction, but through its measurement of disorder as failure to meet familial and employment obligations, the DSM-IV-TR reifies addiction as social transgression.

The Cognitive Behavioural Model of Eating Disorders

Unlike the Alcoholics Anonymous and biomedical disease models, the cognitive behavioural model (CBT) of addiction *does* consider external causal factors in the development of addiction. From an ostensibly non-judgmental stance, CBT seeks to understand the internal logics that reinforce habitual or regularized behaviours. Cognitive Behavioural Therapy combines the central tenets of behaviourism and cognitive therapies.[36] Behaviourism's theories of classical and operant conditioning, developed by Pavlov and Skinner, respectively, generally refer to "process[es] by which a previously unimportant or irrelevant stimulus becomes important or relevant."[37] Developed by Beck in 1976, cognitive therapy posits that "what is important for the individual is not the experience itself, but the meaning that the individual attaches to the experience."[38] The interactions between experience and meaning attachment processes become CBT's focus of modification for individuals with "unwanted or challenging behaviours,"[39] like binging and purging, for example. The CBT approach argues that such behaviours become reinforced, at least initially, by desired outcomes and "distorted"[40] perceptions of those experiences. This interpretive framework is the most widely used approach to treating eating disorders.

However, even though CBT recognizes eating disorders as learned behaviours, it defines such behaviours as inherently maladaptive responses. Consequently, treatment seeks to reform the anorexic to deal appropriately with overwhelming and internalized cultural pressures. While a productive tool in terms of its *application within* a systemic analysis of addiction, the cognitive behavioural model *in practice* does not incorporate a meaningful and sustained analysis of systemic factors to which people adapt. If symptomatic responses to underlying power structures are deemed 'maladaptive,' then it is implied that there is a set of behaviours that constitutes 'normal' or 'acceptable' ways of adapting to the same conditions. In other words, the maladaptive behaviours are still the focus of study and reform rather than the structures of power. As Mebbie Bell's work demonstrates, therapeutic conditions often reproduce and intensify the very power relations that lead to disordered eating, a process explored in chapter 3 through Ibi Kaslik's *Skinny* and Kevin Patterson's *Consumption*. The chapter examines how cognitive behavioural therapy fails to register causal, intersectional influences of gendered, classed, and racialized norms in ways that reinscribe patriarchal, capitalist, and colonial ideologies.

As such, CBT-based treatment places the onus of disorder on individuals, even if social factors are acknowledged. Adaptation, self-control, and coping skills are the buzzwords of the CBT approach, while systemic factors are either unquestioned, or understanding their role is assumed to be tangential to the therapeutic process. The works examined in this study configure structures of power as intimately and insidiously connected to the protagonists' suffering. Like the disease models of addiction, the CBT approach avoids in-depth analysis of the relationship between the user and her political economy.[41] Celia Kitzinger and Rachel Perkins' argue that Western psychological approaches "teach us to privatize, individualize, and pathologize our problems as women [and always serve] to obscure larger social and political issues ... [by] converting them into individual pathologies [through] an insistent focus on the personal;"[42] this is exemplified by CBT positioning transformation as a solely personal matter. A broader consequence of such depoliticization, as *Heave* and *Skinny* suggest, is that the rhetoric of maladaption proliferates within social and institutional discourse around addiction, which implicitly serves to normalize conditions of inequality. As each of the following chapters will argue, the therapeutic claim of adaptation and success through self-transformation is highly problematic and often untenable, while structural inequalities such as poverty, patriarchy, and settler colonialism remain active in people's lives.

The Cultural Studies Model of Addiction

Cultural studies of addiction are generally concerned with questioning the relationship between social structures and the user. Perhaps the two most enduringly influential cultural analyses of addiction are Jacques Derrida's "The Rhetoric of Drugs" and Felix Guattari's "Socially Significant Drugs." Their respective epistemologies of the drug user offer ideologically opposed analyses of the relationship between the addict and society. While each traces the sociopolitical context of drug addiction, they offer conflicting causal analyses, resulting in starkly different prescriptions for its eradication: Derrida advocates for the severing of addicts from society, while Guattari argues for a sociopolitical reorganization that would transform the society in which addiction arises.

Derrida asserts unequivocally that "drug use threatens the social bond" and should be prohibited on the grounds that it is both "desocializing, and contagious for the socius."[43] Positing that the user "cuts himself off from the world,"[44] Derrida cites the addict's conscious control over his acts of ingestion as justification for positioning the user outside or even antagonistic to a society comprised of citizens who manage to be "conscious, vigilant, and normal subject[s], master[s] of [their] intentions and desires."[45] Ultimately, Derrida privileges the maintenance of civil society over the inclusion of all individuals. His anxiety surrounding the systemic "restructuring and ... repoliticizing"[46] such an inclusion would require reflects his opposition to institutional reform, and this raises the question of "who qualifies as a citizen?" when belonging (or being 'socially bonded') is predicated on obedience. Despite his declared commitment to condemn any "attitude ... which, directly or indirectly, cuts off the possibility of an essentially interminable questioning, that is critical and thus transforming,"[47] Derrida exempts the 'social bond' from the reach of this questioning. While rejecting biological ideologies that seek to preserve the sacredness of the physical body, he remains resolutely committed to the sacredness of the body politic but resistant to interrogating the ideologies and practices that shore up its cohesion. These are the ideologies and practices that would potentially create and/or exacerbate the incidence of drug addiction, as suggested by the works of fiction examined in this study, as well as by critics such as Felix Guattari, Roland Chrisjohn et al., and Christopher B.R. Smith.

Guattari's theory clarifies the limitations of Derrida's stance that implies society cannot prohibit or eradicate the drug without also ostracizing the user. Guattari calls this a chemotherapeutic response to the problem of drug addiction which, in fact, creates a sociopolitical atmosphere in which the individual is forced into either "a solitude without recourse,"[48] or complete dependence on a system contingent on individual subordination. His essay begins by calling for "a new non-repressive approach, and therefore a new relation of power between the people involved and political power"[49] – a system in which the suffering of drug users is not justification for "repression and police control."[50] Clearly elevating the well-being of all individuals above protecting existing social bonds between an exclusive or delimitable group of citizens, Guattari argues that "it is only on the level of a political reconfiguration that would take social, individual, and aesthetic objectives into account that we will be able to alter the situation of drug addicts."[51]

The political possibilities implied by this analysis are exciting because the locus of the problem of addiction shifts to include socioeconomic circumstances. Yet Guattari's analysis is limited in two significant ways. First, his advocacy for changing the person through changing their situation disregards the notion that it is not merely the situation of the "drug addict" that requires attention. When causal lines are drawn between micropolitical fields and someone already labelled Addict, addiction still retains its status as a pre-existing individual disease. Guattari's theory implies that the effects of addiction may be ameliorated by a nurturing sociopolitical environment, but the category of addiction-as-disease remains intact. One must consider, though, that when connections are made among the situations of all citizens, forms of social suffering, and forms of social success, epistemological perceptions of the Addict alter fundamentally. As a result, treatment possibilities swell to contemplate the transformation of circumstances that give rise to addiction, rather than narrow to pursue the most effective methods of triage. Second, Guattari does not clarify or historically locate his terms. Although his model for understanding and 'solving' drug addiction presents a more complex interaction among the user, civil society, and drugs than that offered by Derrida, Guattari's final comments need further contextualization and testing. He argues that "it is necessary to arrive at a kind of logic, not dualistic, but triplistic, multiplistic, polyvocal, that gives both *a full responsibility* and *a full irresponsibility* to individuals, according to the micropolitical arrangement through which one considers them."[52] Perhaps constituting a call to readers to define their own micropolitical arrangements, Guattari's theory is nonetheless abstract in a way that must be demystified. Given his influential work on the subject, it is curious that he does not use the word capitalism to talk about "the situation of drug addicts." Systemic interpretations of addiction are not so evasive.

Central to the analyses developed in this book is an exploration of how each novel's representation of addiction emerges in relation to ideologies and structures of capitalism, as well as patriarchy and settler colonialism. This intersectional analysis interrogates how addiction appears within matrices of inequality and circulates as a symptom *of* inequality. Significantly, it is one of many symptoms, but not an inevitable, predetermined, or universal one. In other words, while inequality emerges as a predictor of addiction, it is by no means a socioeconomic gene. The implications of such a working hypothesis, then, inspire two investigative shifts away from the cultural analyses of addiction. First, as Jane Lilienfeld argues, instead of "focus[ing] primarily on symbolic meanings of the cultural phenomenon of addiction," literary analyses of addiction must address narratives that articulate "how alcoholics and addicts experience themselves and their needs and choices."[53] Second, the approach in this book attempts to localize and historicize narrative – and specifically, representations of addiction – in micropolitical arrangements of late capitalism in Canada.

Depicted as largely post-industrial, the economic structure of late capitalism in the novels also includes resource extraction and production (as seen in *Consumption* and *Monkey Beach* in relation to colonial practices), as well as consumer practices, media saturation, and information technology. The dialectic between the structural and ideological will be elaborated in each chapter, but the major way in which late capitalism shapes the fictional worlds of the novels is through classed and racialized social relations. For example, relations between the poor and affluent in *Heave*[54] and *lullabies for little criminals* suggest that "perceptions and self-perceptions are shaped by the social need to cloak [the class] polarities."[55] Moreover, the relative affluence of the protagonists in *Skinny* and *Consumption* draws an analysis of their anorexia as affective responses to estrangement triggered by normalized middle-class expectations. As well, the struggles of the protagonists in *Monkey Beach* and *In Search of April Raintree* are directly and indirectly shaped by the dismantling of traditional Indigenous practices, which occurred partially through residential schooling and government-corporate partnerships of resource extraction. Emotional survival for the protagonists comes to mean economic survival. I examine depictions of habitual substance use and self-harming behaviours as "needs and choices"[56] within these various settings – settings that have clear limits to socioeconomic possibility.

The Systemic Analysis Model of Addiction

A strong, though comparatively small, body of critical work on the political economy of addiction assesses the methodological limitations of many of the dominant theories examined above. Studies such as Rajeev Bhargava's *Individualism in Social Science: Forms and Limits of a Methodology* (1992), Sylvia Tesh's *Hidden Arguments: Political Ideology and Disease Prevention Policy* (1988), Kitzinger and Perkins's *Changing Our Minds: Lesbian Feminism and Psychology* (1993), and Jo-Ann Episkenew's *Taking Back our Spirits* (2009) explore the extent to which logics of capitalism, patriarchy, and settler colonialism shape psychiatric, legal, educational, and social service interventions. They go on to argue that the resultant stigmatization, pathologization, and criminalization of individuals perpetuates both self-harming behaviours and neoliberal ideologies. Roland Chrisjohn et al.'s *The Circle Game: Shadows and Substance in the Indian Residential School Experience in Canada* provides a particularly influential and explicit deconstruction of the intersections between capitalism and addiction discourse. The authors contend that the scientific methodologies employed by twentieth-century, Western biomedical studies of addiction are "driven by a pathological ideology"[57] of Methodological Individualism (MI). Positing that the first aspect of MI is the belief that "all phenomena (including drug addiction) must be accounted for in terms of what individuals think, choose, and do,"[58] Chrisjohn et al. argue that this focalized drive arises from the sense that political economies are external variables that hold no statistical significance in the study of disease. However, they insist that historical and material circumstances are "not ... variable[s]: [they are] constants."[59] The consequence of what they view as the reductionism of biomedical methodologies is that constants like colonial legacies and social, gender, and economic inequalities become distilled down to "personal, internal, and individual characteristics."[60] This leads to the assumption that the individual is the inevitable site of the problem, thereby "deflecting scrutiny away from inquiries into systemics."[61]

In other words, Chrisjohn et al. argue that, even if cognizant of causal socioeconomic factors (such as Canadian colonial and corporate capitalism in Indigenous communities), psychological investigation ultimately does not include these constants in theories of addiction or recovery because traditional scientific methods cannot measure such factors. They therefore contend that "scientific investigation" becomes "ideologically bound to develop at best an incomplete, inaccurate understanding"[62] of addiction. Such methodological limitations inevitably localize the source of addiction on the individual, leaving systemic constants underexamined and unchallenged. The authors also discuss the political and ideological expedience of the scientific method's procedural omissions. By tracing the ways in which MI is central to the "imaginary relationship of individuals to their real conditions of existence,"[63] we can understand MI as an essential tool in the naturalization of capitalism through the investigative deflection that it performs. This study hopes to contribute to existing denaturalization strategies by resisting methodological individualism that categorizes 'addiction' within the pervasive reaches of capitalism, heteropatriarchy, and settler colonialism.

Harm reduction discourse also frames drug and alcohol use within such sociopolitical contexts. It is the most prominent counter-narrative for abstinence-based approaches to addiction treatment. As Toronto social worker Sarah Prowse explains, "its attitude of acceptance and compassion really *is* radical, within the treatment world anyway, and certainly in my harm reduction therapeutic practice, and that of all the practitioners I know. The hegemonic factors leading to and supporting ongoing drug use are what we talk most about, and what we argue most about with our clients who have bought into the personal failure model wholesale."[64] Broadly defined as "a set of compassionate and pragmatic approaches for reducing harm associated with high-risk behaviors and improving quality of life"[65] for individuals, their families, and their communities, harm reduction recognizes that people will continue to use drugs and alcohol despite attempts at prevention and cessation. Not strictly limited to healthcare related fields, harm reduction policies "span various fields, including public health policy, prevention, intervention, education, peer support, and advocacy."[66] Safe injection sites, low-barrier subsidized housing, and wet shelters are each non-punitive approaches to supporting people who use drugs and alcohol to reduce the likelihood of overdose and ensure access to various social services, regardless of user status or compliance with addiction treatment.

While harm reduction seeks to reduce the immediate harms (e.g. physical, mental, emotional, financial, social) associated with drug and alcohol use on individual and community levels, it also understands and challenges the criminalization of drug use and users under conditions of prohibition. As Mark Haden notes, "the marginalizing processes of drug prohibition on drug addicts are both obvious (employment cannot be pursued from a jail cell) and subtle, as exclusionary societal attitudes can be very indirect."[67] Although none of the novels examined in this study depict harm reduction practices or philosophy, literary critics and teachers should be familiar with this systemic view of drug and alcohol use in order to flesh out the social and political consequences of abstinence-based, punitive depictions and treatment of addiction. In so doing, educators can move towards action-oriented pedagogy by identifying harm reduction as a framework within which people and institutions challenge stereotypes of people who use alcohol and drugs through changing policies, behaviours, and language that rely on these stereotypes.

By striving for conceptual clarity, I endeavour to move my analysis of addiction discourse beyond the realm of deconstruction to attend to the subversive qualities of the addiction narratives examined. From the analyses of different views of addiction above, in which addiction is either assumed to have a concrete meaning or is operationally defined with or without the acknowledgment that addiction is a concept, it is clear that definitions matter – and the definition of addiction is a contested one. Sedgwick seeks to clarify the conceptual basis of addiction attribution during late capitalism,[68] a historical moment in which the parameters of addiction have expanded to include food consumption, sex, exercise, and work. She locates the processes by which acts became identities and the identity of the Addict became a "species"[69] as occurring "under the taxonomic pressure of the ... [late nineteenth-century] medical-juridical authority ... and in the context of changing class and imperial relations."[70] Sedgwick concludes that the will is the focus of attribution. Conlin's, Kaslik's, and Robinson's novels perform cunning reshapings of the "species" named "addict" that imply a will operating in reaction to external stimuli. By unpacking the circuitry informing such reactions, I examine the specific strategies the authors use to refigure addiction as a form of social suffering instead of individualized pathology. The provocations performed by these novels are paradigm shifting. Each variously represents addiction not as willed acts in a vacuum, but rather as a complex set of behaviours, which are often contextually useful in the perceived or actual mitigation of socially inflected pain, as well as the pressures, contradictions, and injustices of living under capitalism, patriarchy, and settler colonialism.

The recognition of these structural inequalities that informs my analysis of substance use should not be confused with determinism. That is not to argue that all marginalized peoples, by virtue of experiencing inequalities, will use drugs or alcohol to cope. Rather, I am pointing out that the dominating views of addiction as pathology, as moral contamination and failure, and contradictorily, as completely within the control of the addict to defeat, is a politically expedient stereotype that shores up class, race, and gender oppression to justify the punitive and often criminalizing treatment of those who use substances to adapt, escape, or cope with their experience of such oppression. It is beyond the scope of this study and my expertise to formulate a working hypothesis about the degrees of agency associated with substance use. However, the works of fiction I examine trouble dominant stereotypes that cast addicts as incapable – and often unworthy – of articulating their experiences and needs. If I am making any argument about agency, it is that individuals should have autonomy over our means of coping and/or pleasure while minimizing harms.

The Literary Analysis Model of Addiction

Literary criticism, like several of the addiction discourses above, tends to take a methodologically individualistic approach to analysing addiction. This critical predilection has conditioned the limits of epistemological inquiry into depictions of addiction, as well as produced a specialized field in which the scope and genres of examination also appear restricted. What this work adds to these approaches is a different theoretical lens through which to examine the production, reception, and significance of literary renderings of addiction; a lens that considers how and why the Addict has become a political category of identity, and a lens that asks how addiction itself emerges within personal and social power relations. Situating this analysis of habitual behaviours in relation to matters of class, gender, and colonialism also attends to creative subversions of dominant discourses of addiction, and contemplates the methodological developments needed in literary criticism to pursue intersectional analyses and sociopolitically accountable future methods of interpretation.

In her analysis of anorexia narratives, Isabelle Meuret employs the kind of narrow methodology I seek to expand. Meuret's *Writing Size Zero: Figuring Anorexia in Contemporary World Literatures* (2007) strives to interrupt pathologizing medical, social, and cultural interpretations of anorexia by affording anorexics the power to define their own experiences. The author also argues that anorexia has become "a medical and literary hit"[71] by exploring the ways in which critical attention in these disciplines arrives from a place of fascination to the point of becoming epidemic. In this way, she figures the study of an already pathologized experience as pathology in and of itself – and significantly, one described as a marketable pathology. But it is Meuret's focus on the linguistic figuration of anorexia that is troubling. Largely "expound[ing] on the grammatology of anorexia,"[72] Meuret contends that the "signifying practices" of starving and writing are "inextricably linked to a compulsive obsession with words."[73] She provides evidence for this thesis with meticulous close readings of world literatures thematically categorized into explorations of the erotic, perfection, profanity, and famine, among others. Claiming that the book's title *Writing Size Zero* (which becomes her term for anorexic writing), "reconciles *textual* and *corporeal* practices,"[74] Meuret concludes by reframing anorexia as a writing disorder, driven by a pursuit for "harmony."[75] Meuret is attentive to textual engagements with or refusals of dominant social discourses about anorexia that articulate dissonances between experience and popular beliefs; however, she offers little insight into how such information can be mobilized to find resistance strategies against the development of anorexia or its pathologization. In addition, her methodology exerts an individualized notion of empowerment, or harmony. This lens inevitably shapes Meuret's central contention that, because "anorexics are dying for words, which they concretise in a self-engendered flesh, … the will to live overpowers the longing for death … [by] embrac[ing] a creative role."[76] The implication is that only through their isolated utterances do anorexic writers[77] (arguably) achieve authentic expression of or liberation from their suffering. And significantly, such resolution is purely symbolic. Such imaginative resolutions of textual contradictions must be contextualized socially and historically for readers, or else they "leave the real untouched."[78]

Szabados and Probert's *Writing Addiction* also exemplifies the problematic rigidity of common epistemological assumptions in its axiomatic claim that "addicts are internally compelled to do what they decide not to do, as body and desire, the biological, in opposition to reason and will, articulate the self."[79] Arising from this concept are studies interested in the metaphorical richness of addiction symptomology. Thematic doubling, for example, which is taken to symbolize a self divided against itself, has become a central trope identified and examined in addiction criticism. Other conceptual preoccupations with literary representations of addiction concern ideas of desire, consumerism, confession, and transcendence, as well as analyses of connections between addiction and writing.[80] Such metaphors for addiction are interrogated for the ontological, philosophical, and aesthetic issues raised by the physiological aspect of addiction, the causes of which are assumed to be pathological or elided in order to contemplate the effects of dependence and compulsion.

More routinely, however, literary critical work on addiction is interested in theorizing the act of writing as a form of addiction and interrogating the symptomology of addiction as comparable to creative processes. Symptomology is the key term here. The texts that attract the most persistent critical attention are those which describe the habits of the addict and the depths of depravity to which he (usually he) goes for a fix. According to William S. Burroughs, reading "sickness … often [reveals] repulsive details not for weak stomachs."[81] Burroughs' words seem a provocation to readers to toughen up, to face the truth of addiction head on, to eat vicariously the naked lunch.[82] And yet, criticism tends to treat the "repulsive details" or symptoms as de facto manifestations of creative obsession. Sue Sorenson expresses a similar criticism of the Szabados and Probert's collection, arguing that the "essayists give themselves over ... automatically to the notion that addiction and writing are analogous."[83] The critical tendency to treat addiction as a philosophical springboard deflates the harsh realities of chemical dependence and reproduces a narrowly empirical view of addiction as a compelling cluster of symptoms.

The reduction of addiction's meaning into a series of symptoms has also shaped which narratives and genres predominantly receive critical attention. The focus of literary criticism's engagement with addiction can be grouped into two broad categories: masculinist trip narratives and biography. The literary mystique of the male addict-writer genre arguably reached its fever pitch with the Beat writers and Burroughs in particular. *Naked Lunch* prompted a Marxist analysis of addiction by positing addiction as a metaphor for the capitalist economic order. Central to Burroughs' idea in *The Algebra of Need*[84] is the claim that capitalism creates dependencies, or the virus of need. Products, through repeated consumption, become necessary to consumers on physical and emotional levels. Junk, in Burroughs' estimation, is "the ultimate merchandise. No sales talk necessary. The client will crawl through a sewer and beg to buy;" as such, addicts, or "dope fiends," are figured as "sick people who cannot act other than they do."[85] Critics are persistently interested in the provocative connection Burroughs draws between habits of consumerism and habits of addiction; indeed, his insinuation that we are all addict-consumers constitutes a rather damning – if deterministic – critique of capitalism. His "basic formula"[86] of junk, however, has produced a similarly reductive or narrow consideration of addiction. For example, Allan Johnston[87] concludes that the Beat writers sought to transcend or subvert the algebra of need through transcendent trips, while simultaneously leaving unexamined (as does Burroughs) the circuitry that unites drug and fiend, and romanticizing the writer-addict for his ability to be creative in spite of his dependency. While the narrative innovations of trip narratives are fascinating, neither the narratives nor the majority of critical analyses of them seems particularly interested in interrogating the representational politics of aesthetic tropes in trip narratives. Lindsey Michael Banco's *Travel and Drugs in Twentieth-Century Literature* (2010) provides a rare departure from this trend by deconstructing the romanticization of trip narratives through interrogating connections between 'tripping' and reassertions of "neo-colonial subjectivities" and commodifications.[88]

And yet, critics have tended to neglect the "before" – or history – of the Addict in trip narratives, and instead rely on a capitalist logic of drug supply and demand. However, I would argue that is because the texts that draw literary attention are typically those that, as Allan G. Borst astutely notes, plot the "addict-subjects … mired in the daily drudgery of managing their habits."[89] My argument here, then, is that literary criticism of addiction narratives is too narrowly focused on symptoms and the trip, which assume a particular definition of the Addict. Even when trip narratives explicitly draw connections between capitalism and addiction, those connections are examined in terms of the shared symptomology of each process of consumption. In some cases, this could arise because the narratives themselves do not provoke a deeper analysis. For example, Ann Marlowe argued in her autobiography that "copping" for heroin is "not so different from centering your life around shopping or making deals. Same activity, different aesthetic."[90] This common, yet cursory metaphor seems uncritically accepted and reproduces a view of the Addict as fiend, as diseased, as compulsive; even if the user and consumer are metaphorically comparable, prevailing literary criticism does not seem interested in the mechanisms that subject the user, rather than the consumer, to stigmatization and criminalization. Perhaps this is not a compelling notion because the sample size is small: literary criticism overwhelmingly focuses on the literary works of authors who also have addictions. Criticism of works including *Fear and Loathing in Las Vegas*, *Under the Volcano*, and *Naked Lunch*, for example, are not concerned with social determinants or political consequences of addiction because Hunter S. Thompson, Malcolm Lowry, and William S. Boroughs are not primarily exploring addiction within such frameworks.

Perhaps as a continuation of this trend, literary criticism has also focused its attention heavily on the lives of writers who have struggled with addiction. Biographies of infamous addicts are popular and tend to be interested in the connections between inebriate experience and literary production. For example, Gordon Bowker's *Pursued by Furies: A Life of Malcolm Lowry* (1993) repeatedly asserts the "two tyrannies"[91] of Lowry's life were "the pen and the bottle"[92]; he also cites Earle Birney as confirming Lowry's persona as a "spree drinker and … spree writer"[93] in order to mythologize Lowry's creative process as "recklessly"[94] heroic. Robert Morrison's *The English Opium Eater: A Biography of Thomas De Quincey* (2010) is also interested in the dynamic between writing and addiction. Morrison, however, seeks to redeem De Quincey from pervasive impressions of him as simply "a famous 'addict' who happened also to be a writer".[95] Arguing that De Quincey's *Confessions of an English Opium-Eater* played an inaugural role in the genre of addiction narratives authored by addicts, who "consciously aimed [their work] at a broad commercial audience",[96] Morrison traces the scope and reach of De Quincey's literary influence from the Victorian era to the twenty-first century. Casting De Quincey's addictions as neither heroic nor indulgent, Morrison instead argues that, despite the periodic debilitating nature of De Quincey's habit, he managed to shrewdly identify and capitalize on the creative and commercial potency of writing about addiction in ways that captured the imaginations of a wide audience. While an important contribution to the literary history of addiction literature, Morrison's biography follows in a critical tradition of privileging primary works written by addicts that centrally deal with the pleasures and pains of addiction. Such works certainly "speak directly to our ongoing fascination with habit, desire, commercialism, and consumption";[97] yet, their focus on symptomology – the "during" of addiction – invites a similar critical focus, which fails to contend with the politics of representation, regardless of the author's intentions or user status.

It is significant to explore why the focus of literary addiction studies holds steady on biographies, autobiographies, and trip narratives. Within the field of Canadian literature alone, representations of addiction and eating disorders proliferate,[98] featuring both central and peripheral characters, including alcoholic parents, aunts and uncles, cousins, the burn-out older brother, anorexic and bulimic daughters, and homeless addicts. What emerges is a much more complex and diverse landscape of fictional portrayals of addiction and drug and alcohol use that demands attention to their individual and shared textual meanings, as well as how and with what effects they evoke, contest, and/or confirm broader discourses of addiction.

This study focuses on realist Canadian literature, written in the last twenty years, which features young female protagonists coming of age between 1980 and 2000. It is also attentive to peripheral characters, whose experiences offer nuances to the revisions targeted in the texts. The focus on realist fiction rather than science fiction, fantasy, experimental, or otherwise non-realist narrative allows for realism's depiction of recognizable settings, characters, and issues, and offers specific possibilities for self-reflection, social critique, and transformation. Of course, as David Creelman reminds us, "texts are not mirrors of societies. They do not simply reflect a region's concerns, and they cannot be read unproblematically as sociological documents."[99] My methodology does not treat the novels as such. Rather, I see realist fiction as both participating in the construction of "common sense"[100] and destabilizing it. Realist texts allow readers, critics, and students to "explore the various competing assumptions embedded in a text"[101] – assumptions each of us holds about individual morality, choice, free will, social responsibility, deviance, and redemption – and interrogate their logics and broader social consequences. Non-realist texts grapple with such questions of power, identity, and otherness, in part through radical defamiliarization of our recognizable world. Such an analysis is beyond the scope of this project, but it is an exciting possible area of study in relation to subversive depictions of addiction. In her development of the term "visionary fiction," for example, Walidah Imarisha points to a branch of science fiction "that has relevance towards building new, freer worlds … with the arc always bending towards justice."[102] I bend my critical and pedagogical approach towards justice by focusing on texts that feature familiar characters questioning familiar, often unchallenged, structures of power. By no means a comprehensive study, this book does seek to provoke an expanded focus and methodology in critical approaches to Canadian literatures depicting addiction through its choice of texts that share strong thematic and structural subversions of dominant views of the Addict. The contested meanings of addiction and the implications for marginalized communities, in particular, are of central critical concern.

Towards an Intersectional Analysis of Addiction

This relatively brief survey of prevalent addiction discourses leads to the central hypothesis guiding my engagements with literary representations in the chapters that follow. By unearthing how treatment plans rooted in the disease model potentially exacerbate that which they purport to cure, and interrogating the concept of addiction as a construct within capitalist, patriarchal, and settler colonial systems of power, we can trace the ways in which select contemporary depictions of addiction work to articulate and challenge the oppressive logics of those systems. Therefore, this study pursues an intersectional literary analysis of addiction. Kimberlé Crenshaw developed the intersectional approach to analysing and combatting violence against women of colour by tackling the limitations of identity-based politics that so "frequently conflates or ignores intragroup differences."[103] Consequently, as she points out, feminist and antiracist practices focus on patriarchy and white supremacy as though they are separate rather than interrelated categories of power that intersect in diverse ways in the lived experiences of women of colour. While chapters 2, 3, and 4 of this book focus on different forms of structural oppression, the analysis in each case examines how capitalism, patriarchy, and settler colonialism differently correlate to each protagonist's articulation of habitual behaviours. Conversely, the analysis also investigates how those behaviours are met with disciplinary responses that reassert multiple structures of oppression.

This intersectional analysis also understands such systemic forces as interdependent, or what Sherene Razack calls interlocking; that is, "each system of oppression relie[s] on the other to give it meaning, and that this interlocking effect [can] only be traced in historically specific ways."[104] For example, the ways in which capitalism relies on the subjugation of poor women in particular informs my analysis of depictions of addiction in chapter 2. It goes on to examine how poverty and patriarchy impacts young women intergenerationally and argues that, because of each protagonist's class status, they are particularly vulnerable to sexual violence and exploitation. Chapter 3 explores how class norms are also patriarchal, and argues that each protagonist's self-starvation expresses affective responses to intersections between immigrant and colonial experiences, middle-class aspirations, and medicalized, patriarchal surveillance. Chapter 4 analyses Canadian settler colonialism in the late 1990s as uniting with industrial capitalism to disrupt Indigenous kinship relations and appropriate Indigenous land and resources. Substance use in this section is depicted as a response to alienation from not only the means of production, but from connections of kinship and resistance that are strained or severed by colonial capitalism. This intersectional approach more broadly interrogates how each novel develops a critique of the pathology paradigm by tracing how logics and contradictions of capitalism, patriarchy, and settler colonialism produce addiction and treat addicts. By drawing together Marxist, feminist, post-colonial, anarchist, and Indigenous theories to elaborate on how these narratives refigure addiction as social suffering, my analysis traces the moral, economic, emotional, intellectual, and political dimensions of capitalism, patriarchy, and settler colonialism and their intersections with the production, definition, and treatment of addiction that occur in the novels examined.

The subversive nature of contemporary Canadian literary depictions of female protagonists who exhibit behaviours commonly labeled addictive demands intersectional critical attention that lays bare the inadequacies of the dominant models for understanding addiction and addiction narratives outlined above. While such dominant models are perhaps sufficient for other corpuses of literature, they prove unrehearsable in relation to the works examined here. The de-individualizing thrust of these narratives functions in two subversive manners, which concern empathy and blame. If social realist texts often rely on empathy for readers to identify with individual protagonists, these texts simultaneously flirt with the individualism upon which literary affect is produced, and frustrate individualized empathic responses that would seek to disentangle protagonists from the networks of intricate and intimate power relations that give rise to their social suffering. The violence of this process is foregrounded in *lullabies for little criminals* by Baby's description of being sent to the detention centre; she feels "removed from [her] natural environment" to be "studied"[105] like "one of the little fetuses in jars."[106] The simile makes visible the decontextualizing processes by which those experiencing social problems become objects of scientific study. Furthermore, such frustration of decontextualized empathy could risk crystalizing into individualized blame. However, the nuanced articulations of defiance that characterize the rhetoric of many of the protagonists serve to expand the framework of culpability. Serrie's declaration in *Heave* that "it's easier to be drunk and high in the dark than it is to be sober in the horrible truth of your own life"[107] yokes together action and circumstance in a way that provokes a process of contextualization rather than a dialectic of blame versus justification. Consequently, interpretative strategies are necessary to discern the "kind of logic, not dualistic, but triplistic, multiplistic, polyvocal, that gives both *a full responsibility* and *a full irresponsibility* to individuals."[108]

Part of the critical and social literacy that these novels condition involves an awareness of antagonisms they present to competing addiction narratives, both inter- and extra-textually. By moving beyond individualizing modes of interpretation that dissect the aesthetics and symptoms of a given protagonist's addiction, my approach contextualizes habitual behaviours in order to identify the textual representation of extra-textual sociopolitical conflicts. I will then situate the details and stakes of each text's resolution in broader social and historical contexts, steps rarely taken in literary studies of addiction. Interestingly, the parallels between Meuret's analytical method and the biographical studies of addiction examined above suggest that the prevalent literary interest in addiction is with addiction as metaphor, in ways that write over bodily, textual, and extra-textual realities. Textual details are still assessed symbolically, but as Frederic Jameson argues, "the value and character of such symbolic action are now significantly modified and enlarged."[109] By expanding the critical focus to include more than middle-class male narratives of tragic-heroic descents/flights into addiction and establishing a critical intent to ground analyses of addiction in contexts of socioeconomic, gender, and racialized relations, this study aligns with Jameson's view that "only an ultimate rewriting of these utterances in terms of their essentially polemic and subversive strategies restores them to their proper place in the dialogical system of the social classes."[110] In other words, because hegemonic discourses work to uphold ideological values of particular classes, subversive or counter-discursive utterances from various cultural and class locations must be read in dialogue with each other to discern their critiques of normalized power and potential for resistance and social transformation.

The medium of literature is particularly suited to facilitate the ideological deconstruction necessary to discern competing narratives about addiction's meaning in contemporary Canadian society. Fiction can convey a contextual view of social and economic relationships in which characters are implicated – a view often unavailable or elided through clinical interviews, for example, which are inevitably narrower in scope because of their tendency to be elicited for diagnostic purposes that already privilege a therapeutic model. These contextualizing properties of story challenge the individualistic imperatives of capitalism by making plain the historical and material contingencies that shape individuals' relationships to their world and themselves. To that end, each of the narratives examined are rife with metaphors of embodiment that express each protagonist's relationship to her body as an object. Conveyed as attempts to reanimate, numb, punish, emotionally fashion, or defiantly control the physical body, "addiction" describes a process of self-estrangement that seems an extension of Karl Marx's conception of the term, insofar as the body becomes another site of labour necessary to emotional and social survival. The novels studied in the chapters that follow suggest that habitual behaviours marked as addictive are "merely a *means* to satisfy needs external to [addictive behaviours themselves]."[111] The novels thereby yoke the logics of addictive acts to ideological logics and material circumstances that make them appear necessary.

Acknowledging the existence and interlocking grip of historical, socioeconomic forces that shape literary and social representations of addiction, as well as participating in tracking the ways fiction interrogates the role of psychiatric, legal, and medical institutions in a political economy that defines, pathologizes, criminalizes, and surveils the Addict, allows for an important critical perspective. This approach affords scholars and teachers to discern the faulty logic and ethics of locating full causal and recovery responsibility on addicted individuals, when the literature makes clear that addiction often expresses and responds to the systemic dehumanization of subjects within capitalist, patriarchal, and settler colonial contexts. As Rimstead asks, "can we not, as oppositional readers, ask what it means to be the ones pinned to the wall by these generalizations and stereotypes, and if or how these lived experiences are different from the labels which pin people down this way?"[112] The goal of this study is to listen to such experiences as they are portrayed in historicized present iterations by developing and testing a methodology that illuminates contexts within which addiction arises, challenges existing explanatory models that do not, and offers strategies for maintaining intersectional, critical awareness of the sociopolitical echoes of individual acts. This approach forms the structure of each body chapter, both in terms of its literary analysis and pedagogical proposals.

Chapter Two

Poverty, Individualism, and the Meaningful Uses of Alcohol and Drugs in Christy Ann Conlin's *Heave* and Heather O'Neill's *lullabies for little criminals*

"We injure ourselves because of injury."

– Camilla Gibb[1]

This chapter examines how two novels refigure addiction as social suffering by portraying habitual substance use as just one among several behaviours developed to adapt to the emotional, physical, and social strains of poverty and moral regulation. Christy Ann Conlin's *Heave* and Heather O'Neill's *lullabies for little criminals* stress the role that stigma plays in shaping Serrie and Baby's relationship with alcohol and heroin, respectively. Defined as a "*mark of disgrace, associated with particular circumstances, qualit[ies], pe[ople]*,"[2] stigma is depicted in each novel as both contributor to addiction and an obstacle to recovery. In a manner that mimics Margaret Atwood's literary theorization of debt as "the engine … [that] shoves the plot along, changes the mental states of the characters, and determines their scope of action,"[3] stigmatization in these novels becomes a formative aspect of subjectivity. This force produces a distressed "private climate"[4] that shapes each protagonist's assessment of her self-worth, as well as the contextualized meaning of her alcohol or drug use. Through Serrie and Baby's negotiations with the demands of individualism, the novels demonstrate the meaningful uses of their alcohol and drug use as internalized mediations of social evaluations of worth. By attending closely to storyline and narrative structure, this chapter will track the ways in which Conlin and O'Neill break from dominant social, political, and medical scripts for addiction, and thereby compel readers to account for the systemic conditions that tend to be effaced by those scripts. The close reading employed in this chapter is a necessary tool to recast the protagonists' experiences as forms of social suffering that are imbued with meaningful functionality and agency, a process which undercuts pathologizing and disease model understandings of addiction. The closing transformative pedagogy section of this chapter offers strategies for how to guide classroom investigations into how the novels portray poverty, addiction, and stigma in ways that refigure addiction as social suffering.

The novels contend with the interpersonal circulation of stigmatizing cultural and political discourses on poverty that inform the moral regulation of those deemed potentially at risk of or already failing to perform their individual functions within patriarchal capitalism. In a Canadian context, political discourse and social welfare policies demonstrate that the ideological production of stigmatizing views of the poor persist in the nation's popular culture. Addiction is rhetorically linked to poverty through the concept of dependency. A clear example of the political reinscription of poverty and addiction as pathological dependence occurred during Question Period in the Ontario legislative assembly on 4 November 2008. Finance Minister Dwight Duncan was called on by three opposition MPPs to account for the causes of Ontario's "have-not" status, as well as to defend the Liberal responses to it – both financial and moral. The Opposition immediately conflated equalization with welfare, and all Ontarians with welfare recipients. Calling Ontario's position of need and dependency "embarrassing," avoidable, contrary to the province's "rightful place in Confederation," and accusing the Liberals of "spending like drunken sailors" and "pocket[ing] the equalization handouts,"[5] the Conservatives blamed budget mismanagement and weak leadership for Ontario's 'poverty' and demanded an explanation for being transformed from "breadwinners" to "welfare recipients or whiners." The ways in which these associations stigmatize need are clear, and remarkable about the debate is the opposition's near-hysterical tone and the umbrage with which they express their anxieties. Not just morally indignant, their comments are imbued with fear and shame at the prospect of becoming the poor Other (or "poor cousin," as Newfoundland premier Danny Williams so positioned Ontario in the Canadian economy). This expression of shame only reinforces stereotypes already attached to the poor – as welfare cheats, drunks, and undeserving of assistance. The startlingly brazen articulation of these views evidently has cultural currency; spoken in public space and entered on the public record, the MPPs seem to take for granted that their audience will agree that becoming dependent on public funds demonstrates a (moral) failing.[6] By aligning behaviours of the poor as leeching from the employed and as indulging in uncontrolled and short-sighted behaviours (whether spending or drinking), the implication is that people who are poor and people who use drugs and alcohol are, at best, a nuisance, and at worst, expendable.

Literary criticism and pedagogy have the potential to interrogate the stigmatization of poverty and addiction in both the political arena and literature. As demonstrated by Conlin's and O'Neill's novels, literature can intervene to disrupt the perpetuation of symbolic violence against addicts and the poor that intimately and insidiously affects individual lives. The crucial discursive and imaginative disruptions performed by the novels discussed in this chapter occur through their ironic subversions of associations that equate poverty and addiction with personal failure. Neither Serrie nor Baby can depend on any social safety net to provide them with the necessities of life. Rather than dependent "have-nots," they are "forcibly poor,"[7] and both young girls are sexually assaulted when struggling for the means of basic survival. Within such scenes of constraint, addiction or habitual inebriation appears as an improvised mechanism of psychic survival or numbing in order to condition their bodies to withstand violent acts of exploitation.

Significantly, the various forms of rehabilitation with which Serrie and Baby come into conflict do not register the meaningful functions of their drug use. Instead, seeking to reproduce "normal, productive"[8] subjects, treatment and detention centers are represented in both novels as complicit in enforcing class, gender, and moral norms, which initially shape the emergence of each protagonist's adaptive-addictive behaviour. Such regulatory norms disappear from sight under the scrutiny of individualized treatment models of addiction. Moreover, Conlin and O'Neill's novels suggest that the disease model of addiction can become a tool of moral regulation within economic logics of capitalism. Their poverty leaves Serrie and Baby particularly vulnerable to violent institutional responses to their behaviours: each girl becomes incarcerated and must conform to criteria of morality, productivity, and health to be released. The form of incarceration each protagonist confronts can be read as a disciplinary tool of capitalism. According to Karl Marx, capitalism "does not consider [the worker] when he is not working, as a human being; but leaves such consideration to criminal law, to doctors, to religion, to the statistical tables, to politics and to the poorhouse."[9] This characterization describes the social status of those labelled 'addicts' in the novels, and as such, the logic with which these figures are institutionally treated is perhaps most accurately described as a carceral response to addiction. While Marx's formulation describes the situation of the chronically unemployed, this chapter considers those who do not have the opportunity, desire, or gender- or class-status to labour for their existence; these populations come under familial and institutional scrutiny, which identifies them as not only unproductive but a strain on public resources. Conlin and O'Neill's addiction narratives describe familial and personal situations of impoverished and working-class young women, who are barely employment age but subject to a variety of corrective methods – including physical confinement – which seek simultaneously to prepare and discipline them for working-class lives.

Each novel utilizes distinctive rhetorical and structural strategies to expose and subvert dominant narratives of addiction as ideologically necessary to the perpetuation of capitalist individualism. Conlin's *Heave* rehearses the Alcoholics Anonymous script of addiction but problematizes the legitimacy of its central claims through the use of retrospect and synecdoche. O'Neill's *lullabies for little criminals* evokes a common Western literary trope of sacrifice and addiction, which plots the female addict along a path of degradation and contamination by drugs into a state of moral insensibility. However, O'Neill rewrites the sources of infection as stigma, displacement from kinship relationships, and decontextualized interventions of social services. By foregrounding the development of Baby's "habitus" – the process Pierre Bourdieu describes as "the internalization of the structure of social space [which generates] practices adjusted to the regularities inherent in a condition"[10] – the novel exposes social services' failure to recognize the meaningful uses of Baby's habitual forms of psychic departure, whether imaginatively or chemically induced. Both protagonists periodically rail against being caught in such a bind. Yet each novel ultimately scripts the ambivalent isolation of these figures who challenge class and gender norms – the very norms through which the health and wellness of many are sacrificed to shore up the productive fictions of the governing whole.

"I'm no frigging fixer-upper": Subversions of the Alcoholics Anonymous Script in Christy Ann Conlin's *Heave*

As explored in chapter 1, methodological individualism pervades several interpretative approaches to addiction, including those of literary analysis. Early reviews of Christy Ann Conlin's *Heave* uniformly cite the protagonist's alcoholism as the central problem of the novel, and routinely ignore the narrative emphasis on how socioeconomic conditions shape the affective and interpersonal re/actions of multiple characters. Claire Rothman diagnoses Serrie as "an alcoholic" and describes the novel as "an account of her confronting this fact and growing up in the process."[11] According to Alison Calder, "Serrie's life is a series of alcoholic blackouts, leading to damaged relationships,"[12] while for W.P. Kinsella, Serrie is an "alcoholic, prone to erratic and self-destructive behaviour."[13] There is no 'before' to her alcoholism in such formulations, despite the novel's structural emphasis on reflection and historical context. Much like the Alcoholics Anonymous view of addiction, Calder and Kinsella attribute relational and emotional problems to drinking rather than considering such problems as exacerbating drinking habits. Moreover, critics repeatedly decontextualize the novel's characters and describe them according to internal traits and motivations. For example, Kinsella dubs Serrie's father Cyril as a "pleasant but weird" man, who "[gave] up employment years before."[14] This reductive comment is also inaccurate given Conlin's emphasis on Cyril's post-traumatic stress to explain his inability to work. Kinsella's review thus elides one of the most salient qualities of Conlin's rhetorical style: her use of social and historical characterization.

All figures in Conlin's world are introduced according to their economic and emotional histories, which come to symbolize individual aspects of their social realities. In this way, Conlin employs a kind of social synecdoche, through which Serrie's performance of the Alcoholics Anonymous narrative exceeds the confines of its individualizing and essentializing boundaries by articulating the historical and material roots of her identity. The text thereby refuses to artificially sever personal narrative from family and community narratives. The subsequent representation of addiction that emerges in contrast to that put forth by Alcoholics Anonymous is one of adaptation rather than sickness, of survival rather than moral abandon.

Heave's subversive elements destabilize the central tenets of the Alcoholics Anonymous program. The central tenet of its philosophy is that "the alcoholic is a very sick person."[15] As proof of faith in this truth, the Big Book offers a collection of stories from AA members meant "to show other alcoholics *precisely how [they] have recovered.*"[16] In a methodological move similar to that made by many literary critics of addiction, the 'truth' of addiction is already assumed, and so AA's narrative offerings then become blueprints or scripts to discover and confess this truth. As a form of confession, the AA member story works in the disciplinary mode described by Foucault: as practices of often coerced truth extraction, which function in the service of regulatory power. For Michel Foucault, confession is "one of the main rituals [the West relies] on for the production of truth"[17] and, significantly, one that inaugurated a "metamorphosis in literature"[18] from heroic accounts of great social and spiritual import to "a literature ordered according to the infinite task of extracting from the depths of oneself ... a truth which the very form of the confession holds out like a shimmering mirage."[19] However, *Heave* persistently frustrates the AA search for confession.

Building on Carole Cain's analysis of AA's four key narrative markers, this chapter traces the ways in which *Heave* mimics the process of AA confession. Serrie's introspective journey continually spirals out into her family and community, ending in a final refusal to internalize the truth of her suffering as 'alcoholism.' She confesses to nothing that is not qualified by circumstance. Positing that rehearsing the AA story is a process of "identity reconstitution,"[20] Cain implies that the desired identity is a penitent, perpetually striving individual, who, although still afflicted with a disease, has renounced her or his previous state of indulgence in the pleasures and pains of alcoholism, and instead humbly manages a terminal illness. *Heave* forces a schism between the forces of reconstitution and the subject of reconstitution; consequently, the identity of 'alcoholic' is revealed as a performance that must be continually shored up by narrative reinforcement, rather than expressive of an inherent illness. The logic of AA member script is rewritten as a mechanism through which adaptive behaviour is reduced to signify individual maladjustment and dis-ease, with moral, biological, and spiritual dimensions.

Conlin's novel, then, challenges liberal humanist claims of individual autonomy and equality that undergird addiction discourse in three ways: by contextualizing self-harming behaviour within scenes of socioeconomic and institutional power; by juxtaposing Serrie's narrative against imposed practices of formalized treatment, which elide the role of inequality that both informs 'addictive' behaviour and proves a substantial if not insurmountable obstacle to recovery; and by representing these treatment interventions as modes of moral regulation. In these ways, *Heave* mobilizes the structure and language of an internationally recognized recovery program to represent its underlying logic as disempowering, and its promises of recovery as erroneous.

According to Cain, the four narrative markers of the conventional AA member story are: the ritual identification of oneself as an alcoholic;[21] the reinterpretation of one's past to affirm the cause of one's problems as drinking;[22] the description of "hit[ting] bottom";[23] and the testimonial conclusion of describing one's life since finding AA.[24] Conlin's novel rehearses these signature characteristics of the AA disease narrative of addiction in ways that reveal its inability to address the scope and grip of class and gender inequalities, as well as expose the ideology and implications of the practice of its imposition. Implicitly impelled by the AA imperative, Serrie reevaluates her past; however, as she lays the AA narrative over the events of her life, a significant and unavoidable excess of experience emerges that is neither contained nor explained by the disease model of alcoholism. She grows up in thinly veiled impoverished circumstances within a community that actively ostracizes poor people through moral regulation, social surveillance, and stigmatization. These socioeconomic circumstances expose her to numerous forms of emotional and physical suffering – both personally and as empathic witness – from which drinking is refigured as just one method of escape. Thus, while Serrie attempts to plot her drinking history, she instead plots her process of developing ways to cope with socially contextualized traumas, and reciprocally, becoming subject to discipline when those ways of coping threaten her ability to remain a productive member of her community.

Beginning with the ritual identification of herself as an alcoholic in the prologue, Serrie undermines the concept of alcoholism as it is reproduced by Alcoholics Anonymous, her doctor, and her family through the details of her narrative. By juxtaposing the pathologizing terms of its deployment to the different ways Serrie describes her drinking, the narrative conveys alcoholism as one behaviour among others that have meaningful uses for survival within her particular socioeconomic context. The prologue takes place after Serrie has already been through treatment and a period of sobriety. During an imagined exchange with her deceased Grammie, Serrie exclaims, "I'm a twenty-one-year-old drunk with no job," to which Grammie responds, "*Well, now, there's plenty worse things to be ... Like a leper or a goddamn pervert or a hypocrite or a liar.*"[25] This exchange ignites Serrie's self-identification as an alcoholic, a condition tacitly placed within a constellation of diseases with moral, social, and biological dimensions. Her imaginative creation of Grammie's rejection of the narrative that Serrie attempts to rehearse is significant because it undermines the tenor of self-loathing infusing Serrie's claim, while also indicating that Serrie feels self-compassion, even if she can only project such compassion onto an imagined Other. However, the subordination of addiction to leprosy categorizes alcoholism as a physical disease, as well as anticipates the ways Serrie is treated as a social pariah. In this iteration, the first step of AA identity reconstitution is refigured as a process of claiming one's pathologized condition rather than a process of moral awakening or acceptance of disease.

However, the novel goes beyond merely drawing out the stigmatizing implications of self-identifying as an alcoholic. Her acts as a 'runaway' mirror her tendencies as an 'alcoholic.' As she literally bolts from the church in the middle of her wedding, Serrie opens her monologue by saying, "Dearie always said, 'Go tits to the wind.' And I am. Going so fast it seemed as though I was hovering above myself, watching."[26] Conceptually, this image establishes a pattern of behaviour in which drinking appears as just one manifestation of desire for escape from actual or potential suffering – in this case from her wedding to a financially and physically controlling man. Furthermore, both the act and experiential quality of escape strengthen the rhetorical connection between running and drinking: they are each characterized by detached, insensible flight – she runs so fast that the pain of the situation and the consequences of her getaway are not immediately registered. Running "so fast the burn is a memory before it's even had time to hurt [her],"[27] Serrie reflects with subtle defiance on her runaway act, which emphasizes a central quality that is explicitly present in her drinking behaviour: a willful desire to numb experiences of pain. Moreover, she does so in a distinctive way; through either running or drinking frantically, she tries to get ahead of the pain rather than linger in a state of sensibility.

Throughout the novel, Conlin depicts Serrie's drinking as a means of achieving blackout, rather than euphoric intoxication.[28] Longing for "the efficiency of blackouts,"[29] Serrie articulates the uncomplicated terms of her desire to drink after seventeen months of sobriety: "Do I know what I'm doing? Oh, yes, I sure do, no justification of how it's just going to be one drink. I don't give a sweet blessed shit anymore. Feeling this way has got to stop and I cannot wait to get wasted."[30] Expressed with a characteristic tone of defiance, the imagined conversation evokes the Alcoholics Anonymous view of the Addict as self-deluded by her own disease, expressed through promises of moderation or denial. Embracing the functional aspects of inebriation, Serrie rejects this interpretation of her actions. Instead, her drinking has meaningful uses: mainly, escape from consciously registering emotional and physical pain. While the novel's prologue clearly describes Serrie's behavioural patterns as directed towards escape and insensibility, their qualitative similarities to Serrie's drinking are not apparent until the central retrospective narrative begins. Claiming a fugitive identity before an alcoholic one, Serrie's reevaluation of her past begins with "snap[ping] back to [her] first run-away"[31] via a trip to Europe. This retrospective structure systematically traces the circuitry between Serrie's impoverished upbringing and the accumulation of strategies she learns to employ to escape the fear, anxiety, and suffering she experiences growing up. As such, a narrative trajectory is established that often jarringly juxtaposes an emotionally, historically, and economically contextualized set of behaviours against an imposed fiction of an inherently flawed alcoholic identity.

Serrie claims one other identity in addition to that of the runaway and the drunk, which evolves from several confrontations with external imperatives to suppress emotion and conform to social norms: the Stoic. Serrie's mother teaches her to dissociate from fear by "not … cry[ing] but … go[ing] to sleep so it would all go away."[32] Instilled at a young age is the sense that unconsciousness is preferable to experiencing fear induced by circumstances she cannot control. Offered not only as an escape, sleep is also figured as preferable to emotionally and physically experiencing and expressing sadness, as with crying. This imperative to reject difficult feelings is transformed into a desire to not feel at all when, as a teenager, Serrie becomes obsessed with becoming a Stoic; she strives towards attaining the ideal of "apatheia,"[33] which Robin Campbell defines as "immunity from feeling."[34] While the struggle takes the form of numbing behaviour, the motivation comes from external pressures to embody other qualities of the Stoic: "courage and endurance, self-control and self-reliance, upright conduct … and obedience to the state."[35] These ideals form a portrait of an individual willfully invested in silently withstanding hardship, in whatever form, through controlling her feelings, depending on no one, and fulfilling her obligations to society. Ironically, Serrie's idealization of the apatheic Stoic – the ideal, conforming citizen – informs her pursuit of insensibility, highlighting the ways in which societal pressures inform individual behaviours.

Significantly, it is the women in Serrie's family who persistently instruct her to be stoic in the face of hardships. As Serrie screams and cries on the first day of school, her mother insists, "You'll get used to it";[36] when Serrie experiences her first menstrual cramps, her aunt Gallie disdainfully notes, "it's not like you just got a suntan. You'll get used to it";[37] and when Serrie's father loses his job and her family is tensely and barely getting by, Grammie reasons that, "you just ha[ve] to go about your business, even if you fe[el] bad," arguing that "the Spinster's roses had outlived the Spinster, and [Serrie] had to be like the roses."[38] The events she is told she will "get used to" are presented to her as inevitable; it is her reaction that others insist can be controlled. The phrase is both an imperative and a maxim: Serrie will get used to it because there is no other option, but she will also get used to it because everyone does; it's natural. To be like the roses implies the usual gendered expectations – Serrie must be pretty, ornamental, constant, and quiet, and she must do so effortlessly, as though it were part of her nature. The simile is also ironic because roses need rich soil and space to grow, but these are not the intended or received connotations. While Serrie retorts, "I'm no plant"[39] in a brief but characteristic expression of resistance, her inability to stoically adapt to her surroundings becomes a source of shame.

Drinking, pursing apatheia, running, and working all become methods of emotional numbing and detachment in reaction to both external events and the suspicion that Serrie is flawed because she cannot adapt. If *Heave* can be read as testing the durability of the AA narrative to name and contain the sources of the problems that afflict the alcoholic, then the first convention of self-diagnosis is destabilized through the assertion of several possible and reasonable identities that may describe Serrie's experiences. Whether Serrie ultimately accepts or rejects "drunk," "runaway," or "Stoic" as sufficient labels of self-expression, the shared underlying reasons for her impulses to blackout, escape, and avoid feeling remain unaddressed. Rather, by paralleling the adaptive function of the behaviours distilled into these identities, Conlin's novel appears to suggest that so long as Serrie suppresses her emotions through means other than alcohol, she will evade censure from her family and community. Ironically, the set of escapist behaviours she develops to cope with difficult circumstances is interpreted as the willful inability to conform – *to cope properly*.

The second defining feature of the AA narrative that the novel subverts is the reinterpretation of the past through constructing a "drinking history." This phrase clearly delineates the parameters of the required self-reflection: the only pertinent evidence of alcoholism is drinking behaviour, and the identity transformation of the drinker into the alcoholic can only occur if the AA member takes account of all instances of drinking as evidence of his or her disease. This second step is predicated on the member making the "appropriate connection between alcohol and the problems it has led to."[40] Serrie's narrative reverses this formula in ways that suggest the novel constitutes an attempt to conceptually redefine alcoholism. Baker and Hacker argue that the process of conceptual clarification requires an examination of "the complex grammatical structures in which [the word 'alcoholic'] occur[s] (and those in which [it] cannot significantly occur)."[41] Conlin's narrative highlights several incongruities between iterations of the word "alcoholic" and representations of drinking behaviours by contrasting social context against identity codes. An asymmetrical pattern of representation emerges that dramatizes a disconnection between conceptual and empiricist understandings of alcoholism. When Serrie describes a traumatic incident from her past that explicitly conveys the gendered, economic, and accumulated qualities of her social suffering, it is inevitably followed by a declarative statement – by her or someone else – which inaccurately re-interprets the trauma as a consequence of her drinking. For example, from a psychiatric hospital bed, Serrie recounts an earlier drinking binge with an old acquaintance. Their encounter triggers a sense of their shared impoverished and socially excluded status in Foster. Overwhelmed by thoughts "about [her] father and [her] mother … [she] start[s] that stupid boo-hooing into the glass."[42] Her self-mocking tone denies the legitimacy of her feelings and again reinforces her drinking as a reaction to unpredictable inner turmoil rooted in a history of tangible traumas. She imagines her sadness as a "thrash[ing] … fish on the dock with the hook in its eye,"[43] evoking an emotional experience akin to being jerked out of a relatively calm state, blinded and left to die slowly. Drinking to the point of black out is depicted here as an attempt to literally put herself out of her misery.

And yet, when she wakes up in the hospital afterward, she concludes, "you knew you were a drunk and a doper, you knew that for sure after hearing Dearie fill in the details."[44] The deeply complicated social and emotional context of her drinking are whittled down to her behaviour and then transformed into an identity. While highlighting the extent to which calling herself "a drunk and a doper" fails to capture the complexity of why Serrie drinks, the scene's articulation of the self-diagnosis reinforces her internalization of pathologizing views of drinking. Significantly, the second-person address echoes the sentiments of her family and friends, as well as suggests that Serrie relates to herself as an aberrant Other when she understands her actions as an indication of her intrinsic identity. However, the mode of address also potentially situates the reader as diagnosed addict, who is privy to a drinking history that emerges as a result – rather than as the source – of social suffering. In Baker and Hacker's terms, Conlin depicts the insufficiency of the terms "drunk" and "doper" to describe the logic of alcoholism by juxtaposing the contextualized moments of inebriation against an ad hoc decontextualized diagnosis.

The doctor at the hospital also encapsulates Serrie's history within an individualizing discourse. Responding to his open-ended questions, she describes her impoverished upbringing, her father's illness, her mother's resentments and violence, her discomfort with the confines of both male and female gender expectations, and even the circumstances in which she was raped. The doctor responds by saying "*you* will need a treatment program to deal with *these issues*."[45] The diagnosis is jarring and effectively highlights the dissonance between Serrie's experience of alcoholism and its treatment. The phrase implies that the treatment will address her inability to get used to these issues – the poverty and relative powerlessness of her circumstances – rather than validate the trauma and injustice of those issues directly. Recognizing the incommensurability between her story and the doctor's reception of it, she notes that her stories appear as "facts to him, pain to me."[46] This terse equation enacts another instance of the novel's conceptual subversions by demonstrating Serrie's awareness that the medicalized meaning the doctor makes of her drinking eclipses the ways in which it has emerged as a coping mechanism for her socially inflected pain. The degree to which her behaviours are decontextualized is depicted as particularly grievous given the detailed history Serrie shares with the doctor.

In contrast with the doctor's reductive view of Serrie's drinking, Conlin produces a subversively expanded version of her drinking history. The narrative persistently contextualizes her private despair within scenes of economic- and gender-based trauma, and explicitly articulates her drinking as a method of escaping her affective responses to those traumas. Explaining that "it's easier to be drunk and high in the dark than it is to be sober in the horrible truth of your own life,"[47] Serrie implies that such "horrible truths" are ostensibly rooted in her family's history of mental illness and poverty. Perhaps the most heinous of these realities is not fully revealed until the end of the novel, when Serrie rows out to sea to get drunk alone. Before the blackout descends, she recalls being raped by the local antique dealer several times during the months before she flees to London. The disclosure could be read as the climax of a Foucauldian-confession; certainly Kinsella's review reads it as such, claiming that "only in the final pages do we learn what is really bothering her," and arguing that Conlin is ethically remiss for withholding such "vital information."[48] Positing sexual trauma as *the* reason for Serrie's "erratic and self-destructive behaviour,"[49] Kinsella seems indignant that readers might be led to believe that something other than rape could account for Serrie's behaviour. Such a reading actively elides the complex circumstances surrounding the rape that contextualize Serrie's vulnerability to economic and sexual exploitation, which must be addressed as part of the broader circuitry of her social suffering.

The linguistic and structural web of indebtedness surrounding the sexual violence constitutes the most explicit example of how poverty and intimate circuitries of moral regulation inform alcoholism in the novel. Serrie's mother tasks her daughter with quietly selling off the antiques in their attic so they can pay the bills. When Serrie drops an expensive teapot, effectively ruining the value of the set, Mr. Burgess exploits her precarious economic situation and guilt by offering full value for the pot if she will have sex with him. On six more occasions, he offers what he tells her is above market value for the rest of the pieces with "the same arrangement,"[50] attempting to turn an act of sexual assault into a financial transaction. During the relapse scene in the rowboat, Serrie recalls the moment she discovered that the Clichy paperweight Mr. Burgess bought from her for fifteen hundred dollars is actually worth close to fifteen thousand. Pointedly, the first words that come to Serrie's mind are her grandmother's admonition to "always know what you are worth."[51] Implying her internalization of responsibility for the repeated violation, these lines evoke the classed and gendered structure of Serrie's guilt. Grammie's relatively privileged class position is depicted as both a source of comfort and moral regulation in the family. Benefiting from generations of wealthy and politically connected German ancestors, Grammie was a head nurse until retirement, continues to live in a "century home,"[52] and drives a "red mini Austin."[53] As such, she is able to assist her daughters financially in raising their families on below poverty line incomes. As Serrie's mother explains to her children, "we've got nothing, not a pot to piss in, nor a window to throw it out of. If it wasn't for the charity of your grandmother, we'd be on the streets."[54]

Such charitable material support, however, also carries complicated moral demands. Conlin peppers the first half of the narrative with Grammie's maxims and warnings, several of which echo later in Serrie's imagination as reprimands. The phrase "always know what you are worth"[55] evokes an earlier scene in which Grammie repeatedly warns Serrie and her mother Martha to "lock the door"[56] when Mr. Burgess comes by. While not shaming Martha for being "hard up,"[57] she insists "the hard up can do foolish things."[58] But Grammie's understanding of being "hard up" is different than Martha and Serrie's. While Grammie seems to understand poverty as "a psychosocial space" from which to "rise above,"[59] Martha and Serrie experience it as an "everyday struggle."[60] From these different perspectives, "foolish" for Grammie implies poor judgment in light of obvious knowledge, while for Martha and Serrie, it comes to mean acts of necessity despite ostensibly obvious knowledge. "Always know what you are worth" is perhaps a statement encouraging recognition of one's value, but when Serrie hears Grammie's words very close "in [her] ear,"[61] they echo as a haunting reproof for not heeding her warning. In this context, they amount to blaming Serrie for allowing the rapes to occur because Grammie had warned her about Mr. Burgess's "patience" and "rapacity."[62] The implication here is that Serrie let herself be out-negotiated in a financial transaction even though she knew better. Serrie seems to interpret the rape as exemplifying her class-based foolishness or ignorance regarding both the worth of Clichy eggs and her own worth in comparison. In Grammie's formulation of blame, it is the exploited who must disrupt cycles of economic and sexual violence. Even though Grammie's attitude might constitute a recognition of ongoing agency within profoundly disempowering contexts, its individualizing vision of empowerment becomes the underlying source of Serrie's guilt, which she seeks to escape through drinking.

Sexual violence is not the only form of class-based trauma that Serrie experiences in the novel. Occurring in the middle of the narrative – as is typical of AA stories – is the third major characteristic of the AA personal story: the recollection of hitting bottom and finding AA. In AA discourse, rock bottom signifies the moment when the alcoholic has lost everything because of her drinking; finding AA signifies a kind of salvation that must be chosen in light of the alcoholic's recognition that her actions are the reason for her destitution. This narrative marker reinforces the view that the alcoholic can and should take responsibility for her problem behaviour. Serrie's rock bottom moment occurs when she wakes up in the psychiatric hospital without money, without protection from family, and beset by traumatic memories and shame. By this point in the narrative, her parents' economic and emotional histories have been disclosed, and the connection between drinking and escape from the pain associated with uncontrollable socioeconomic circumstances has been established. However, despite her attempts to attribute her problems to alcoholism, the narrative structure and contextual associations prevent the interpretation of Serrie's rock bottom as self-directed. Furthermore, she does not "find AA" – it finds her. Indeed, both her introduction to and experience of AA are characterized by coercion.

Intervening as a tool of social control in *Heave*, AA treatment is imposed on Serrie as a condition of relative freedom. The doctor's response to her initial refusal to participate in AA leaves little room for disagreement; he "says he will take away [her] courtyard privileges and [her] off-grounds privileges, which he is just about to give [her], and that's all for today."[63] His vaguely threatening ultimatum is compounded by his utter power over her: she literally has no choice beyond staying in the hospital indefinitely. The doors are locked, her family does not take her home, and the doctor has the authority to grant or deny her access to the outside world. Within this obliquely disciplinary atmosphere, consenting to go to AA constitutes good behaviour. Furthermore, the condition of her release from the psychiatric hospital is attending a compulsory twenty-eight day in-patient treatment program, which does not officially require attending meetings as "a formal part of treatment," although Serrie learns that "you have to go. Not going is one of the things they will kick you out for."[64] Conlin thus constructs Alcoholics Anonymous as the lone prescribed avenue for recovery in the novel, the prescription of which is disciplinarily endorsed by its institutionalization. As discussed in the introduction, the potential for the pathology model to justify "arbitrary power to intervene"[65] in the lives of those marked deviant is realized in *Heave*'s depiction of AA.

However, the representation of Weeping Willows does not constitute a full indictment of addiction treatment centres – it is here that Serrie learns to identify the sources of her anger and overcome the self-loathing that AA insists is the reason alcoholics drink. While in the facility, she refuses to participate in her friend Dearie's phoned-in, self-involved diatribes that inadvertently insult and silence Serrie. But more notably, given that the entire novel is told in retrospect, Serrie's pseudo-AA personal narrative deploys this evaluation of the roots of self-loathing to the AA experience. Like the other patients, she is told that she has a "disease about feelings"[66] – that the struggle involves coping with her feelings. While this slippage in the AA narrative allows for an understanding of feelings to precede drinking, the broader struggle is still figured as individual disease, from which there is no cure except learning to just "get used to it."

The final narrative marker of the AA personal story is the closing explanation of "what [the alcoholic's] life has been like since [she] joined AA."[67] This is perhaps the convention most explicitly engaged and subverted in *Heave*. AA membership and identity produce a variety of results, which for Serrie are mostly negative: day passes and privileges at the psychiatric hospital; policing and infantalization by her family;[68] and shame during treatment. Despite helping her to quit drinking, at least momentarily, AA does not acknowledge the scope and grip of her economic- and gender-based struggles or provide sustainable coping strategies. The pressure to financially and socially reproduce herself and her family is enormous both before and after treatment, yet these socioeconomic conditions do not disappear when Serrie gets sober. As Serrie reflects, "one day at a time, one step at a time, they say in the Foster AA meetings – the meetings that I never get to now because of my factory work."[69]

However, treatment teaches Serrie socially acceptable and economically productive ways to numb her feelings. After rehab, she works at a factory where she insists, "my life has never been so easy – if I can chop rhubarb, I can do anything. I chop alone until my hand just keeps going, so numb that it belongs to the knife now ... I am becoming a robot."[70] The image of the robot mirrors Marx's depiction of estranged labour as that which leads to "decline to a mere machine"[71] by the selling of "human identity."[72] And yet, this habitual transformation into an insentient, automatic tool of production is refigured as a positive experience precisely because of its simultaneously numbing, empowering, and desocializing consequences. "Consumed with a purpose,"[73] Serrie is "made alive for the performance of [her] functions."[74] Estrangement from her labour gives her a sense of physical mastery, but that physicality is imagined as mechanical and automatic. Only in this guise does she experience autonomy, as well as assert a futurity to her powers – she can do anything if she can work hard. Her sole employment before rehab was as a drugstore clerk, which constantly exposed her to the gaze and gossip of the community. In the comparative isolation of the factory, labour is respite from "being back in the Valley, with everybody knowing everything, every mistake [she's] ever made."[75] Serrie also welcomes the transformational qualities of methodical assembly line work with a similar tone of relief with which she welcomed and pursued blackouts. Conlin lists a sequence of activities that epitomize these functionalities for Serrie: the chopping knife, the cigarette, and running. These acts provoke a similar absence of physical and emotional sensation once they reach an intensity previously equated with the moment of blackout, when "time, as [she] know[s] it, falls away."[76] These sublimations suggest that she still strives for insensibility, while learning to omit drinking from her repertoire of numbing strategies.

Serrie also takes refuge from emotional attachment through her relationship with her boss and hotel mogul, Hans Zimmer. She explains her attraction to him: "It's not just him, it's this whole warm and renovated world I want, where things function, and hard work pays off; I want order."[77] This articulation of desire extends a central metaphor in the novel, through which Serrie's socioeconomic struggles are expressed through her family's decaying house. Over the course of the novel, parts of her childhood home are slowly sold off, the lights and hot water function only sporadically, and the front yard is peppered with Cyril's outhouse collection, drawing ridicule from the entire community. Thus, the terms of her desire for Hans reflect a determination to attain what has eluded her and her family – financial and emotional stability as compensation for their hard work, instead of cyclical unemployment and emotional disability. Marriage to Hans signifies Serrie's desire for metaphorical and literal renovation; she wants his world but also wants him to renovate her. Serrie's interest in Hans, running, and factory work are situated as a single constellation of acts informed by a desire for economic certainty and freedom from pain. Only, unlike drinking, they are not pathologized because they are deemed economically and socially productive, and are rewarded by approval from her family and a reprieve from financial burden. Essentially, AA gives her new tools to emotionally 'run-away' from economic- and gender-based oppression, while those forms of exploitation remain unacknowledged as the source of her compulsion to drink.

And yet AA also teaches Serrie to reflect on her circumstances to assess her level of self-respect. Ironically, this ability to self-assess ultimately leads to her rejection of the AA identity in two ways. First, she rejects the social stigma attached to it. Declaring, "I'm no frigging fixer-upper,"[78] Serrie insists to Hans that she is neither broken nor dilapidated, not property to be bought, sold, abandoned, or renovated to conform to dominant standards of beauty or functionality. Note, too, the connection to Grammie's doctrine to "know your worth." Unlike recalling her grandmother's words when she learns the value of the Clichy egg as accusations of her worthlessness, Serrie asserts her worth to Hans, as beyond market, social, and gendered worthiness, which have always constructed her as lacking, and justified efforts to (punitively) reform her. The declaration also recalls and rejects the basis of her initial attraction to Zimmer and "the renovated world" he initially represents for her.

Another crucial aspect of the AA identity that Serrie rejects is its gendered implications. Feminist criticism of AA takes issue with its "patriarchal culture ... and the self-effacement that is required for working AA's Twelve Steps."[79] Similarly, Conlin's portrayal of AA culture firmly situates men in positions of power over women, while positioning the recovery narrative as requiring a re-narration of the addict's life in ways that can elide significant systemic factors in his or her logic of drinking. *Heave* adds to a feminist critique of AA by creating Serrie's post-AA socioeconomic climate as an extension of AA's patriarchal culture, which ultimately requires a similar self-effacement. Hans is the patriarchal figure who does not care about her past in rehab, which initially comforts Serrie. He repeatedly validates Serrie's AA identity as a sober alcoholic who works hard; he does not judge her for her past because she has "take[n] control"[80] and built "character"[81] through AA. Hans reads her sobriety as conformity to a work ethic, yet he values the gendered nature of her work as housekeeper, as dependent employee, and as domestic partner. His acceptance of her is predicated on erasure. She does not tell him about her past traumas, and he does not want to know. Yet, when Serrie refuses to perform her role as supportive future wife, he strikes her,[82] which provokes a swift succession of decisions that lead to Serrie leaving him at the altar, constituting both the ending and beginning of the novel.

The concluding image of Serrie's emergence from the outhouse symbolizes her ultimate rejection of a moralistic, pathologizing view of her socialized adaptations. On her marriage day, within the confines of the outhouse rather than the Catholic confessional, she rejects the guilt that a confession of sins might produce, enacting instead a repudiation or exorcism of internalized beliefs in her constitutional weakness. She strips off her red bra and the remains of her antique wedding dress, rejecting the outward markers of roguishness and childish deviance, while also rejecting a symbol of restored beauty. No longer restrained by the confines of femininity – symbolized by the bra, as well as the antique dress and veil that get caught in the door – she literally goes "tits to the wind,"[83] a phrase evocative of sexual abandon or freedom, brazen vulnerability, and rebirth.[84]

Through reiteration, the AA member story is intended to culminate in a solidification of the teller's conviction that drinking is the cause of her or his problems. The unmistakable AA story structure of Serrie's recollections implies an attempt to make sense of her actions through reiterating her conversion to AA, and affirming her faith and commitment to working its recovery strategies. As Cain argues, the AA member story is a "cognitive tool" for the teller to self-identify as an alcoholic.[85] In terms of the broader narrative structure, though, we are reminded that this retelling of her life story is all in retrospect: she has accepted the AA identity in the past, but in the present of the novel, her problems have not gone away. Instead of rehearsing and reaffirming the efficacy of AA in attaining sobriety, Serrie situates the organization as an antagonist to her development during her retrospective narrative. In the present, Serrie tells her story under *uncompelled* circumstances. She recollects having gone through the process of reinterpreting her past after undergoing the AA program and maintaining over a year's sobriety – and reevaluates *that* process. Given that each AA marker in Serrie's narrative is subverted by context that exceeds the confines of the AA master narrative, self-identifying as an AA alcoholic would mean denying the legitimacy of her affective responses to the traumas of inequality.

AA intervenes in the narrative as a fully imbricated force in a political economy that both assumes a fully autonomous subject, and enforces social control and moral regulation of those who do not or cannot exercise their assumed autonomy. Indeed, one of the prevailing critiques of AA's discourse of self-help is that it assumes a generic individual experience that transcends consideration of gender, economic status, race, and age. In the preface to the second edition of the Big Book, the authors claim that "alcohol being no respecter of persons, we are an accurate cross section of America, and in distant lands, the same democratic evening-up process is going on."[86] This universalizing model of alcoholism is intended both to demonstrate that alcoholism can happen to anyone, and to empower members to believe that recovery is available to anyone who wants it. Yet, as evidenced in the final two chapters of *Heave*, there are obstacles to achieving and maintaining sobriety that are directly related to class and gender inequalities with which Serrie has not been given adequate tools to deal with in AA. These sections are particularly strained in their reiteration of the AA imperative that the alcoholic view all her problems as arising from drinking, insofar as Serrie faces stigmatization at work and home, as well as precarious employment, poverty, and sexual violence. So even as she works the AA recovery program and stops drinking, her antagonists have not disappeared.

Heave's structural and linguistic subversions of the Alcoholics Anonymous member script transform its narrative's linear, retrospective personal account into a circuitous, cumulative social narrative. Conlin's novel foregrounds and deconstructs the individualizing and pathologizing implications of each AA narrative marker by reversing the causal timeline from drinking that causes the alcoholic's problems, to the problems that lead to drinking that lead to being labeled an alcoholic. Serrie's rote self-identification as an alcoholic does not perform the required consolidation of her problems into a disease because her drinking history is preceded and continuously informed by a social history of her family and community. This history traces the ideological and material realities of poverty that shape the emotional context for Serrie's drinking, in addition to several other adaptive behaviours. Furthermore, *Heave*'s subversion of the AA script 'rock bottom moment' undermines its crucial purpose of reaffirming that the alcoholic's life had become unmanageable because of her disease. Instead, a desire to escape cumulative economic and sexual violence prompts Serrie's particularly aggressive pursuit of blackout. Leading to forced confinement, rock bottom triggers the imposition of AA, which is refigured as a disciplinary measure. The AA narrative essentially writes over Serrie's experience with moralizing maxims that cite the source of Serrie's problems both before and after treatment as characteristic of her disease. The final way in which *Heave* challenges the adequacy of the AA narrative is its juxtaposition of Serrie's life before and after AA. Released back into the same social realities, Serrie is expected to adapt appropriately to economic and gendered constraints. In this formulation, relapse would be indicative of her inability to manage her disease. Instead, Conlin's novel transforms the locus of disease from the individual to the social. Her relapse constitutes a rejection of the AA view of drinking as the alcoholic's Achilles heel, as that which will always be and cause her downfall. Consequently, the implications of the methodologically individualist AA narrative are exposed. Its presence in the novel decontextualizes Serrie's drinking and refuses to take into account – or let the alcoholic take into account – the ideological, economic, and gendered circuitries of power and moral regulation that bring together the substance and the person.

"Just a person standing there without any context": Sacrifice and the Con/textualization of Drug Use in Heather O'Neill's *lullabies for little criminals*

As with all the novels included in this study, Heather O'Neill's *lullabies for little criminals* juxtaposes competing interpretations of addiction. Unlike *Heave*, however, the biological and moral disease narratives of addiction are pushed to the periphery. While arriving periodically at the centre in ways that alter the interwoven trajectories of plot and character development, pathologizing narratives of addiction do not appear as the direct antagonists in the novel, as is the case in *Heave*, *Skinny*, and *Consumption*. Rather, O'Neill places Baby within a complex field of class and gender conflicts, in which the protagonist employs both realistic and fantastic improvisations to actually and imaginatively mitigate volatile circumstances. The narrative sequencing of displacements to which Baby is subjected is integral to contextualizing her use of drugs, as well as discerning the significance of the fantasy elements in the novel. The novel's broader view of prolonged drug use as adaptive response to social factors is produced through the discursive interaction between its realist and fantastic elements – an effect perhaps intended by O'Neill, who has stated that she "wanted to capture this non-judgmental attitude a lot of lower-class kids have to drugs."[87]

As a result, *lullabies for little criminals* challenges sociopolitical readings of addiction that decontextualize drug use as an isolatable deviant behaviour by focusing on its logic and utility in social contexts. Nancy Campbell contends that dominant approaches to drug policy, narratives, and treatment are based on "attempts to know the 'truth' of addiction,"[88] and work to locate such truth in the drug or the individual rather than attending to the particular parameters of the economic and moral fabric that brings the drug and the user together. Such myopic practices, as Campbell argues, "displace other explanations such as economic dislocation or cultural practices that deny agency and efficacy to many people in social contexts where drug use proliferates."[89] O'Neill's novel foregrounds such factors in a compellingly textured representation of urban existence in which drug use and drug-related harms proliferate. The vehicle of this narrative, though, is not instances of drug ingestion by the eleven-year-old protagonist, Baby. Rather, drug use is conveyed as just one of several imaginative measures Baby employs to emotionally and physically negotiate conditions of physical displacement, moral regulation, and stigmatization. By interpreting O'Neill's method of characterization as a process of "habitus" development,[90] the relational nature of Baby's particular survival strategies become evident. In concert with her changing environments, Baby "continuously transforms necessities into strategies, constraints into preferences ... which derive their meaning, i.e. their value, from their position in a system of oppositions and correlations."[91] This pragmatic logic shapes a spectrum of her behaviours, from mitigating social exclusion to negotiating sex for money. For example, whenever she feels "sad and insecure"[92] at school, Baby questions her father Jules about her mother, a "terrible habit"[93] that nonetheless soothes her emotionally because it makes her feel less different from the other children. And similarly, in reaction to the necessity of it "ha[ving] to be done and money was money,"[94] Baby has sex with a john and, because she "didn't really know how you were supposed to ask guys to put a condom on,"[95] she is left unprotected.

Within this framework of "economic possibilities and impossibilities,"[96] which are also shaped by her young age, Baby's drug use – like Serrie's drinking – often functions as a form of escape. However, while Serrie pursues total insensibility to pain through behaviours like (but not confined to) excessive drinking, Baby uses drugs as one strategy among many to induce self-transformation by creating gauzy, fairy tale versions of herself and her circumstances. Indeed, the severity of Baby's drug use escalates – and the fantastical elements of her highs intensify – as her experiences of displacement, disillusionment, and degradation accumulate. Domenic A. Beneventi astutely notes that, "living in a space constantly being violated by outside forces of law and lawlessness, Baby...constricts her sense of home to its smallest possible dimensions, the size of her suitcase and her imagination."[97] As it becomes harder for her to create fairy tale retellings of her home, heroin provides the most reliable insulation against registering the effects of the economic and moral climate of her world, and the means of conjuring an alternative world. O'Neill instead rewrites the tropes of recklessly abandoned addicts to construct Baby as a willful negotiator of class and gender norms. Forces that would discipline O'Neill's female protagonist in the maintenance of a working-class ethos, then, are denaturalized through the narrative's emphasis on Baby's affective responses to poverty and social service interventions seeking to either reform or punish those relegated to positions of systemic expendability.

O'Neill uses various medical and ethnographic metaphors to express ways in which social services pathologizes Baby's survival or adaptive strategies through decontextualization. "Removed from [her] natural environment and brought [to Family Services] to be studied,"[98] Baby is scrutinized as a set of behaviours, taken out of their realm of intelligibility and reinscribed as delinquent. Through this confrontation between contextualized characterization and decontextualized diagnosis, the novel refigures several habitual acts – including heroin use – as social suffering by depicting Baby's desires and behaviours as inextricably tied to her "social structure,"[99] even as they often pursue transport from it. The central motivating desire she has for interpersonal connection is both continually thwarted by forcible displacement and increasingly only subjectively achievable through communal drug use. Situated within a community of actors living out a "fictional existence,"[100] then, Baby's drug use appears as a means of maintaining a serviceable role in various ensemble fictions of adaptation to physical and psychic dislocations.

The novel opens amid a scene of relocation that establishes Baby's characteristic capriciousness. She describes moving into a one-bedroom apartment in the red-light and Hell's Angels district of Montreal with her twenty-six year old father. Yet, any grittiness is imaginatively refurbished through Baby's eyes: the image of "a girl with an oxygen mask holding a tiny baby in her arms" is "pretty graffiti,"[101] and the fake nails of a previous tenant lie in their soap dish "like petals that had fallen off a flower."[102] As she softens the rougher edges, Baby also deflates potential dangers she witnesses through fantastical dramatization. For example, the bikers are a "joy" to see as they "drive by, like a parade, on their way to blow up a restaurant."[103] Baby dresses up the details of her circumstances to achieve an effect similar to that accomplished by those in her community who dress up in Salvation Army clothes: "You could ... buy a pin-striped jacket and stick a plastic flower in the lapel, and call yourself an aristocrat – everyone was living a sort of fictional existence."[104] This fictional existence involves refiguring the necessities of urban poverty as acts of leisured class eccentricity, thereby transforming the realities of unemployment into performances of upper-class indolence.

Far from innocuous or whimsical, such role-playing serves deliberate functions for Baby. Jules's "terrible stories"[105] of his rural upbringing, which are filled with incidents of familial violence, neglect, and schoolyard poor-bashing, are to her "like Grimms' fairy tales ... The stories about Val des Loups helped [her] to feel better than other kids.

Unlike them, [she] had come from a country of great mystery and pain."[106] Casting herself as heroine in a grander adventure becomes Baby's immediate method of emotional survival. Her fictionalizing lens enables emotional survival in the face of (initially) ineffable experiences of social exclusion. The stories also constitute the foundation of her connection to Jules. By locating her experience within a fairy tale plot, however "tragic" and "creepy,"[107] Baby ensures that figures and experiences within that plot are usually conveyed as ridiculous and exciting, or affectionate and meaningful, rather than neglectful, violent, and disempowered. Paralleling the eventual triumph over adversity that characterizes fairy tales, Baby can, at least initially, envision an escape from poverty. Therefore, as drugs become a kind of lubricant to maintain her fictionalizing lens and as she self-consciously narrates her logic for using, Baby subverts tropes of female addiction in which drug use is characterized by a "loss of will."[108]

The volitional nature of Baby's fictionalizing perspective is emphasized at precisely the moments when the setting and characters within her fiction are threatened. Early in the novel, O'Neill indicates that Jules is more entrenched in his fictional existence than Baby is – or is allowed to be. Baby must continually negotiate multiple social circumstances – particularly school – that contest the shared imaginative view of the world that Baby and Jules construct. Yet, the effects of such material and moral intrusions are kept at bay in the opening chapter. Although it might seem apt that Baby and Jules call their home the Ostrich Hotel, neither of their heads is completely buried in the sand. As Baby's opening account of "life with jules" unfolds, she matter-of-factly relates numerous somber details that indicate her firm grasp on reality, the most notable of which is her revelation in knowing the truth behind Jules's insistence on calling his heroin "chocolate milk."[109]

It is at this point that drugs first begin to figure in Baby's narrative as variously symbolizing escape, community, and alienation. Jules literally pushes Baby away when he and his friends decide to get high in the middle of her twelfth birthday party. Feeling like she could "even sort of feel the sidewalk rocking under [her] feet"[110] without her founding connection with Jules, she wanders to a local kids' hangout in the housing projects. She finds other kids eating a jar of maraschino cherries because they think they're soaked in whiskey, but Baby is excluded from their make-believe because Jules told her it was "bullshit."[111] She returns home to find Jules propped up next to Lester and the now-docile Kent, high on heroin, looking like "Wynken, Blynken, and Nod:

three little boys who were tucked in together, about to sail off into the starry universe."[112] These scenes reflect Baby's early associations with drugs: using drugs seems like a game for those around her, in which the users appear joined in a kind of insular, blissful experience, but they are experiences in which Baby cannot participate. And yet, Baby is oddly comforted through interacting with these inebriated communities. She tells the kids in the park stories about her doll, Roxy, and their laughter confirms her confidence in being a "survivor"[113] via her identification with the doll. And her comparison of Jules, Lester, and Kent to Wynken, Blynken, and Nod further reflects the underlying use of Baby's reinterpretative strategies: they are harmless children with access to alternate worlds in which fishing from the stars is a legitimate and possible enterprise.

Clearly exerting a will within circumstances largely beyond her control, Baby's drug use unfolds as a conscious, functional habit. This habit can be located on a continuum of imaginative acts that constitute Baby's primary means of adaptation to the central displacements to which she is subject. By tracing Baby's cumulative reactions to repeated experiences of separation, alienation, and re-identification, her drug use can reasonably be read as functional and meaningful in terms of the senses – however illusory – of safety, community, and empowerment inebriation brings her. While Serrie desires to terminate perception completely, Baby uses both imagination and drugs to see herself and others anew. Significantly, this self is "cool and gorgeous"[114] and "heroic"[115] – an adored and powerful character in a larger fictional existence in which anything is possible. Yet, the plot of the novel is driven by the effects of poverty, the circumstances of which increase Baby's self-loathing through internalized stigmatization, separate her physically and emotionally from her father, and regulate her sexuality and class status through institutional forces. These conditions resemble what Joan Sangster calls "overlapping processes of 'private and public policing,' in which the family, the dominant culture, and medical and welfare surveillance, as well as the state, are all involved in prescribing the proper behaviour for young women … [and] the appropriate discipline if they transgress society's norms."[116] The social world of *lullabies for little criminals* dramatizes such multidirectional scenes of moral regulation of young women. The fact that Baby hovers between childhood and adolescent is a vital aspect of the plot. Like Serrie, she experiences the confines and dangers of burgeoning sexuality; unlike Serrie, Baby does not have a kindly, if stern, grandmother to tell her she is normal. She has Jules, who anxiously and violently prescribes norms of feminine behaviour and disciplines transgressions. Jules subjects Baby to social control in a manner akin to educational officials. She is female, poor, and increasingly labelled delinquent. So while subject to increasing pressure to socially reproduce themselves as autonomous and morally acceptable subjects, Baby and Jules struggle to find the "means or the capacities to discharge the responsibilities of citizenship and social reproduction."[117] Significantly, like Serrie, Baby too polices her own behaviour in attempts to be "normal." Inebriation, then – whether imaginary fantasy or drug-induced hallucinations – becomes a mechanism of self-governance.

By the time she turns thirteen, Baby experiences seven displacements, which alternate between the separation and reunion of Baby and Jules. The two become increasingly disconnected with each move, and the conditions that precipitate their moves become more intrusive and permanent, stemming from the accrued conditions of poverty and stigmatization. The second section of the novel – and the first example of the repeated narrative pattern of displacement, alienation, and reidentification – begins with their abrupt separation when Jules is hospitalized for tuberculosis. Precipitated by his precarious socioeconomic status and history of impoverishment,[118] Jules is left with little choice but to put Baby in foster care. The section serves to subvert views of drug use as self-absorbed and self-indulgent by depicting Baby's drug use as developing along a continuum of behaviours intended to establish and maintain meaningful social connections. The simultaneous separation from Jules and encounters with other children, whom she calls "losers,"[119] is devastating for Baby. She is "humiliat[ed] to have the same schedule as a bunch of strangers,"[120] a schedule which includes the intimacies of watching television, eating, and sleeping together – all activities that she shared with Jules. The forced identification with other children is complicated by her sense that she is still different from them. When she learns that Jules will be hospitalized longer than expected, she says, "I didn't know anyone whose father lived in a hospital."[121] She begins to physically mark her difference by wearing stickers on her face, stealing mascara, swearing, and committing petty vandalism.[122] Eventually, however, she becomes a "part of all [the] sad little rituals"[123] of the other foster kids. Like her, they have all developed imaginative worlds and identities. Linus Lucas, for example, fancies himself a recovering heroin addict on methadone, who has known such poverty that he always checks his drinking glass for cockroaches. Baby responds to Linus because he makes "everything exciting, like this was the place to be."[124] And indeed, it is for Baby. Her close friendships with the boys – who are much like Jules – are formed around communal strategies of reinvention and escape. These goals are accomplished not only through the relationships with the boys, but also through drug use in the absence of these relationships of reinvention.

The foster home setting also provokes Baby to confront her own stigmatization. In a rare shift of narrative focus, Baby is narrated through the eyes of social services when she overhears her foster mother tell a social worker that

> Baby is completely out of her mind … the child is wild. It's not her fault. But she'll never be normal … There was rotten food in the fridge, clothes all over the floor … You just wanted to throw out all the things that she had in her suitcase and give her a chance to start all over again … And she smelled.[125]

Stereotypes of poor people abound in this description, the negative valences of which are emphasized by the tone of the speaker. Appalled by Baby's former dirty and disordered living conditions, the foster mother also extrapolates such adjectives to describe Baby's mental and moral condition. Significantly, the woman expresses a sentiment that thematically anticipates the problematic *deus ex machina* at the end of the novel: that Baby can be saved by removing all physical markers of deprivation. Such an interpretation of Baby's circumstances eclipses her persistent desire to be with her father, which the narrative suggests is ultimately untenable both under conditions of poverty and if she is to be lifted out of them.

Their alienation from one another also occurs as a consequence of his stay in rehab. As in *Heave*, rehab in *lullabies for little criminals* is represented as a site of social isolation and moral regulation. However, O'Neill's novel is more ambivalent about the effects of rehabilitation on the addict and his family. Like Serrie, Jules finds relief in being separated from the pressures of daily life. The Doorway, where he's been sent, is "supposed to be the opposite of a heroin addict's natural environment,"[126] which for Jules involves striving to find the legitimate employment required to provide for his child despite having little market use-value. Despite his complaints of the difficulties to stay sober given that dealers sell outside the facility gate, Jules decides to extend his stay at rehab, where he is being encouraged to "reinvent" himself.[127]

Conversely, Baby experiences their meeting as an ending to their shared fictional existence. Acutely aware that they do not share a context anymore, she also reels from Jules' rejection of "the old times"[128] they shared together. Baby's realization that she is independent is not an empowering moment; instead it inaugurates a moment of existential loneliness: "Jules and I had always been best friends. When he was broke, I was broke. When you considered his situation, you also had to consider mine. I had somehow stepped out of his world."[129] By describing her ties to Jules as both financial and situational, Baby expresses her dependence on him, as well as the comfort of class solidarity they shared. The equality and solidarity that Baby experienced in her relationship with Jules provides her with a kind of protection: so long as she is in Jules's world, she remains somewhat insulated from the grittier realities of their life by the fictional existence they create together. Furthermore, with Jules she is part of a socially recognized unit, but without him, she feels like an orphan, unable to "plead for any rights because [she] didn't have any."[130] Her realization that they are no longer friends is therefore understandably hurtful and terrifying; but her skewed sense that she is the cause – that she has "stepped out" of Jules's life – suggests that she blames herself. She redirects this internalization of powerlessness into a relentless pursuit to regain his company through identification with his community.

O'Neill depicts this change in her social structure as the source of a perhaps childish but inherently logical wish to be "on drugs, too."[131] She recalls how Jules's junkie friends adored her and how they all shared in a common vision of her future as a famous and beautiful singer.[132] "Very firm in the idea that [she] would become a drug addict too now,"[133] Baby cooks up mushrooms with Felix and waits "to be anointed cool and troubled."[134] Evoking an implicitly masculine view of drug use, as the habit of rebels with or without a cause, Baby's motivation is bound up with wanting to emulate her father in order to gain access to his emotional life again. More broadly, to be elevated to the status of tortured outcast would at once induct her into a community of other misfits and validate the extent of her troubles. As well, to seek anointment also implies a view of the self as martyr, as worthy of spiritual elevation. Her first drug trip, then, is motivated by a desire to have her pain and alienation recognized both socially and spiritually.

Unexpectedly, however, Baby rejects the whole drug experience. Her hallucinations are enjoyable enough: thousands of snowflake-sized origami cranes fall and swirl softly from the ceiling,[135] but she ultimately concludes,

> everything in the world was dead and quiet and calm. You wouldn't be stunned by anything in this state ... There would be nothing horrific in life, but then again, there wouldn't be anything wonderful either. It made me nervous that I wouldn't give a damn about brushing my teeth in the morning, or remembering to put my homework in my bag ... Some people wanted to feel this way, but I didn't. This separation from feeling was Jules's remedy to life. But I was going to have to find other things to make me feel good and confident in life. I was just going to have to start being my own person.[136]

This passage is especially remarkable for its portrayal of drug use as a survival mechanism. Though she does not judge Jules's choice, she wants to remain open to joy even if it means experiencing pain. The dead, quiet calm of the high unnerves her in its unreality. She also expresses her anxiety at such complete detachment in terms that belie her sense of social obligation surrounding routine, hygiene, and commitment to education – all concerns that challenge the terms upon which she is subsequently identified and stigmatized as poor. Finally, she equates confidence and joy with the pursuit and attainment of autonomy – the very goal that she and Jules share when he returns from rehab and the practices of which separate them.

The narrative associates Jules's process of individual reinvention in rehab as the source of the "war" Baby feels Jules has declared between them.[137] In light of Beck and Beck-Gurnsheim's assertion that "most of the rights and entitlements to support by the welfare state are designed for individuals rather than for families,"[138] Jules' reinvention of himself as the burdened breadwinner makes sense. Baby becomes to him a dependent who threatens his ability to survive. Acutely aware that he will be judged by social services for her moral and financial safety, he begins to act in ways that indicate growing anxieties surrounding Baby's morality and sexuality. Jules seems to feel his responsibility to Baby more acutely, but in ways that situate her as a leeching dependent who compromises his reformed and autonomous identity: "'Fuck it all,' he said quietly [to Baby]. 'I'm going to get the classifieds and find myself a tidy one-bedroom apartment. I'll save some money without you.'"[139] This moment is made all the more traumatic for Baby because a middle-class friend from school overhears it and tells all their classmates, the social echoes of which ostracize her completely.

O'Neill constructs the subsequent scenes in which the kids at school peek at her in a bathroom stall, accuse her of seducing the music teacher, and bombard her with questions about her appearance, exposing the illogical nature of stereotypical associations between poverty, addiction, and moral degeneracy. They taunt Baby with "questions that weren't really meant to be questions, but were meant to be insults," like "how come your pants are falling off your hips?" and "how come you have a jacket that's like an adult's jacket?"[140] Pointing out physical markers of hunger, undernourishment, and dependence on second-hand clothes, the kids also call her "learning disabled … [and] a drug addict too."[141] Baby's verbatim recording and mystified responses to these associations emphasize the scope and force of the stigma she is made to endure – socially contaminated by her father's reputation, she is also seen as an addict and intellectually deficient, despite her excellent grades. Baby's tone also highlights her inability to gloss over or fictionalize the terms of her exclusion. These two scenes figure prominently in the development of her drug use.

Although Baby's social torment is somewhat escapable, her ostracization at school, and increasingly at home, establishes the emotional value that drug use will come to hold for her. Without the economic means to leave Jules even though her emotional survival becomes increasingly dependent on it, Baby responds to relationships that release her, however briefly, from Jules's financial and emotional violence. But it is towards those relationships that Jules most strenuously exerts moral regulation. When Baby begins receiving the attentions of Alphonse, Jules calls her a whore and threatens that he "should just throw [her] ass out and move into a one and a half."[142] Claiming that he "gave [her] the best of everything," he declares, "you don't get it from me!"[143] Having clearly internalized sexual and moral imperatives that are especially leveled at poor people, he relinquishes responsibility for her to protect his (however illusory) sense of social standing.

Already socially isolated, Baby is frequently left physically alone by Jules while he pursues alternative sources of income, a situation which precipitates her connection with Alphonse. With this deep disruption of her social structure, in Bourdieu's terms, Baby again "transforms necessities into strategies, constraints into preferences."[144] The necessities and constraints most felt by Baby are existential. Desiring companionship and recognition of her worth, she seeks a connection with

Alphonse that is rooted initially in feelings of empowerment through class solidarity and love, however insincere or imperfect. Regardless of the degree to which he is focused on getting her to work for him as a prostitute, she acutely responds to his imperatives to "fuck all that prisoner shit. You know what you want. Don't let anyone fuck with your soul."[145] He supports her "delinquency" as acts of resistance against the injustice she feels daily at school and home. When they drink together, she resolves to be "a heroic drinker"[146] to impress him. Significantly for Baby, Alphonse is also attractive because he is not disgusted by her sexual maturity.[147] Jules's disgust persists, however, and results in a brief but deeply influential interruption of Baby's relationship with Alphonse when Jules follows through on his threats to disown her and reports her to social services for "sleeping with a pimp."[148]

Increasingly, drugs supply the means by which she simultaneously escapes social life and dulls her senses enough to endure sex with Alphonse, and eventually her johns. While she and Alphonse do have a relationship of reinvention, pot and wine are necessary lubrication for Baby to maintain their imaginative and physical connection. So, in the grip of economic and social constraint, Baby responds to his suggestion to try heroin next with a kind of relief. Reasoning that her guardian angel would be happy with her choice, this fairy tale perspective allows her to live in an imagined narrative of benign protection, watched over by a fairy who wants her to feel no pain. And indeed, Baby feels no pain: "When I was stoned, I wasn't cold or sad. I saw things in a lovely way, where everything was brand-new and meaningless."[149] Unlike her initial mushroom trip, the meaninglessness offered by heroin is preferable to the unpredictability of experiencing happiness and suffering.

The irregularity and variability of Baby's drug use constitutes a significant subversion of dominant tropes of addiction when examined over the course of the narrative. Instead of unfolding as justification for "writ[ing] off"[150] Baby over the course of her development, the protagonist's drug use is portrayed as imbricated in a biopolitical circuitry of regulation, emphasized by her moments of reflection before ingestion. Through its depiction of drug use as aspirational, adaptive, and socially contingent, *lullabies for little criminals* affords Baby the capacity for reflection that is not undermined by her drug use. Conveyed as one of several provisional strategies of adaptation, or in Bourdieu's terms, continuous transformations of "necessities into strategies, constraints into preferences,"[151] Baby's drug use is an option rather than an inevitability – a strategy rather than a compulsion – in relation to the ideological and material constraints of her environment. And yet, while O'Neill's portrayal of a pre-pubescent girl with a heroin habit challenges stereotypical figures and explanations of addiction in popular culture, the novel's most crucial disruption of dominant tropes of addiction is its explicit critique of an institutionalized, scientific, empirical approach to treating social problems more broadly.

lullabies for little criminals consistently juxtaposes the development of Baby's habitus, or her strategies for social and emotional survival, against external and superficial interpretations of her appearance, behaviour, and class. The social worker at the first foster home and the children at school verbally paint for Baby a picture of how she appears to them – ragged, dirty, promiscuous, stupid – which articulate well-rehearsed stereotypes of the poor. However, these scenes, in concert with the Family Services intake scene, foreground the ways in which Baby's "private climate"[152] is structured to insulate herself from such judgments. These confrontations create rhetorical fissures in her consciousness that re-inform her strategies of emotional survival. Moreover, these scenes draw parallels between social forms of stigma and institutional approaches to social welfare. During the Family Services intake scene, Baby reflects, "I felt as if I were in formaldehyde, one of the little fetuses in jars … I'd been removed from my natural environment and brought here to be studied … Lots of times when children draw a person on a blank piece of paper, they don't draw any background at all, just a person standing there without any context. That was me."[153] As with each novel examined in this book, the intrusions of institutional forms of reformation situate the protagonists in interpretative vacuums, or within ahistorical narratives of deviation. Unique to O'Neill's text is her use of medicalized metaphors as social critique. Baby's interpretation of the social services gaze is both surgical and anthropological, situating her as simultaneously diseased and foreign. Considering herself a biological curiosity and social specimen, Baby instinctively knows to protect herself from their "prognosis"[154] because it cannot include an understanding of her context. O'Neill's characterization of social services' client assessment techniques as akin to simple preschool drawings emphasizes the inadequacies of decontextualizing interpretive practices by suggesting they are juvenile and inexperienced. And yet, these practices situate Baby as a subject to be studied, experimented on, and released back into her perceived natural environment – "Bobo Academy"[155] – where her new status as "a system kid"[156] requires new strategies of emotional adaptation. In this way, drug use is refigured as social suffering in O'Neill's novel.

Heave and *lullabies for criminals* develop subversions of pathologizing addiction narratives by simultaneously portraying addiction as a perfomative identity, and featuring protagonists who refuse to perform it in the ways expected by dominant social and medical scripts. The novels challenge the logic of pathologizing views of the Addict by depicting a performative dynamic between the user and her social context. Serrie and Baby's forms of habitual inebriation are constructed as adaptive responses to individualistic pressures of stigma. Each novel can be read as an evocation and critique of addiction narratives that pathologize the addict as maladaptive through their respective suggestions that addiction serves inherently logical functions within ideological and material frameworks that demand particular codes of conduct. Conlin and O'Neill also represent addiction treatment as a method of moral regulation that reinforces values associated with individualism, such as personal responsibility, "self-control and emotional stability in everyday life."[157] According to Alan Hunt, anyone can be an agent of moral regulation because "liberal models of government promote active engagement of individuals in this project rather than top-down discipline."[158] For example, long before the protagonists express addictive behaviours or encounter treatment programs, their families, teachers, and friends encourage, lecture, shame, coerce, and often model for them values of reliability, self-control, and emotional reserve. Consequently, when the protagonists' behaviours are judged as failures to exert or maintain – or refusals *to want to* exert or maintain – such values, institutional forms of regulation are imposed, while the systemic forces to which they sought to adapt or survive within remain intact.

Discovery, Resistance, and Transformative Pedagogy

Heave and *lullabies for little criminals* could appear on various Canadian literature syllabi. They could be studied as poverty narratives, fiction featuring adolescent girls, contemporary urban and rural fiction, father and daughter fiction, English writing in Quebec (*lullabies*), or Atlantic Canadian fiction (*Heave*). Whatever the focus when teaching these novels, students will identify Serrie's drinking and Baby's heroin use as factors affecting plot and characterization. The question for educators is how we can recognize when students introduce potentially charged topics "not to critique them but to reaffirm their opinions about them …

[through] appeal[s] to common sense."[159] While this section explores strategies for teaching the novels as addiction narratives, it is also useful for instructors who seek ways to transform generalizing student comments about addiction and addicts into productive interrogations of familiar literary tropes, as well as address how unexamined beliefs affect reading practices and civic engagement. Conlin and O'Neill's novels may trouble the pathology paradigm of addiction, but students will not necessarily be willing or critically equipped to discuss how or with what significance they do so, let alone how to apply such critiques outside the classroom. This section will consider strategies for breaking down, or undoing, common sense views of addiction. It will also consider ways in which to mobilize student perceptions of the novels' social critiques embedded beyond the classroom, thus moving from a critical to transformative pedagogy.

Reading addiction in order to undo it – to defamiliarize and deessentialize it – is to evaluate constantly what we think we know about it by detecting discursive patterns, differences, and contradictions, as well as listening to how various texts refigure its causes, effects, and social meaning. Towards these ends, before moving into direct literary analysis, teachers could start with a discovery exercise designed to externalize student impressions of addiction into a forum for collective, critical interpretation. This activity asks each student and the teacher to write a poem or a list following a prompt that begins with "Addiction is."[160] It can be as long or as short as there are responses to the prompt. As students read aloud sections from their poems, the teacher records on the board keywords and phrases. They then facilitate a class discussion that questions where such depictions or impressions emerge from, what causal definitions of addiction they imply, and how such depictions might affect the lived reality of people using substances habitually. These responses can be arranged in four columns on the board.

The notion that there is one truth of addiction is destabilized by the visual representation of multiple perceived truths together. Yet, the point should be clearly made that the exercise is not meant to demonstrate the relativity or absence of truth, but rather to investigate how stories about addiction are generated, and to spark critical assessment of those stories, their dissemination, and their social impact. If student responses to the poem are recorded on the left side of the board, the immediate column to the right could indicate, in the students' words, from where the idea may have come. For example, if the phrase is "Addiction is sickness," the student might cite news programs as supporting this claim.

Various visual media will likely be listed in the second column, as well as school, doctors, books, music, and personal experience. Central to the teacher's role should be asking how the stories compete, contradict, and/or complement each other, teasing out how students understand the personal and social consequences of each view of addiction, and providing critical language and frameworks within which to pursue these questions. The discourse analysis in chapter 1 of this study is useful background for the educator in this regard. While no one view of addiction cited on the board is privileged over another, teachers should ask which are more commonly circulated or given authority in our culture. This opening discovery exercise seeks to establish literature and literary analysis as important contributors to collectively building a critical understanding of addiction. When asked to analyse how *Heave* and *lullabies* each depict addiction, students will have several images of addiction to use as comparative reference points. After the exercise, teachers could collect the poems, repeat the exercise at the end of the course, and assign a short written reflection about how the two pieces compare. The essay would illuminate whether or not readings, class discussion, and experiences outside the classroom may have provoked any change in the student's perspective and why.

This discovery process, of course, is not without its perils. Inviting students to speak their truths about addiction will mean they bring experience into the classroom, in terms of their individual struggles with addictions or through relationships with family or friends with addictions. The issues this raises are threefold (at least). One, while teachers are not psychologists, the fact that students will be triggered[161] or activated by classroom discussion is unavoidable and must be thought through as such. To discourage disclosure is, as Krista Ratcliffe argues, to "deny the realities of students' lives, the realities that they will write into their reading and writing assignments whether teachers ask them to or not."[162] Other common approaches to supporting students' emotional engagement with course content include clearly listing campus and community resources for mental health and addiction supports on the syllabi, as well as alerting students that the course material and discussions will directly engage with addiction and its consequences. Nevertheless, no easy formula exists for compartmentalizing emotional responses in the classroom. Most universities offer workshops and training for teachers regarding supporting students with mental health issues; while essential training, fewer resources exist for educators to develop skills to negotiate emotionally charged discussion in the classroom that is not necessarily a matter of mental health, but rather inevitable reactions to difficult material. This challenge should continue to be addressed in teaching and learning development centers as a crucial aspect of assisting teachers in pursuing active, critical pedagogy.

A second way in which students' personal experiences can impact critical approaches to teaching addiction narratives concerns inter-student dynamics. Most teachers have witnessed students rolling their eyes or otherwise discrediting or dismissing anecdotal or personal responses to class material. Even if anti-oppressive principles or shared values have been established in the classroom, the tension between reason and emotion can play out in ways that tacitly silence students who try to make sense of material by telling personal stories. Moreover, in making themselves vulnerable through sharing their stories of addiction, students risk judgment, pity, or outright hostility from classmates. Sherene Razack offers important interventions in these power dynamics that are applicable here. She identifies the stories of marginalized peoples – and in this context, addiction and addicts are labels and identities that marginalize people – as essential to social change because they articulate "experience[s] of the world that [are] not admitted into dominant knowledge paradigms."[163] Yet, because these stories often entail tellers talking across differences from their listeners, students and teachers must explicitly discuss how storytelling can lead to oppression for the teller, and call on students to acknowledge that "we work from the basis that we all have only partial knowledge, and that we come from different subject positions."[164] As chapter 4 will explore, employing Peggy McIntosh's influential approach to identifying privilege[165] is a powerful discovery exercise, which would establish a reference point for educators when reminding students of the influence of positionality. One immediate method I have used to validate student experience as valued knowledge is to model active listening. After thanking the student for sharing, I rephrase the students comments to confirm I heard accurately and then pull a strand from the story that raises crucial questions for the class to consider in our ongoing investigation into depictions of addiction, indicating that we may have missed this opportunity without their contribution.

Democratizing the Authority of Experience

When students bring their emotions and personal stories to bear on literary analysis, the challenges can be complicated and require vigilant facilitation by teachers to ensure such responses are not undervalued.

However, teachers must also be aware of when articulations of personal experience in the classroom become overemphasized and deployed to silence any critical interrogation of addiction. A crucial aspect of responding to student disclosures is to never deny the effects of addiction. It is a given that addiction can have destructive effects. As many educators have encountered, students can be resistant to contextualizing issues perceived to be personal failings that have detrimental social effects because they worry their participation in such discussions will excuse the problem. However, when experience is leveraged as the absolute truth, educators need tools to balance validation and sustained analysis. bell hooks traces the dynamic web of power and oppression that constructs such claims to an "authority of experience."[166] For marginalized students whose voices "have been neither heard nor welcomed,"[167] hooks points out that asserting experiential knowledge can function as perceived empowerment or a "survival strategy."[168] Conversely, for more privileged students, articulations of experience as irrefutable truth express ways of seeing the world from positions of privilege that have never been challenged, and reassert the primacy of those positions.[169]

When facilitating class discussions about how Jules's stay in rehab affects Baby in *lullabies for little criminals*, I observed these competing assertions of experiential authority. A student who identified as Indigenous characterized rehabilitation as "another form of jail" that broke up her family; another student insisted that rehabilitation is the only option for addicts, citing the fact that a private facility in Southern Ontario helped his brother. Both students refused to analyse O'Neill's depiction of treatment because their respective claims to truth made such analysis moot in their eyes. At the time, I did not have the language to frame this dynamic. I strove to validate each student's response while also transforming their claims into questions for the class to consider in relation to the text. By immediately remarking that both students raise the issue of how our experiences affect our interpretations of the novel, I asked the class why they thought that might be the case. It was not a smooth transition, but attention was refocused on the scene when Baby visits Jules in rehab.

I continue to question how I could have handled irrefutable claims to experience differently; I worry my reframing dismissed each student's experience, thereby also communicating to the rest of the class that personal insight is inappropriate in the classroom. hooks' work on the classroom politics of experience have been instructive. She reasons that "if experience is already invoked in the classroom as a way of knowing that coexists in a nonhierarchical way with other ways of knowing, then it lessens the possibility that it can be used to silence."[170] Her approach to establishing such epistemological equality to circumvent the assertion of essentialist, racialized knowledge could be adapted to literary analysis of addiction. Similar to hooks' invitation for students to write an autobiographical statement about an early racial memory, teachers could assign students (and themselves) to write a paragraph about a moment that shaped their understanding of addiction. This exercise validates personal experience as a legitimate aspect of critical inquiry – though just one aspect that everyone can lay provisional claim to, but not at the expense of learning from others or critically and collectively approaching depictions of addiction.

Contextualizing Choice

Undoing addiction in the classroom means problematizing notions of agency. On this front, teachers will encounter resistance to analysing addiction, perhaps more forcefully than or in concert with claims to experiential authority. Even if students provisionally accept that problems are not solely a matter of individual pathology or choice, they often deduce that the only other interpretation of addiction is to accept social context as *the* determining factor. Inevitably and understandably, they want to talk about choice and where to locate agency. Central to facilitating this inquiry is recognizing that students want to think of themselves as autonomous, free, and empowered. Naming oppressive structures and their intimate effects on personal agency can be emotionally threatening, as well as intellectually challenging. A problem-based pedagogical approach foregrounds this resistance by asking students to reflect on their reactions to texts that suggest choice is compromised by external variables. Yet, when choice is examined specifically in relation to addiction, the act deemed addictive is the narrow focus of inspection. As a colleague exclaimed in reaction to *Heave*, "Okay, okay, Serrie's oppressed. She can still choose not to drink."

One strategy I have found particularly effective in widening the circle of inquiry around the literary addict is to divide the classroom into two groups; one builds a case for how a text depicts addiction by applying the notion of individualism, and the other of contextualized choice. For reference, a PowerPoint slide provides definitions for individualism – the perspective that "all phenomena (including drug addiction) must be accounted for in terms of what individuals think, choose, and do"[171] – and contextualized choice – the perspective that behaviours are "improvisation[s] within scene[s] of constraint."[172] I redeploy Butler's theory of performativity as describing choice; a useful alternative if teachers are not convinced of performativity's applicability to addiction is Razack's assertion that "a mesh of material relations surrounds our capacity to be autonomous."[173] Students then present their findings to the class. During discussion, the teacher asks further questions that draw out the distinction between the two analytical lenses, including "What aspects of Serrie's experience are omitted or highlighted?," "What perspective do various characters seem more aligned with?," "Does Serrie's gender, age, and/or class status shape her relationship with alcohol?," and "Does the novel suggest Serrie could have chosen to act in ways that would have made her situation better?"

While this group work is problem-posing and dialogic in practice, it may not be the most effective way to pursue analyses of addiction as social suffering if students seem particularly resistant to analysing choice and socially contextualizing addiction. The three suggestions that follow are more creative approaches to prompting students to identify and question individualism as a lens through which to read narrative. First, journaling can provoke the kind of private, reflective space and slower pace that is often necessary for self-reflexive analysis. Paired with an incremental reading assignment, journaling also leaves a written record of analytical development. For example, consider assigning students to read only fifty pages of O'Neill's novel per week, after which they must reflect in writing on how setting and plot interact with Baby's characterization. Unencumbered by the knowledge that Baby will start using heroin during their sixth week of reading, students may pay closer attention to the novel's depiction of poverty, choice, and Baby's emotional and imaginative world. The last written stage of the assignment is a reflection on how O'Neill depicts the logic of Baby's heroin use. The formal and thematic elements of the text strongly suggest that *lullabies for little criminals* constitutes an important systemic critique, which is achieved through focalizing the story through the eyes of a subject who is particularly vulnerable to the constraints imposed by external forces.

Creative intervention can also be employed to prompt students to isolate and problematize choice as a guiding analytical framework. Such an assignment could require students to rewrite sections of *Heave* or *lullabies for little criminals* which they identify as moments of choice for Serrie and Baby, according to what students perceive to be preferable alternatives to each protagonist's behaviour. The only assignment guideline is that the plots cannot be altered in any way. They are prompted to consider whether their creative interventions value certain ways of coping over others. By putting students in the position to rewrite individual behaviours, they will have to interrogate how much agency is possible when circumstances are beyond Baby's control, the nature of Baby's needs, and how she could otherwise fulfil them.

In addition to engaging student resistance to the challenges posed by subversive depictions of addiction, teachers can also implement action-oriented strategies designed to encourage students to move their knowledge into the world, to reevaluate and intervene in mainstream depictions addiction, and seek out counternarratives. One example of this type of assignment is asking students to initiate conversations with friends or family about stereotypes of alcoholism and reflect on these conversations in a course journal. Such reflections might include thinking about the differences between using the term 'addict' or 'alcoholic' and using the term 'people who use drugs or alcohol'; noting tensions, questions, and feelings that arise for them during and after such conversations; and questioning whether the nature vs. nurture debate is a helpful framework within which to discuss drug and alcohol use. Other sample assignments could have students design a reading list for a directed readings course on alternative to DSM and AA analysis of addiction; interview a harm reduction worker; or keep a record of depictions of drug and alcohol use in popular culture, and submit a final essay that compares and contrasts these portrayals to one of the novels studied in the course.

Whether or not students conclude that addiction is not a mark of individual weakness or pathology, these pedagogical approaches provoke students to question their assumptions about choice, reevaluate their understanding of how systemic factors shape individual lives, and encourage social action. The novels feature protagonists whose agency resides in their refusal to play out the accepted script that casts them as diseased and degraded. Serrie's reevaluation of the AA member script constitutes a denial of its fundamental construction of the addict as penitent, while Baby's persistent contextualizations of her drug use as psychically freeing disrupt notions of the female addict as morally compromised or contaminated. Underlying both socially and institutionally endorsed views of the Addict is the requirement that they are fully responsible for the disease. But notions of pathology and personal responsibility are challenged by each text's refiguring of addictive behaviours as adaptive negotiations of uncontrollable conditions of poverty. Given Sedgwick's and Valverde's analyses of the social construction of addiction as a disease of the will, one value being asserted through such dominant addiction discourse is self-control, or a healthy will. Because the logic of Serrie and Baby's habitual substance use cannot be disentangled from their socioeconomic contexts, their expressions of will cannot be disentangled from the demands of those contexts. By reframing the limits of responsibility as emotional survival, Conlin and O'Neill characterize and challenge the fundamental logic of pathologizing treatment models as an expectation that the Addict simultaneously transcend the grip of her socioeconomic contexts and admit her failure to do so in the past.

Chapter Three

Anorexia and the Production of Economically Oriented Subjects in Ibi Kaslik's *Skinny* and Kevin Patterson's *Consumption*

"The imprint left on her mind by the long famished body that had seemed in the darkness to consist of nothing but sharp crags and angles, the memory of its painfully defined almost skeletal ribcage, a pattern of ridges like a washboard, was fading as rapidly as any other transient impression on a soft surface."

– Margaret Atwood[1]

Countering the view of anorexia as the "rich, spoiled, white girl's disease,"[2] Ibi Kaslik's *Skinny* and Kevin Patterson's *Consumption* refigure anorexia as social suffering by portraying the protagonists' physical wasting as the mitigation of desires that are incommensurate with the productive logics, or ideologies, of patriarchal capitalism and colonialism, respectively. *Skinny*'s discursive domain is characterized by individualism, while *Consumption*'s is distinguished by tropes of consumption. Emerging from these narratives is a critique of the embodied consequences of economic subject formation within specifically capitalist and settler colonial contexts. By reading Giselle (*Skinny*) and Marie (*Consumption*) as "economically oriented subjects,"[3] I incorporate analyses of capitalism into the ways Judith Butler's theory of gender performativity has been deployed to undo pathologizing, stereotypical views of anorexia.

Neither Giselle nor Marie 'does' her class, culture, or gender alone; she is "always 'doing' with or for another, even if the other is only imaginary."[4] Kaslik and Patterson depict historicized, familial relationships as instrumental in their protagonists' relationship to their bodies. In *Skinny*, social success is framed in terms of persistent, reiterative striving towards individual achievement, which must also be paternalistically sanctioned. Giselle's mode of self-fashioning develops in response to the demands of this economy; her anorexia is depicted as an attempt to suppress her hunger for emotional and physical intimacy – a hunger that she perceives as incommensurate with fulfilling her parents' class and gender expectations. As such, the logic of Giselle's anorexia echoes the logic of individualism developed in the novel. In *Consumption*, however, social belonging is portrayed as either participation in or rejection of consumer, colonial capitalism. Marie's mode of self-fashioning is passive; her body literally wastes within an economy that demands she find satisfaction through individual consumer practices rather than interdependent kinship relations. Anorexia is refigured as not so much a rejection but a symptom of frustrated human hunger for intimacy and authenticity that is either a threat to success within or foreclosed by conditions of patriarchal and colonial capitalism. As with other novels in this study, treatment is depicted as an antagonistic force that misunderstands and pathologizes the contextual meaning of the protagonists' behaviours. The terms of treatment rhetorically echo the ideological influences that originally shape the women's actions. In these ways, the novels examined in this chapter refigure anorexia as a condition of social suffering rather than individual pathology.

Skinny and *Consumption* share similar literary strategies in their development of this critique. Both authors situate their protagonists as inheritors of generational legacies of pressures to conform or adapt to ideological conditions of class advancement and consumption. In other words, each novel evokes history as what Louis Althusser and Étienne Balibar call the "absent cause"[5] of each protagonist's malaise. Giselle's parents are Hungarian, immigrating to Canada under duress, while Marie's mother is Inuk, and her father is a white settler in Rankin Inlet, Nunavut. The politicized histories of both Giselle's and Marie's parents are represented as part of the "complex organization of the whole"[6] story of their anorexia. Ultimately, history in each novel is presented as that which "refuses desire and sets inexorable limits to individual as well as collective praxis."[7] Each protagonist's father signifies a history that shapes his daughter's emotional desires; each daughter's attachment to her father is depicted as a barrier to forging connections with others. In addition, both authors employ narrative juxtaposition to foreground and parallel the ways in which different subjectivities negotiate shared socioeconomic rationalities. While the internal logic of each protagonist's anorexia is portrayed as one among several ways of adapting to the ideological framework depicted in each novel, it is the anorexic, like the addict, who becomes a target of discipline, whose suffering is deemed irresponsible and maladaptive. This section will also examine how the representation of inpatient treatment in each novel is conveyed as reproducing the conditions of causality in both novels, which ultimately situates treatment as a disciplinary technology that defines and demands appropriate forms of social adaptation and reproduction.

Consequently, Kaslik's and Patterson's novels challenge pathologizing logics of contemporary explanatory and treatment models for anorexia nervosa, as well as expand feminist analyses of anorexia as primarily a dis-ease of cultural consumption. In its earliest uses, the term anorexia meant simply a "want of appetite,"[8] which could arise from any number of causes. With the addition of the qualifier "nervosa," it has become a mental illness. According to the *Diagnostic and Statistical Manual of Mental Disorders*, Fourth Edition, Text Revision (*DSM-IV-TR*),[9] anorexia nervosa signifies a volitional attempt to lose weight provoked by intense fear that one is or will become overweight, "even though underweight."[10] This shift in medical terminology reflects a shift in locus of control from possible external influences to psychological pathology, echoing the methodologically individualistic pressures of clinical diagnostics discussed in chapter 1. Such treatment models for anorexia nervosa are developed in response to essentialized descriptions of the illness. Even when the thinness ideal[11] is recognized as a precipitating factor, anorexic responses to the ideal are categorized as extreme, exceptional, and irrational. Therefore, when cognitive behaviour therapy (CBT) treatment models are applied to anorexic patients, causal influences of gender, class, and colonialism are downplayed or ignored in ways that cannot only limit the efficacy of treatment, but also reinscribe patriarchal, capitalist, and colonial power. These anomalous representations of anorexia provoke a deeper class analysis of eating disorders, as well as expose the ways in which treatment models assume the stereotyped version of the anorexic.

Skinny and *Consumption* also trouble a pervasive stereotype of anorexics as white, heterosexual females, from privileged circumstances, with perfectionist tendencies and overbearing mothers. Susan Bordo argues that such typecasting has simultaneously produced the erroneous view of anorexia as a "'bizarre' disease" borne of "dysfunctional family dynamics,"[12] and eclipsed the fact that "many young college women, of all races and ethnicities"[13] are restricting, bingeing, purging, and otherwise exhibiting problematic and self-harming practices in relation to food, exercise, and body image. By isolating anorexia as a rare disease typical of affluent young girls, "clinicians failed to see how normative [anorexic] behaviour had become."[14] The two novels make compelling corrections to this distorted view of anorexia. Giselle is a twenty-two-year-old queer daughter of recent Hungarian immigrants. Marie is an Inuk-English-Scottish teenager living in Rankin Inlet, Nunavut. Also, aligned with Kaslik's plan to make Giselle "sexed up,"[15] the character expresses her sexuality actively and without shame, which undercuts a myth of the fearful, sexless anorexic woman who attempts to avoid sexual maturity. Most remarkable, however, are the ways in which Marie's and Giselle's starvation is narrated as means to emotional ends rather than an active striving for thinness or fear of becoming fat.[16] The young women in the novels do indeed share a "want of appetite"[17] for food, but the authors juxtapose each woman's literal anorexia against her hunger for intimate connections that she perceives as impossible within her particular social economy. In Sue Saltmarsh's terms, anorexia in each novel is portrayed as an economic subjectivity, a rescripting that produces a critique of the naturalized economic rationalities which each woman negotiates through food restriction and in reaction to which each woman eventually chooses suicide.

Skinny and *Consumption* also incite expansions of feminist, race, class, and queer analyses of the stereotyped profile of anorexia. Such critiques occur on three interrelated political fronts – causal, methodological, and preventative[18] – and have collectivized and politicized the meaning of eating disorders. Causal explanations have moved away from individual pathology and family dynamics to articulate the influence of media, class, race, and patriarchy. However, a persistent assumption underlying these arguments is that eating disorders arise from the consumption of images or representations of body types encoded with hegemonic gender, class, and race ideals. The basic narrative of these representational theories centers around issues of consumption and reiteration: the subject consumes and internalizes normative images of femininity, judges her body against such images, and engages in repetitive practices of body modification to achieve the attributes of normative personhood, which are established as demarcating certain bodies and attributes as less than human. The various ways theorists narrate this process produce different views of the anorexic: she is either an unwitting, pathological, or biologically vulnerable subject, an active protester against feminine norms through the performance of hyperbolic femininity, or a symbol of failed rebellion. Susan Bordo famously refers to the "awesome power of cultural imagery" as "the empire of images," in which "there are no protective borders"[19] to prevent consumption. Feminism's account of this empire builds on Naomi Wolf's claim that "*the beauty myth is always actually prescribing behaviour and not appearance,*"[20] which insists that popular Western images of women are imbued with values that idealize behaviours that shore up patriarchal power. Women's cultural consumption of these values through media informs behaviours that feminist theorists read as hyperbolic reiterations of normative ideals that expose the impossibility of the norm being achieved. Susie Orbach articulates this bind as akin to a positive feedback loop, in which the media simultaneously creates the problematic aspects of female bodies and provides the solutions. By depicting bodies as "sites for (re)construction and improvement,"[21] Bordo argues that advertisers "leave us with the sense that our bodies' capacities are limited only by our purse and determination."[22] Thus, the viewer becomes caught up in this cycle of failure, striving, and consumption.

However, there is more to the story of consumer capitalism than the consumption of products and images; in fact, in neither novel do media representations of thinness or beauty figure at all. In addition to their subversions of medicalized anorexia narratives, *Skinny* and *Consumption* also complicate a premise underlying dominant feminist, class, and race analyses of anorexia, which implies that feminine ideals are internalized through cultural consumption. In this model, self-starvation is situated as a method of affective adaptation to material and ideological realities. By exploring these dimensions of consumer capitalism, Kaslik and Patterson betray the problematics of reading anorexia as either an intrinsic pathology or primarily a disease of cultural consumption. My analysis proceeds from a definition of consumption that expands on extant corporeal feminist theory. In the Marxist sense, consumption shapes all identities within capitalist economies. Its processes shape relations between people and with the self. In this tradition, Sue Saltmarsh "consider[s] consumption as a constitutive process, in which one's participation in consumer culture is imbued with meanings about who one is and might become."[23] Similarly, I argue that the anorexia of the protagonists is shaped by their perceptions of the means, limits, and future of belonging within discursive fields thematically characterized by individualism and consumption. The novels therefore refigure disordered eating as an attempt to regulate desires seen to impede social acceptance or success (*Skinny*), or emotional needs perceived as impossible to fulfil within social conditions defined by consumption and individualism (*Consumption*). I read Giselle and Marie as "actively and continually shaped as consuming" – and individualized – "subjects of the global marketplace, often at the expense of more meaningful forms of social relations."[24] *Skinny* and *Consumption* ultimately suggest that an analysis of the material and ideological conditions of capitalism and colonialism, as well as patriarchy, must be part of explanatory models of disordered eating.

'This hunger is DNA you cannot undo': Anorexia and the Influences of Social and Biological Individualism in Ibi Kaslik's *Skinny*

Skinny begins with Giselle's release from an inpatient treatment program for anorexia into the care of her widowed mother and fourteen-year-old sister, Holly. Interspersed among her attempts to resume 'normal' functioning, Giselle recounts significant events that led to her hospitalization, including the emotional and physical expectations of her father, the surveillance by her mother, and the demands of first-year medical school, during which time she stops eating and sleeping until she eventually collapses. Structurally, the novel is similar to *Heave*, in that the protagonist tells her story of descent into self-destruction after her release from a treatment facility, a trajectory that contextualizes Giselle's anorexic behaviours, plots those details against an imposed biomedical treatment narrative, and foregrounds obstacles to recovery that echo the pressures that contributed to her anorexia. These are precisely the aspects of the novel that produce challenges to spectacularizing and pathologizing portrayals of anorexia. The trope of inheritance in the novel situates Giselle's behaviours as coherent within a historical continuum that has naturalized through the paternal enforcement of ideals of patriarchal individualism.

Kaslik's narrative alternates between the perspectives of Giselle and Holly, which has a twofold effect. First, this juxtaposition of viewpoints invites a necessary and useful critical engagement with the ways in which capitalist individualism and patriarchal medical authority differently intersect with each sister's practices of self-formation. Informed by Mebbie Bell's analysis of panoptic femininity and Paula Saukko's critique of normative femininity, my reading of *Skinny* describes how the novel represents Giselle and Holly as subject to such regulatory pressures, to which each sister adapts through physical and emotional discipline. Second, the alternating points of view produce a contrast between Holly's opinion of Giselle as a tragically flawed, morally weak woman who cannot (but should) rise to the demands of adult self-sufficiency against Giselle's first-person account of striving for pristine emotional autonomy. In effect, Holly becomes an active participant in the disciplinary circuitry surrounding Giselle. Finally, I argue that Giselle's resistance to reformation, in the end, is conveyed as an internalization of biological and moral pathology, factors that become part of the reason she views reformation as an unsustainable option within the available versions of personhood pressed upon her.

The first way in which the novel refigures anorexia as social suffering is by situating Giselle's family history as a proximate cause of what are essentially Giselle's "technologies of … self."[25] Her father Thomas, and mother Vesla, are Hungarian immigrants, who, before their escape to Canada, were having an affair while her mother was engaged to an influential Communist leader, Misha. Thomas's social position as a Hungarian immigrant, as well as his uncertain status as Giselle's biological father, profoundly shape his expectations and treatment of his family, and Giselle in particular. The short passage called "The Story of Your Flight,"[26] which Giselle has ostensibly compiled from Thomas's personal papers, expresses his political reasons for leaving Hungary. Believing that the social fallout of the Soviet intervention in the 1917 Bolshevik-led October Revolution is little understood among Canadians, "he will try to explain that success, in medicine, in academics, in any field, was reserved only for those with Communist connections, with money, or those willing to become good Communists."[27] Giselle imagines that, after emigration to Canada, Thomas commits wholeheartedly to the ideals of capitalism and its promises of social and economic mobility for those who work hard enough. However, these ideals of individual striving and class mobility also influence his treatment of his daughters and, in particular, they are portrayed as directly shaping Giselle's relationship with desire, food, and her body.

This legacy is explicitly tied to Giselle's analysis of why she began starving herself. Early in the novel, she reflects on how her parents' political history is tied to her sense of embodiment:

> I'd inherited Thomas's mind. I couldn't squander that. But I'd inherited something else too: their suffering, which has brought me to this place. Born between these worlds that waged war on my ragged little teenage body … I conceded only to working hard at school and bringing home good grades.[28]

Ironically, working hard becomes both a scholastic and physical endeavour for Giselle, as she prepares her body and emotions for the demands of her career and her parents' expectations of success. Imagining her parents' expectations that she succeed in Canada as an assault on her body establishes a corporeal metaphor that is sustained throughout the novel. Viewing herself as genetically obligated to live up to her father's intellectual capacities, she rebels against their gendered expectations that she take "extracurricular lessons" and dress in "expensive feminine clothes,"[29] and agrees only to focus on scholastic success. This battle is what Giselle perceives as bringing her "to this place," in which the deterioration of her body is an inevitable price to pay for academic success[30] – which echoes one of the fields in which Thomas believes personal talent should lead to advancement. The language of inheritance through which Giselle describes her relationship to her father also reinforces the ways in which the narrative situates Giselle's suffering as a generational condition. However, it is not actual genetic imprinting that determines behaviour in the novel but the strength of each character's belief in biological determinism.

For example, the ambiguity surrounding Giselle's paternity is revealed very late in the text, which highlights Thomas's investment in biological lineage. The revelation also causes Giselle to reinterpret persistent memories of Thomas's treatment of her as explanation for how she has come to associate her physicality with her sense of worth. She recalls "black cords ... on [her] and a soft white noise fill[ing] [her] nose like ginger ale."[31] Her father subjected her to multiple EEGs to try to find out if Giselle was epileptic; because Misha was also epileptic, a positive test result would lead Thomas to conclude that Giselle is not his biological daughter. Either outcome is symbolically significant. For Thomas to claim Giselle as his 'own,' even if she is not genetically related, is to accept into his family a reminder of his communist past. To claim Giselle as genetically related to him implies a patriarchal relationship of ownership between them. Consequently, Thomas's anxiety surrounding this directly informs Giselle's sense of identity: in one of her few attempts to explain how she became anorexic, Giselle claims, "he started the whole mess with those icy-blue eyes that kept me begging for my right to exist."[32] Referring to her anorexia as the "mess," she understands her condition as a kind of reiterative begging and seeking of approval, as well as striving towards a state of being that "needs no one."[33] Echoing the sense of indebtedness she feels to both her parents for their "suffering"[34] to bring her to Canada, Giselle interprets

Thomas's behaviour as an appraisal of her worth, and worries that she may not prove constitutionally capable of fulfilling his expectations.

The anxious relationship between Thomas's expectations and Giselle's anorexia is further emphasized by his reactions to her attempts to please him. The scene in which a twelve-year-old Giselle informs Thomas that Holly is unexpectedly performing above average at school conveys the long-term impact of his surveillance and discipline on Giselle's process of self-formation. Haunted by Thomas's disappointed sobbing after four-year-old Holly is diagnosed with hearing loss and a learning disability, Giselle helps Holly learn to read a year ahead of her peers. After proudly announcing the news to Thomas, she recalls how "his eyes examine my oily preteen moon face … He fixes his eyes on my thick calves … Then he does something awful. He reaches out and squeezes my thick leg, pinching the fat next to the knee."[35] Registering that Thomas values physiological perfection, Giselle expects "compliments on [her] patience and dedication"[36] for helping Holly overcome physical limitations and for proving that she can be the agent of such mastery. Instead, she is punished and degraded: for indirectly challenging his medical and patriarchal authority by exclaiming, "the doctor was wrong"[37] about Holly, for having pride in her accomplishment, and for expecting recognition for helping his favourite daughter. By belittling her actions with a punitive physical act, Thomas initiates a complex association for Giselle between her physicality and her emotional desire.

This recollected scene provides crucial context to Giselle's central description of how she equates her physical body with her emotional aspirations. Earlier in the narrative, Giselle reasons:

> I had let too much go: I was too tall, too awkward, my belly was too bloated, my arms too thick. It got so I couldn't harness my own growing appetite for their desire, but I could make my stomach flat, I could starve myself until I felt my flat hipbones protrude and I could place my thumbs into the indents at the top of my narrow pelvis. I learned to control my desire for people, for food. And this is how I discovered a new intimacy which required no one.[38]

Here, in effect, Giselle reenacts Thomas's evaluative measures of physical excess, which comes to signify a threatening excess of desire and ambition – a desire that leaves her open not only to punishment but an emotional dependence on others for validation. She learns to control her sexual and emotional appetites through controlling her body, and measures her success by measuring the contours of her body. Furthermore, she frames desire as need, not choice. By equating people and food as desires that must be controlled, the novel constructs the human body as innately social, as well as hungry, but also compelled to negotiate a social realm that only allows for a certain type of expression and fulfilment of those appetites. The trope of control[39] that runs through eating disorder discourse is thus refigured in *Skinny* as self-regulation intended to adapt to social pressures that demand a suppression of emotion. Deborah Tolman and Elizabeth Debold theorize that anorexia develops in response to dominant cultural representations of beautiful passive women, like Snow White, that convey the message that "the desirable woman is the woman with no desire."[40] According to them, the regimented and willful practices of muting sexual appetite signify the pursuit of no-body, for disembodiment, for liberation from negotiating sexual economies. *Skinny* complicates this theory: Giselle's pursuit of a no-body is indeed predicated on muting desire, but it is a desire for people, or connection. She is not reacting to threatening moralized sexual imperatives; rather, the desire that she represses is intolerable because it is incommensurate with the kind of self-reliance that is both necessary to social survival and modelled and enforced by the individualism of her father.

Skinny's fictional world thus emerges as what Mebbie Bell might call a "sociocultural panoptic[on],"[41] within which Giselle internalizes and responds to capitalist-inflected patriarchal and biological imperatives to attain self-reliance, professional success, and social and familial belonging. Such pressures produce one central conflict for Giselle: her desire for emotional intimacy and love threatens – and indeed seems incommensurate with – accomplishing those goals. This conflict expresses itself physically through attempts to form a desireless, self-contained body. Feeling disemboweled by the unrequited love she feels for her father, Giselle envisions that "the nerves and guts have seemingly been packed away, sewn in and cleaned up so as not to make all the innocent bystanders uncomfortable."[42] Externalizing her body as "the" rather than "my," Giselle imagines her internal organs as representing an excess that must be concealed so that it does not tax others; yet, the unpredictability of "nerves and guts" as traditionally masculine metonyms for bravery and rebellion suggests that Giselle's need for others is only "seemingly" contained by attempts to starve it away. Such emotional surgery eventually leads to her hospitalization and ultimate death. Bell argues that patriarchal regimes collude with medical practice to punitively reform anorexics to reproductively and behaviourally appropriate standards of femininity. Diagnosis, in Bell's model, is refigured as assessment of failed or rogue femininity, upon which the anorexic is then "drawn into the Panopticon of inpatient medical treatment ... [and] becomes patient/prisoner of [patriarchal] medicine's panoptic force."[43] Giselle is a patient/prisoner *before* she enters treatment: under the appraising and punitive gaze of her father, who is also a doctor, Giselle both strives to achieve the standards of femininity he imposes and rebelliously attempts to emulate the striving individualism he models as a means of survival and asserting her "right to exist."[44]

The second way in which *Skinny* refigures anorexia as social suffering is by employing narrative juxtaposition. Through alternating points of view from within the same discursive field, Kaslik foregrounds Holly and Giselle's respective practices of self-formation in the context of their father's paternalistic expectations for their individual success. Characterized by self-regulation of desire, the regulation of bodily proportions through restriction and purging is Giselle's way of seeking autonomy and self-reliance. Saukko posits that such striving is culturally enforced and shapes even feminist discourses on eating disorder treatment: "The ideal end state is imagined in terms of attaining the bounded, autonomous, masculine self, independent from the influences of tradition, family members, consumer culture and constraining gender roles."[45] Achieving this state of selfhood is complicated: the self must strive for autonomy but not appear to be exerting any effort. Giselle sees this self as necessary to her emotional survival and social success; indeed, she sees both qualities embodied in Holly and envies her "utter detachment,"[46] "swaggering ease and immortal confidence,"[47] and automatic skill.[48]

Significantly, this ideal is not particularized to the anorexic woman in the novel, as Holly also seeks to deaden her bodily responses to chaotic external conditions. As she explains, "I have to knock my head against the wall ... I need to jump fences, throw myself off the edge of this spinning core. Sometimes I land so hard my head stops making its noise."[49] Expressing the same compulsion to regulate feeling as her sister, Holly similarly seeks control through what could be read as acts of physical self-harm. Moreover, as a competitive track and field athlete, Holly strives for a particular type of physical self-formation that gives her a sense of pride and superiority over others by treating her body as a means to an end: "There was still a lot of work to do on my body ... and

I would continue to do it, despite the constant ache in my knees and back."[50] However, the sisters' conceptually comparable acts of self-regulation are different for two reasons: first, the body types that emerge from the respective practices of self-formation are differently valued within the sociocultural panopticon; and second, the sociocultural panopticon works punitively to regulate the older sister, while protectively supporting the younger. Because the end result of anorexia might be death, the differential treatment might seem necessary; however, the point here is to examine the constitutive trajectories of behaviours similar in their intent, rather than only to focus on speculated consequences of those behaviours.

Both sisters' technologies of self can be read as self-destructive. Without presuming that any joy Holly derives from physical pain is inherently dysfunctional or immoral, the narrative parallels each sister's desire for an embodied autonomy as underlying their respective bodily practices in ways that foreground the relative degree of their acceptability. Unless Holly's actions impede her ability to play sports, she will not be subject to pathologization because of the social value of her athleticism, while Giselle's attempts to fashion her body to meet social demands trigger disciplinary responses. While Giselle's body is marked as diseased, Holly's is elevated for its strident autonomy. The novel indeed problematizes the "thinness" ideal that still characterizes much of the eating disorder theory; however, *Skinny* also exposes how the athletic female body is emblematic of female autonomy defined and controlled in patriarchal terms. In this way, the novel also suggests that there is a privilege attached to even being given access to the athletic realm. Both Giselle's and Holly's success are framed as contingent upon patriarchal support.

The differential protection and regulation of each sister is signified by the haunting presences in the novel. Both sisters are visited by apparitions: Giselle sees an ever-emaciated version of herself, who berates her when she eats and taunts her with 'reminders' that no one will love her if she is anything but skinny. In contrast, Holly is visited by the ghost of her dead father, usually during moments when she needs his moral support. She imagines that he appears during a track meet and that he anxiously wonders if she hears his cheering. His presence ultimately reinforces Holly's sense that she is entitled to such support. As she reflects, "*I had called him and he had come*."[51] And yet, she recognizes that she cannot "want him too much"[52] or he will not return again. Even though she is his favourite, Holly, like Giselle, learns that too much desire is undesirable. Patriarchal support here is figured as contingent on adoration without expectation. However, Holly's ghost is relatively protective, in comparison to Giselle's tormenting companion.

Giselle's ghost is an externalization of her belief that survival is utterly contingent on the relentless surveillance and control of her appetites. Indeed, the ghost is there to catch her in moments of 'weakness' and keep her on track. After a binge, Giselle reasons that she is entitled to be like other people, to "eat and work and love. That's what they do, that's what I do."[53] Recognizing that her pursuit of self-reliance has taken her beyond even autonomously belonging to the mundane world of meals, work, and family, Giselle tries to reclaim the right to exist, but this time from her self. But the ghost replies, "*not us, we are stripped clean of want, we move like lean lions.*"[54] Ironically, through her desire for self-reliance, Giselle is no longer an "I" but a "we," eternally attached to a murderous other, whose reproofs hyperbolically echo her parents' demands of emotional control. "*You'll clean that up and starve that away, young lady,*"[55] the creature warns, after Giselle "gorge[s]"[56] and attempts to purge. Reinforcing the narrative's construction of starvation signifying emotional control, Giselle's creature also polices her physicality by reminding her of the strength skinniness is meant to embody. The creature is pared down to bone and sinew; it does not desire like a human but stalks like a lion and carries no excess weight that could threaten survival. The image also seems to imply that only a kind of entitled consumption, a hunger that demonstrates prowess rather than need, is permissible. Like Holly, Giselle has internalized their father's interdiction to strictly regulate desire and attain physical and emotional self-reliance. While their ghosts do not resemble one another in form or tone, they each embody the specific way in which a paternal and classed authority has shaped their respective processes of self-formation.

Tolman and Debold speak to the question of patriarchal influence and protection in their analyses of eating disorders. They argue that a woman will "try to live within her impossible confines, because she holds the power to attract men's desire and to garner the protection of a man in a sexually violent world."[57] They also point out that "the illusion of protection by one man is absurd, given … the fact that the perpetrators of this violence are frequently the very men who are supposed to provide this 'protection.'"[58] While Tolman and Debold focus exclusively on the sexual politics of starving oneself, we can see how a broader understanding of protection, as well as the double jeopardy of that protection, works through the ways in which Giselle and Holly are differently affected.

Protection, in *Skinny,* is an economic and social process, as well as physical and sexual. Holly receives relatively more protection and support in all these areas, while Giselle is left vulnerable. The mirroring of the sisters' experiences emphasizes the implications of Giselle's lack of protection: like her sister, she seeks to excel within a highly competitive field characterized by self-discipline, perfectionism, and individual achievement. Thomas is essentially the gatekeeper to the medical field for Giselle. His refusal to let her touch his medical bag,[59] coupled with his consistent derogation of her efforts to impress him, signifies his power – but refusal – to facilitate her success. In contrast, Holly's success is framed as contingent upon patriarchal support, which she experiences as protection by her (male) coach and her father. The necessity of their support is emphasized by Holly's confrontation with her principal, who takes issue with what he perceives as her un-feminine self-confidence. Asking if she think she "need[s] a different set of rules" because she think she's "so special,"[60] the principal threatens that those who assume they are exceptional "die in car crashes, in drug overdoses."[61] His threat seems to equate Holly's ambition with a reckless form of adolescent masculinity, which offends the principal and provokes simultaneously a disciplinary and protective response to provide "guidance"[62] in the absence of Holly's father. Although Holly's coach intervenes to legitimize her ambition and autonomy, the principal's objection to her "swaggering ease and immortal confidence"[63] indicates that she – like Giselle – must negotiate paternalistic views of acceptable expressions of female success. The sisters' respective abilities to do so profoundly inform their processes of self-formation.

While Holly experiences her body as a site of curiosity, openness, and strength that is *hers*, Giselle experiences her body as a constant threat to her autonomy and as a feral animal – somehow not human, or mutatively so. As her practices of regulating desire lead to emaciation and incapacitation, she is admitted to the hospital for anorexia, and, like Serrie from *Heave*, is treated according to a disciplinary logic that fails to address the conditions that got her there in the first place. Furthermore, from her socially admired position, Holly ends up becoming an agent of disciplinary control over Giselle, and part of the social circuitry that blames, infantilizes, and pathologizes her. As Bell points out, the release of the patient/prisoner is merely a "transition from the medical Panopticon to sociocultural panopticism."[64] Elements of the classic

Panopticon evident in the inpatient setting are also reproduced socially, including: omnipotent and invisible surveillance; standards of conformity whose details are kept hidden from the patient/prisoner; and the use of "disciplinary agents" who are both "the gazer[s] and gazed on."[65] The doctor, in Bell's theory, is the ultimate patriarchal authority, who works through primarily female nurses who "advocate for normative femininity."[66] *Skinny*'s treatment and recovery narrative aligns with Bell's analysis, while also complicating it in one crucial way.

Holly and her mother can be read as the advocates or disciplinary agents described by Bell. Significantly, their judgment constitutes one of the obstacles to Giselle's recovery because they reinforce the same normative and individualistic imperatives that initially created her dis-ease. Indeed, Giselle's post-treatment experience of disciplinary panopticism is more confining once she has been marked as anorexic. Released into her family's care under the condition that she continue her apparent commitment to "heal herself,"[67] Giselle is greeted by both her mother and Holly with thinly veiled blame and resentment. Her mother tells her, "your father and I came to this country so you could eat, so you could have choices. And look at you now, you look like a prisoner. You have to promise me you're going to eat with us and be good."[68] In a direct expression of the ideological tension at the heart of the text's immigration narrative, Vesla's words frame Giselle's behaviour as a conscious and unfathomable betrayal of her parents' efforts to secure their children's survival and freedom. Vesla's moralistic language also implies that the autonomous subject has a responsibility to the group to be self-reliant and productive, but this (obligatory) flow of care only works one way. Care of the individual by society, as Bell and the novel suggest, is reformatory. The unequal reciprocity of this social relationship is rendered blatant through her mother's reaction to Giselle's continued weight loss: "You promised me this bullshit was over ... I'm putting you back in the clinic if you continue to lose weight ... Do adults have to be badgered to eat properly? ... [or] constantly monitored?"[69] Implying that Giselle's restrictive eating habits are akin to throwing a childish tantrum, her mother wields the threat of confinement as a form of 'time out' for bad behaviour, which reinforces the portrayal of treatment as a site of behavioural modification.

In addition to such moralizing pathologization of anorexia, Giselle also faces Holly's complicated mixture of anger, pity, and biologically-inflected infantilization. The novel allows us into Holly's process of interpretation: after Giselle is hospitalized and Holly "hear[s] it was a sickness,"[70] Holly turns to pop psychology books entitled *The Perfectionists' Daughter* and *The Girl Who Thought She Had No Stomach*[71] for clarification. Not surprisingly, she comes away with the 'knowledge' that anorexia is a pathological behaviour caused by a biologically based cognitive disease whose symptoms include perfectionism and false-perception. Holly then refines this knowledge according to her interactions with Giselle to conclude that, while she is "sick…mentally"[72] and a "madwoman,"[73] Giselle is ultimately exploiting her sickness to act "crazy"[74] and like a "baby."[75] The implication is that, even if 'legitimately' sick, Giselle has the choice to indulge in her sickness or attempt to reform. Holly's diagnostic process therefore parallels at an interpersonal level the social consequences of the stereotypical anorexic described by Bordo. From the books Holly consults follows a process of isolation and moral regulation, which figure anorexia as pathological willfulness or psychological disease.

Moreover, Holly and her mother seem to be operating under a version of what Saukko describes as the time-based expectations of recovery from eating disorder, in which "the anorexic is defined as having 'false consciousness,' projecting a development from this state of falsehood towards genuine health and/or emancipation."[76] Through their admonitions, Holly and her mother attempt to convince Giselle that she is not thinking right and until she does, she will not act right. And "right," as Giselle understands it, means more than just working hard; it means eating her "mom's carefully prepared food," participating in "the extracurricular lessons she expected [her] to take," and wearing "the expensive feminine clothes she wanted [her] to wear."[77] It also means keeping up appearances – participating fully in the fiction that one should be athletically competent and aesthetically pleasing in ways that shore up binary gender norms, a myth which is often at odds with the pressures to eat sustaining meals. "Right" means performing these acts as proof that she is conforming to normative femininity. As she attempts to recover – which, for her doctors and family, means that she will eat right and gain weight – she attends group meetings, volunteers at the hospital, attends all of Holly's various sporting events, and begins to date an old high school acquaintance. She strives to fulfil female gendered roles that emphasize nurturing, heterosexual romance, and familial responsibilities.

In these ways, *Skinny* works to expose sociocultural factors that contribute to the development of eating disorders, as well as to undermine dominant and pathologizing explanations for anorexia that ignore their own complicity in upholding those sociocultural conditions. The ending of the novel works to further destabilize portrayals of the anorexic as pathologically ill by foregrounding how the anorexic comes to internalize such biologically deterministic views. The medical directives throughout the narrative enact a major influence on the way in which Giselle understands herself as inherently diseased, morally weak, and pathologically needy. Most importantly, despite her reflections on the socially meaningful nature of her practices of self-formation, Giselle ultimately experiences her anorexia as a constitutional weakness. The externalized version of all her internalized normative imperatives becomes, as she says, "my hungry, doubting companion. She's always with me, like a jealous streak, a trick knee, a weak stomach, a bad heart, this hunger is DNA you cannot undo."[78] While she understands hunger as innately human, she equates it with a sickness or social and biological impediment to self-reliance: "jealous" implies need for another; "trick," "weak," and "bad" body parts signify weakness that could require help. Also, the contradictory diction is evocative here – she understands her dis-ease as genetically determined, but the context in which her eating patterns unfold only emphasizes Giselle's misunderstanding of her physical manifestations of social suffering. So in addition to plotting the sociocultural obstacles to recovery, Giselle's narration of the final days of her life suggests that the internalization of capitalist and gender imperatives, as well as views of anorexia as a pathological emotional and cognitive state, coerce an internal logic that, in effect, carries biomedical discourse on anorexia to a logical conclusion.

Skinny contests stereotypical accounts of anorexia that cast anorexics as bizarrely fixated on attaining the thinness ideal, or as directing perfectionist tendencies inward in reaction to uncontrollable external circumstances. While both of these commonly held notions presuppose the involvement of societal factors as the cause of anorexia, the anorexic is still disproportionately identified as the locus of the problem. The novel's troping of genetic and political inheritance, as well as its parallel narratives, construct a portrait of anorexia that tips the axis of causality away from the anorexic towards historical and socioeconomic contexts. Lending support to feminist arguments that "cultural emphasis on thinness simply [is]n't the primary factor,"[79] *Skinny* suggests that intersecting capitalist and paternal ideologies can shape the logic of anorexia. Giselle's father's emigration to Canada away from a communist regime is predicated on a desire to attain the promises of a democratic, capitalist society, which suggests that hard work is rewarded monetarily and socially. Kaslik therefore depicts Giselle's physical starvation as a deliberate attempt to repress emotional need she perceives as incommensurate with her father's demands of middle-class individualism and self-reliance. Thomas's influence on Giselle's sense of embodiment is the main way in which *Skinny* refigures anorexia as emerging within a biopolitical circuitry of social suffering.

In addition to *Skinny*'s interventions in theories of causality, the novel also constructs a critique of cognitive behavioural inpatient treatment by paralleling its ideologies of self-reliance, normative femininity, and individualism to those that explicitly inform Giselle's anorexic practices. In this way, the novel depicts the in-patient "sociocultural Panopticon"[80] as an intensification of a pre- and post- treatment sociocultural Panopticon, a thematic echoing which highlights the regulatory properties of eating disorder treatment. However, *Skinny* offers a crucial amendment to Bell's analysis of women within the Panopticon as advocates for normative femininity. While Holly's investment in monitoring Giselle's eating habits and social behaviours certainly has a disciplinary logic, she vacillates between blaming Giselle and trying to "forget that [they're] bound together in bone and blood in this big messy life."[81] At times, she manages the depth of her concern and frustration by aestheticizing Giselle's "misery … [as] terrible and beautiful, like stained white cotton dresses."[82] Holly's role in coercing Giselle's reformation appears predicated on decathecting from her in order to reinforce her own individuality. In the process, she is relegating Giselle to a position of soiled femininity, an image that gains potency and a sense of inevitability from the plural "dresses." Instead of an anomaly, Giselle has for Holly become a symbol of irreversibly flawed femininity. So, while the sisters' parallel narratives provide strategic insight into their respective methods of negotiating similar demands of normative female individualism, the juxtaposed points of view emphasize how processes of individualization foreclose possibilities for mutual insight and support. Holly's role as disciplinary agent of femininity is not so much invested in policing gender norms, but rather emerges as a by-product of delineating her own boundaries of autonomy.

The critical contribution I seek to forward through this argument concerns both dominant medical views and feminist critiques of eating disorders. By analysing the middle-class, patriarchal "discursive domain"[83] created in *Skinny* as producing "self-fashioning," "economically oriented subject[s],"[84] I read Giselle's anorexia as a deliberate practice of self-fashioning, which shares a similar rationale of self-regulation with Holly's socially acceptable forms of bodily control. The argument here is not that Giselle's life-threatening behaviours should also be read as socially acceptable, but rather, because the novel foregrounds the shared context and affective logic of the sisters' processes of self-formation, it is that socioeconomic and gendering context that must be addressed in the treatment of Giselle's anorexia. This is the basis for my critique of the CBT explanation for anorexia; through its focus on realigning the individual to adapt 'normally' to social realities, the hierarchies and injustices of those realities remain unchallenged. Furthermore, given *Skinny*'s portrayal of anorexia as intricately tied to class expectations and intimate forms of surveillance, feminist and cultural critiques that call for changes in representations of women as sustainable methods of prevention also fail to address the ways concrete, interpersonal realities of economic and gender power relations produce contexts in which self-starvation comes to mean emotional survival.

Consumption, like *Skinny*, challenges biomedical explanatory models for anorexia by extracting the thinness ideal out of the realm of causality. *Consumption* in particular refuses to equate the thinness ideal with Marie's condition. While the novel is interested in the impact of Western media on Inuit communities, the beauty myth is conspicuously absent as an import of celebrity media in Rankin Inlet. Instead, systemic, historical, and interpersonal dynamics, which reproduce and enforce ideologies of individualism and consumption, are presented in both novels as positioning the protagonists as economically oriented subjects. While Giselle attempts to "advantageously locate"[85] herself within her matrix of gender and class privilege and oppression by starving herself into what she perceives is the most economical physiological and affective state, Marie struggles to successfully orient herself to the individualistic requirements of consumer culture. Her starvation is symbolic of the lack of nourishment she derives from consumptive practices. Both novels represent anorexia treatment as reinforcing values associated with individualism and consumption, thereby structurally and thematically producing a view of anorexia as an affective and embodied response to institutionalized ideologies of capitalism. Moreover, *Consumption* explores the colonial function of treatment, situating it as a contemporary practice of assimilation. Examined together, these novels necessitate an understanding of anorexia beyond the "empire of images"[86] approach forwarded by Bordo.

'We're all so hungry for the authentic': Dis-eases of Consumption in Kevin Patterson's *Consumption*

Consumption portrays Marie Robertson's progressive lack of appetite as a somatic symptom of dis-ease within domestic and socioeconomic circumstances characterized by colonial and capitalist influences. The meaning of Marie's wasting is thematically linked to the central theme of the novel. Consumption, in multiple thematic iterations, recurs as the central consequence of a compelled transition from a nomadic to a static lifestyle reliant on an economy shaped by colonial practices of corporate resource extraction. Signifying both disease and the basis of social belonging, consumption in the novel refers to processes of resource extraction, tuberculosis, the preparation and ingestion of food and drugs, and the idealization of celebrity culture. By producing a genealogy of consumptive practices along three interwoven narrative strands – territorial, generational, and individual – Patterson situates Marie's anorexia as a rejection-response to alienating conditions of consumer capitalism and acculturation.

The novel's thematic structure and Patterson's strategic manipulation of a third-person omniscient narrator each function to refigure Marie's anorexia as social suffering. I will support this claim in three ways. First, I argue that the historical structure of the narrative traces the "absent cause"[87] of Marie's anorexia – the forces that might be said to be invisibly consuming her – as a legacy of economic and colonial expansion in Rankin Inlet. The narrative does so by drawing parallels among the course of Marie's weight loss, the steady industrialization of her town, and the assimilation of her immediate family. Second, I contend that Patterson refigures anorexia as social suffering through his method of characterization. Habits of consumption in the novel act as a mirror to various aspects of each character's individuality and terms of social belonging. This strategic representation of consumer identities becomes crucial to contextualizing Marie's malaise. Juxtaposed with the fulfilment other characters seem to derive from their consumer investments, it brings Marie neither individual fulfilment nor familial belonging; in fact, it is the incessant drive of those around her to consume or be consumed that produces her sense of alienation. Third, after establishing how forces of colonial and industrial assimilation shape Marie's anorexia, I argue that Patterson portrays eating disorder treatment as hyperbolically misreading Marie's condition in ways that betray such treatment's underlying colonial assumptions. A narrative fissure opens between the portrayal of Marie's progressive malaise and the imposed medical interpretation of her weight loss, which exposes the inability of decontextualized pathology paradigms to adequately explain and treat eating disorders. Consequently, the colonial logic of eating disorder treatment is portrayed as reiterating the values that underlie Rankin Inlet's narrative of 'progress' through territorial and individual consumption. Anne McClintock characterizes the "ideology of 'progress'"[88] as colonial beliefs in the colonized as symbolizing "primitive pre-history, bereft of language and light" (85), from which they are saved through the advances of the Enlightenment and industrialization. Moreover, Jo-Ann Episkenew argues that settlers' continued investment in the mythology of progress "confers upon them privileges that have become normalized ... [and] rationalizes the settlers' seizure and occupation of Indigenous lands."[89] *Consumption* exposes the acculturative force of this ideology by depicting the sacrificial logic underlying the choices characters must make to survive in the face of medical, economic, and environmental changes. Like several other protagonists discussed in this study, Marie ultimately encounters a choice between adaptation and suicide.

Set in Rankin Inlet, Nunavut, between the early 1950s and 2003,[90] Patterson's novel establishes the territorial meaning of consumption by foregrounding the initial incursion of the Hudson's Bay Trading Company into the area, the rise and fall of the nickel mine, and the development of a diamond mine. The consequences of these territorial transformations based on resource extraction are portrayed as directly shaping the Inuit peoples' relationship with the land, their intergenerational relationships, and their individual forms of consumption. Marie's Inuit grandparents, Emo and Winnie, her Inuk mother, Victoria, and settler father, Robertson, are all affected by these incursions; and, by the time Marie's anorexia becomes a narrative event, her family history has been contextualized in ways that situate her malaise as a consequence of colonization in Rankin Inlet.

The historical scope of the novel forms its ideological setting. The opening chapters track the rather efficient transformation of Rankin Inlet from a nomadic space to a site of industrial resource extraction. The central characters are introduced through their negotiation of this transition, involving their compelled conversion from nomadic hunters into static, dependent consumers. The novel begins with 16-year-old Victoria's removal from Rankin Inlet to The Pas, Manitoba, in 1962 to be treated for tuberculosis. Until then, Emo and Winnie, like most

Inuit in the area, "remained for the most part on the land"[91] but went to the coast in the summer to fish and trade with Hudson's Bay trading ships. The doctors on board a visiting "government ship"[92] detect that Victoria has tuberculosis, at which point the narrative splits into two parallel strands. One follows the impetus and effects of Emo's decision to come in off the land to work in the Rankin Inlet nickel mine, and the other traces Victoria's experiences at a sanatorium, and later living with a Cree family in The Pas. The contrast in settings highlights different pressures of early capitalist and colonial assimilation faced by each family member. While Emo is primarily compelled into a system of economic consumption, Victoria learns southern forms of cultural consumption. In both contexts, however, assimilation is portrayed as insidious coercion to modify behaviours and practices because of perceived or actual lack of alternatives and immediate, short-term benefits.

Marx defines consumption as fundamentally impelled by production and as an act that gives meaning to both the product and the consumer. Within a capitalist mode of production, in the moment that the consumer consumes the product, the product's meaning is defined as necessary. Likewise, in the act of consumption the consumer is "return[ed] to himself, but returns as a productive and self-reproducing individual."[93] Within a capitalist context, the productivity of workers is not only established by their labour, but also through their acts of consumption, which signify belonging. In this way, Marx formulates a mutually dependent relationship between industrial capitalism and individual actors within that system. Patterson establishes the unbalanced nature of this dependence by depicting how the nickel mine "produces the object of consumption, the manner of consumption and the motive of consumption"[94] for Emo and other Inuit who were compelled to come in off the land. This context establishes a crucial aspect of Marie's patient history that later eludes "the infectious disease service's"[95] evaluation of her symptoms.

Because the nickel mine in Rankin Inlet has led to a marked decline in caribou population, the nomadic lifestyle of the Inuit is increasingly difficult to sustain. Drawn to the town by rumors that the "mine owners were providing wooden homes to Inuit men who were prepared to work there, to live in one place and eat bannock and tinned meat,"[96] Emo seeks employment. This is in defiance of Winnie's objections that "their dignity would not be preserved, living in shacks the mining company had built, tucked close to one another like dog pens."[97] The terms of Winnie's resistance are ironic. Much is made of the significance of the sled dogs – they warn of danger, are part of the family, perhaps inconvenient but valuable – but Emo ends up not even being treated with the care extended to dogs. Emo's labour indoctrination scene suggests that the nickel mine's particular mode of capitalist production generates a particular kind of worker – not only an efficient one but also a uniform and dependent one. The mine owner first "took his name,"[98] assigned Emo an Anglicized one, along with an employee number, and handed him work clothes, the costs of which all come out of his pay; then he "gave"[99] him a house. The family becomes more dependent on "Kablunauk," or southern, food because there were "too many men in one place scouring the land all around for food."[100] Questions of cultural disintegration aside, the emergent colonial-capitalist social formation is portrayed as meeting the material needs of the families in a sparse way. As such, Patterson takes care to highlight the internal logics of coerced dependency of an economy formed around resource extraction. The mine establishes an economic base in Rankin Inlet that creates the conditions for it to be perceived as necessary. But then abruptly, the mine closes.

At this point, Patterson's analysis of the long-term socioeconomic consequences of exploitative capitalism becomes explicit, and constitutes the historical background to which Marie's anorexia is related. The irresponsibility of the mine owners who abandoned the Inuit women they married is presented as symptomatic of a larger ethos of opportunistic and delinquent capitalism. It is one that creates the conditions for its own legitimacy by transforming the economic, social, and cultural conditions of Rankin Inlet in irreversible ways – in ways that create need at basic levels of survival. Following the mine closure, Emo looks at the sky, at himself, and his "neglected dogs,"[101] gestures that suggest he seeks but cannot find a symbiosis among them that would point towards a return to nomadic life. The omniscient narrator then extrapolates Emo's experience to all "the hunters who had become miners,"[102] whose reliance on "paycheques"[103] and "snow machines"[104] had "atrophied [the] extensive and particular [skills] necessary to make one's way on the tundra."[105] Patterson's portrayal of Emo's compelled transformation into a worker/consumer suggests that those habits of consumption render his earlier nomadic skills inapplicable to his new circumstances and physical return to pre-dependence impossible. Indeed, the entire region is being settled by "the mine, the Church, the government."[106]

Victoria's return from The Pas emphasizes the generational consequences of this transition. Woven within the narrative of socioeconomic assimilation in the North are reports of Victoria's physical and cultural progress in the South. She eventually recovers from TB and is taken into the home of a Cree orderly, Donelda Pierce, who counsels her that "the only way to get smart [is] to stay interested in the world."[107] Victoria comes to think of the tundra home of her early youth as "almost an abstraction"[108] because she only knows it as a space on the map "above the dashes marked *treeline*."[109] For Anglophone settlers from southern cities, The Pas might be construed as the "North," yet for the Inuit of Nunavut, it is more southerly without being the urban "South." So, Patterson depicts Victoria's interpretive lens as complexly shaped by cartography. Her experiential knowledge is almost entirely eclipsed by an image of the North as a seemingly empty expanse above the treeline, a visualization of North that Sherrill E. Grace describes as participating in several narratives of Canadian nationhood, which are predicated on the erasure of First Peoples' presence. Maps that represent the space as empty may "construct an image of the North as inimical to human habitation,"[110] yet they also produce an image of the North as ripe for exploration and resource extraction.[111]

Victoria's appraisal of images of the North is one among several modes of consumption depicted as crucial to Victoria's acculturation, which anticipate her eventual affinity with Robertson, the diamond mine developer. With the combined discouragement to speak Inuktitut and encouragement to educate herself in English, Victoria listens to local, American, and BBC news, and explores other worlds entirely through fantasy novels like *Lord of the Rings*. The dramatic irony of Victoria's cultural experiences is that it has simultaneously assimilative and alienating consequences that become more glaring after she returns to Rankin Inlet. The underlying impetus for the transformations that her family and the region have undergone is unintelligible to her because the news she consumes is from a colonial perspective. And so, even as she lives in Rankin Inlet, her efforts to seek out newspapers and world news take her further away from her family despite their cohabitation, leading her to become involved with Robertson, the manager of the HBC store, the location of one of the few radios in the town.

The historical/generational structure of the novel establishes a contextual circuitry between Marie's anorexia and the impact of assimilative pressures of consumer capitalism on her immediate family. The town has been formed and the algebra of needs[112] inaugurated, whether in accordance with or as resistance to the forces of physical and emotional necessity established in the region. Victoria and Robertson's three children respond differently to the ongoing changes in Rankin Inlet, exemplified by the promised diamond mine. Marie's brother, Pauloosie, rejects the further deterioration of traditional hunting practices and his father's involvement in establishing the mine, and consequently spends increasing amounts of time out on the tundra; their sister, Justine, embraces celebrity culture and plans her escape from Rankin Inlet to Toronto as soon as she comes of age; and Marie is initially presented as ambivalent. Symbolically, Patterson seems to develop a genealogy of assimilation here: Pauloosie resists it, Justine finds direction in its promises, and Marie seems to value harmony between tradition and change, which is signified by her integral role as peacemaker between her parents. Indeed, her combined panic when they argue and her delight when Robertson returns from business trips produce her only overtly social acts before her "malaise" becomes apparent. In particular, her connection with her father, an important factor in her experience of anorexia, is emphasized through short, emphatic phrases: "Marie especially"[113] welcomes him home, and later whispers, "it's nice having Daddy home."[114] Their bond is significant to note in relation to the representation of the relative degrees of assimilation experienced by the Robertson children. Marie derives meaning from strong kinship ties because they provide safety and comfort within a broader community characterized by increasing cultural and material transformations. It is when these bonds are disrupted that Marie begins to wane.

Patterson's method of characterization also serves to emphasize the basis of Marie's dis-ease, or social alienation, within the colonial, capitalist context of the novel. Marx's ultimate conclusion that "production thus creates the consumer"[115] grammatically emphasizes his argument for socially defined identities. The juxtaposition between noun and verb implies that processes of capitalist production create individual identities, not just behaviours, which are defined by their habits of consumption. Patterson's novel plays on this conceptual relationship. Each figure, whether Inuk or settler, is characterized by a unique style and focus of consumption: Robertson is a diamond mine developer; Johanna is obsessed with gourmet food; Penny hunts off the land; Justine saturates herself in celebrity culture; and Dr Balthazar ingests morphine. Moreover, these individual traits of consumption are the basis upon which relationships are forged or disrupted in the novel. As Robert G. Dunn argues, consumption links "the satisfaction of material need and want to the production of meaning, identity, and a sense of place and social membership."[116] Similarly, Patterson describes the relations between the characters in the novel as constituted through shared habits of consumption, which are tied to place and desire. For example, Robertson and Victoria's initial attraction to one another is established through listening to international news radio, and Johanna and Doug share an expensive passion for gourmet and imported cuisine that fuels their long-distance emotional and sexual relationship.

The basis of connection between these couples symbolizes a mutual investment in sustaining and growing their identities as productive and cultured members of the northern community; in effect, they are aligning themselves with "progress." Patterson presents Victoria's choice of a settler partner as a logical choice in the novel, given her early socialization; the nature of his work and the conflict it produces in his family deeply shape Marie's experience of home and kinship, as does her brother's attempts to live more traditionally. Pauloosie and Penny's mutual desire to live autonomously but together on the tundra symbolizes a rejection of not just personal participation in consumer culture, but a rejection of social and familial connection; as such, Marie begins to lose another source of comfort. A causal connection is drawn between Marie's longing for male protection and her weight loss when Justine asks her abruptly why she "never eat[s]."[117] Taking this as a suggestion that Marie might have "ano-rex-ia ner-vosa,"[118] and fearing that she is fat, she responds in one breath, "I'm *not fat*," and in the next, "I really miss Pauloosie."[119] Her simultaneous rejection of corporeal motivation and affirmation of emotional yearning persist until she is admitted to the eating disorder clinic; this dialectic constitutes the basis of the narrative's explicit critique of contemporary eating disorder treatment.

Consistent with Patterson's method of thematic characterization, Marie is also introduced through her habits of consumption. Her "enthusiasm was Weetabix,"[120] which she "inaccurately"[121] spoons into her mouth because she is so tired after a late night of reading *The Chronicles of Narnia*. With a passion for fantasy worlds so engrossing that sleeping and eating are secondary considerations, Marie initially appears a typical bookish, shy teenager. However, in contrast to the other characters, Marie's social status is determined by both her inability to participate in broader social habits of consumption, and her inability to form connections with others based on her unique interests. The narrator later explains that, because Marie is "not conversant in popular music,"[122] as evidenced by her blank locker walls, and is "too skinny, too boyish, and ... too much like a Kablunauk with her white-white-white skin,"[123] she does not have any friends. The details of this passage explain her failure to make relationships based on mutual consumption, heterosexual attraction, and perceived cultural affinity. However, the impact of Marie's social alienation is subordinated in the narrative to the isolation she experiences within her family.

Significantly, the narrator abruptly draws back from close character observations to describe the Robertson family's domestic situation during the onset of Marie's withdrawal. They are portrayed as individually consumed by interests that dis-integrate the family unit: Pauloosie is "out on the land,"[124] Justine "lay[s] in front of the television fantasizing,"[125] and Robertson is busily overseeing land developments because, as the narrator explains, "anyone trying to make the North more like the south has to spring continuously."[126] Each family member reaffirms his or her own sense of identity and social belonging by pursuing consumer activities, while Marie sits alone in her room reading. Instead of relying on internal monologue to explain Marie's motivations – which otherwise Patterson does consistently in the novel – he employs observational juxtaposition between Marie's behaviours and the Robertson family's activities in order to contextualize her malaise as an inability to attain fulfilment through consumption. The consumer habits of each character not only function to develop a thematic critique of consumption as formative of individual identities; Patterson's technique of characterization also conveys a critique of capitalist consumerism that emphasizes its exploitative, as well as its simultaneously unifying and alienating, functions.

The generational transmission of colonial and, increasingly, corporate values to Marie from her parents is symbolized by the houses in which they live and their eating habits. Initially, the Robertsons live in a prefabricated house like all the others that have been imported from Montreal, in which the walls are thin and space is cramped, creating more interaction between family members. The larger, more palatial home Robertson buys with his mining consultation earnings isolates the family further from each other and the community. "The only log house ... seen North of the treeline,"[127] the design is "just like in the magazines,"[128] which reinforces the idea of the North being subsumed by southern values and Robertson in particular risking "backlash from the community"[129] by facilitating such transformations. The house itself forces the sisters and Victoria apart, with "bedrooms – one for each of the children ... twice the size of those in the old house."[130] Moreover, the family is increasingly divided according to eating habits: Pauloosie insists on eating "country food" like "frozen char while the rest of the family ate roast."[131]

However, whether "char, fish sticks, toast, beans, roast: nothing moved [Marie] to eat."[132] The verb describing her motivation here is telling: she prefers neither the traditional nor the imported southern food because she is not inspired or impelled by the choices. She is "skinny"[133] because she is listless, rather than actively striving to remain thin. The grocery items symbolize consumer success, but represent for Marie the progressive dismantling of kinship based on shared relational values and roles: a movement away from a collective to an individualized identity. Specifically, the wider Rankin Inlet community and the Robertsons in particular have had the "bedrock of primary relationships within Inuit Culture"[134] shaken, including their relationships to "land, and by extension their culture ... to one's family ... to his or her own inner Spirit ... [and] to one's social grouping."[135] Consequently, Patterson's technique of characterization depicts Marie's anorexia as a rejection of consumer-based relations that have alienated her more broadly from territorial, spiritual, familial, and social belonging.

Contrasted to the context in which Marie's social suffering is portrayed are the diagnostic process and logic of eating disorder treatment imposed on her. Patterson emphasizes the confusion surrounding the diagnosis of Marie's condition in ways that ultimately expose the dangerously imprecise yet universalizing application of eating disorder treatment. His use of third-person narration establishes what becomes a pattern of uncertain interpretations of Marie's problem. While providing reliable insight into each character's thoughts, the narrator withholds Marie's illuminating inner monologue until her final hours. Leading up to that climax, the narrator instead focuses on characters' speculations regarding Marie's weight loss, all of whom search for a physiological cause for her thinness: tuberculosis, malabsorption,[136] or clinical depression.[137] The only other possible explanation according to Dr Balthazar and the Winnipeg doctors is an eating disorder, and yet Marie's condition is interpreted as anomalous in two significant ways. Because it is not a willful weight loss, Marie's condition does not match the essential criteria for anorexia nervosa. She is not willing herself to starve, and she does not express any fear of becoming fat. She just says she is not hungry. Also, her ethnicity challenges accepted theories of the typical anorexia patient. The latter issue is raised continually in the novel and constitutes a key structural irony: the cultural, economic, social, and epidemiological changes in Rankin Inlet are presented as results of southern agents actively transforming the North in the image of the South. Confusion that an Inuk girl could develop what is understood to be a southern disease highlights ways in which the realities of ongoing colonization are masked by the ideological gravity of discourses of progress and their attendant de-contextualization and historical myopia. As Marie's thinness comes under scrutiny of the Southern doctors, the questions they ask about her condition attempt to account for the cultural anomaly she represents to their diagnostic criteria for anorexia.[138] Ironically, these gestures towards cultural specificity identify a significant factor in what the reader understands as informing Marie's anorexia; that is, it is an intimate legacy of colonial and capitalist transformations that pose significant obstacles to her emotional fulfilment. Yet, the doctors' and dietician's recognition is empirical rather than contextual. Treatment is not fundamentally altered by acknowledging her cultural heritage because it is understood as a trait, rather than a historical, racialized, gendered, and classed subject position. As such, the affective, relational logic of her starvation goes undetected and, instead, treatment reinforces promises of healing through acculturative consumer practices, thereby exacerbating Marie's sense of alienation.

When Marie is eventually admitted to an eating disorder unit, the gap widens between the ambiguous but emotional logic of Marie's thinness and the decontextualized logic of the treatment, which is expressed through the dietician's monologue to Marie. In attempt to normalize her apparent anxiety, Carol assures Marie that most girls are "a little bowled over ... when they come in the first time."[139] But Marie's silence during the scene emphasizes the disconnect between Carol's assumptions regarding Marie's disease and the unspeakable realities of her suffering – unspeakable because Carol's treatment framework enforces the boundaries of what is considered the cause of Marie's anorexia. She explains that, "a big part of what I do is education. And the best way to start that is to talk about what you eat."[140] Her assumption that Marie struggles with a fraught relationship with food contradicts the reader's knowledge that Marie is obsessed with neither food nor losing weight. Carol also reassures Marie that "char or caribou" can be "flown down"[141] for her, an offer that misunderstands the realities of food distribution and consumption in the North.[142] Finally, the dietician attempts to entice Marie to begin eating with promises of "great shopping over at Portage Place" mall,[143] which again situates consumption as a reward for participation in treatment. Marie's silence in response to the dietician's comments, as well as the lack of any narrative insight into her inner thoughts, foreground the cultural ignorance encoded in the dietician's application of eating disorder treatment. Assuming that Marie lives "just from the tundra"[144] and eats only locally hunted game, the dietician demonstrates no knowledge of the colonial transformations of the North. Her ignorance participates in a kind of medicalized assimilation,[145] while she figures health in terms of consumption – eating and shopping.

Constituting what Chrisjohn et al. frame as another tactic "deployed to bring about the 'normalization' of Aboriginal Peoples,"[146] therapy is depicted here as perpetuating the myth of colonial (and capitalist) progress through paternalistically assuming the superiority of its techniques and procedural goals. Its techniques misdiagnose the colonial and capitalist underpinnings of Marie's anorexia as pathology, while its assumed indicators of health signify successful assimilation. The implications of this methodologically individualistic approach to treating Marie's anorexia have interconnected systemic and specific implications. The assimilative logic is evident, but so too is the logic of "damage control."[147] Instead of pursuing the purposeful "liberation" of the "client," therapy has the effect of "camouflaging ... chains, psychic or otherwise,"[148] thereby reinforcing the legitimacy of its diagnostic criteria and treatment methodologies.

It is those methodologies that underscore the misdiagnosis and mistreatment that lead to Marie's suicide. Her actions before she falls to her death symbolize the failure of consumerism to alleviate her suffering and confirm the role of treatment in reinforcing the basis of Marie's social suffering. The imperceptible roots of Marie's anorexia – or "absent cause"[149] – reside in the contrast between colonial and capitalist assimilative pressures undergone by her community, and the false notion that we have no colonial history. Marie's trip to the mall signifies her final attempts to mitigate with shopping the force of her real desires for "company and ... safe[ty,] ... to be sitting at the supper table, her dad and her mom passing around the food."[150] Her desires are not met at the mall. Her longing to eat with her family ironically undercuts the dietician's belief that she does not want to eat or needs to be educated on healthy practices of food consumption; rather, Marie longs for the comfort and safety of the familial rituals of eating. While ostensibly a contradictory act – if she longs for familial connection, she would logically seek out her family's company – her choice to insulate herself from them by immersing herself in books (and music) can be read as a means to escape the progressive alienating qualities of the Robertson family dynamic.

Marie's withdrawal is noted during a time when Victoria is the "only constant presence in the house,"[151] although Marie rarely sees her family; instead, she only hears "the doors emitting and admitting her family during all hours."[152] As each Robertson is immersed in their particular consumer habits, Marie finds solace in music. In this way, consumption works as a coping mechanism for Marie. Therefore, the fact that she cannot buy the CDs she has already listened to at a store but "longed to own"[153] signifies a frustrated attempt to attain affective autonomy, reinforcing her sense of isolation and powerlessness. The meaning of her frustrated attempt to soothe or empower herself becomes clearer in her final reflections:

> Ten seconds before the last of her thoughts, she had not contemplated ending them. She had been standing on the bridge, stung by the unfriendliness of the mall, and by her unprecedented anonymity. The water looked just like it does in the north, except greener maybe, more algae. She could not buy the music she wanted, she could not make her way in this place, the only alternative to Rankin Inlet, not without help. There was no help … Locked in the hospital room. Locked in Rankin Inlet. Alone and fighting tears in the Portage Place food court, with nothing to eat and no money to buy anything.[154]

The accumulated rush of these thoughts overwhelms any hope that she can escape the causes of her suffering: the "unprecedented anonymity" and social isolation of the mall are intensified echoes of the isolation she experiences in the North. The image of the water as the same as that which flows up North symbolizes how similar the North and South have become. Marie experiences them as mirror worlds: in Rankin Inlet, she is locked in her room and shunned at school because she looks too white. In Winnipeg, she is locked in a hospital room and shunned at the mall because she is too "Indian."[155] The final lines of the passage above seem to suggest that even basic participation in normal activities at the mall would have made a difference. Her inability to adapt to naturalized economic rationalities reinforced by treatment are not depicted as failure, but rather the consequence of separation from her family to the South, where her class status is drastically different, though her racialized status quite similar, to her situation in Rankin Inlet. Furthermore, without "money to buy anything,"[156] her anonymity is confirmed. If, as Nikolas Rose contends, "every choice we make is an emblem of our identity, a mark of our individuality,"[157] then Marie's inability to complete the consumer exchange means she cannot distinguish herself as unique through her consumer choices, even if this supposed mark of individuality is illusory. As such, the physical and emotional experiences of the hospital's eating disorder unit and the mall combine into an expression of perceived incarceration. Treatment has reinscribed the colonial view of her as Other, when she is in fact largely, though uneasily, assimilated into consumer capitalism because of the Canadian colonial project.

Unlike Giselle's behaviour, Marie's refusal to eat and ultimate suicide are framed not as motivated acts, but as psychosomatic consequences of hungering for more than the promises an individualizing consumer world can offer. The narrative's dialectic of hunger is captured by Johanna's comment that "we're all so hungry for the authentic."[158] She utters these words in the midst of discussing with her boyfriend how to make their exotic food "look like it does in the pictures in the recipe books."[159] Her words resonate as a moment of clarity in which she recognizes that she and Doug can only ever create and consume a simulation of genuine Italian or Thai food, in the absence of the original sociocultural context. They seek a true, organic experience through means that only ever foreground their distance from such social relations. Marie's hunger is also for authentic intimate connections, but unlike Joanna, Justine, Dr Balthazar, and others, she cannot sufficiently invest in the simulacra of connection to the point that her hunger is quelled.

Consumption develops a complex genealogy of colonial capitalism through depicting an array of characters who portray a variety of consumptive practices. A critical aspect of this lineage of consumption is forged symbolically between Victoria and Marie. Victoria's consumption is directly caused by contact with traders and treated by removal to a southern sanatorium where she learns to desire particular forms of cultural capital. Two decades later, her daughter's wasting is caused by a lack of emotional nourishment within a family fractured by individual pursuits of consumer identities. She is moved to a southern hospital for treatment, where she fails a final time to find belonging in the symbol of consumer culture – the mall. Together, these lineages of consumption produce a view of anorexia as a contemporary capitalist disease of individualism, which is treated with the chemotherapeutic[160] approach of removal and treatment. This approach actually reproduces or intensifies Marie's unbearable alienation within conditions of settler colonial, consumer capitalism.

As in *Skinny*, the primary way in which *Consumption* refigures anorexia as social suffering is through the depiction of treatment as an imposition that reiterates the causal logic of Marie's malaise. Therefore, like *Skinny*, *Consumption* similarly constructs anorexia as a response to coercive ideological and material forces of individualism and consumption, respectively. Marie's starvation, however, is a rejection-response, whereas Giselle's is more accurately characterized as a striving-response. It is the dynamic of coercion and response that is particularly significant to Marie's case. I have argued that Marie's wasting can be read as an embodied consequence of social relations that seek to force upon her the qualified subject position of dependent consumer. This analysis runs the risk of divesting Marie of agency given the passive representation of her starvation; the broader consequences of that divestment would be to rehearse a critical construction of Indigenous, female colonized subjects as powerless within the insidious narrative of colonial progress. However, I do not argue that Marie's anorexia is a matter of incomplete assimilation (i.e., that her essential problem is her inability to replace kinship ties with consumer relationships). While perhaps a negative form of agency, her anorexia represents both a refusal to perform fulfilment within such consumer relationships, and a mourning at the seeming inability to re-capture or re-forge nurturing, vitalizing bonds of kinship.

Teaching Literary Depictions of Anorexia

Teaching *Skinny* and *Consumption* in Canadian literature courses provokes a paradigm shift in our understanding of relationships between the individual and society, culture, and structures of privilege and oppression. While *Heave* and *lullabies for little criminals* certainly recast habitual substance use as a method of adaptation to systemic conditions, the boundaries between character and setting, person and society, are perceptible. The distinction between the anorexic and her circumstances is considerably less defined in Kaslik's and Patterson's novels. Economic, cultural, and gendered values are expressed through the bodies of Giselle and Marie, along with each of the other characters populating these novels. 'Doing' one's identities is as much a corporeal dynamic as it is psychological, emotional, and behavioural one.

By depicting self-starvation as one among innumerable forms of self-fashioning, *Skinny* and *Consumption* fundamentally challenge pathologizing, essentialist claims that underpin biomedical and stereotypical explanations for anorexia. Guided by the foundational principles of critical pedagogy, educators can employ discovery exercises before closer study of these novels that challenge students to reflect on their assumptions about both eating disorders and the influence of culture on individuals. Shereen Siddiqui's dissertation "Teaching to Transform: Toward an Action-Oriented Feminist Pedagogy in Women's Studies" is an excellent resource to guide course assignment.

The exercises I propose are designed to trouble definitions of anorexia and eating disorders so they become a problem for students to interrogate. They also seek to facilitate *conscientização* – critical consciousness – insofar as students come to discern how they are each "rooted in temporal-spatial conditions which mark them and which they also mark."[161] Through these introductory methods, the stage is set for considering how *Skinny* and *Consumption* are counter-hegemonic depictions of anorexia and why they matter personally and politically.

Beginning with an exercise similar to the "Addiction is" prompt discussed in chapter 2, teachers can assign students to write an "Anorexia is" list of associations or definitions. Having students brainstorm their knowledge of anorexia[162] is an important exploratory exercise because, through verbalizing what they know and how they know it, they are engaged in perceiving contradictions or gaps in knowledge, as well as preparing to view the novels as adding to their investigation. Responses might include, "Anorexia is a disease, starving yourself to death, disturbing to watch, tragic, frustrating, gross, weird, a psychological problem, rare, or lonely." After a collective list has been built on the board, teachers should ask how we know or have come to have the impressions expressed in each definition. After accruing a list that likely covers various media, celebrity stories, personal and interpersonal experiences, and psychology courses, teachers could then pose a crucial question: "What do these definitions suggest about the cause(s) of anorexia?" While the DSM-IV definition asserts psychological causality, other narratives are not so straightforward in the causes they imply. Such collective interrogation is extremely fruitful for several reasons: it illustrates that contradictions exist in explaining eating disorders, thereby destabilizing claims to one truth of anorexia; it fosters critical reflection on just how many cultural locations produce these narratives;

it potentially breaks down dichotomous views of eating disorders as an affliction of the few to consider restricted eating and the desire to be thin as culturally pervasive, as factors that vary in degree and expression; and it prompts more questions about how thinness comes to mean something so intimately consequential.

These last two questions of cultural and personal significations of thinness forms the structure and intention of a second exploratory exercise. We might call it "Reading the Empire of Images" to articulate the values encoded in cultural depictions of thin and fat bodies. Model resources for this kind of critique are endless, particularly from a feminist perspective. A well-known example is Jean Kilbourne's *Killing Us Softly* documentary series,[163] which has been widely screened across Canadian and American universities in feminist, media studies, sociology, psychology, marketing, and health sciences courses since the 1980s. In fact, an entire genre of documentaries exists that examines the various ways in which media influence gender norms and inequalities. Therefore, teachers and students likely know that media critique exists and/or have some degree of skill in undertaking media critique. Many teachers across disciplines have likely shown music videos and advertisements to students to provoke critical literacy surrounding how images of female and male bodies depict and subvert gender norms; and many students are familiar with the feminist blogosphere,[164] which has normalized at least a cursory awareness of how mainstream media depicts gender and sexuality.

And yet, while employing a feminist media critique is of course foundational, the goals of "Reading the Empire of Images" are to expand the terms of analysis to include class, race, and ability, and position such critique in the context of matrices of privilege and oppression. When female thinness is read as variously signifying ambition, self-control, confidence, meanness, vanity, and health, these codes must be analysed in terms of their classed, racialized and ableist meanings, as well as their gendered implications.

Dworkin and Wachs[165] provide an instructive example of such intersectional analysis. Particularly concerned with the ways in which female athleticism has become an imperative just as inflected with capitalist, patriarchal, homophobic, and racist implications as the thinness ideal, they describe magazine covers that transmit "the meaning of the words 'health' and 'fitness,' singing it to you through rippling muscles … [and] cover models' eyes [that] look back at you with pride. 'Hard work,' you hear the implied whisper. All of you can do it."[166] The associations with capitalist work ethic are clear, as well as the moral imperative attached to the encouragement that such fitness is attainable. Similarly, in *Skinny*, Holly's body is characterized by muscularity, leanness, agility, and confident sexuality, and she is validated by her coach, teachers, and family for working so hard to excel. By guiding students to interrogate codes of thinness and fitness in various media, teachers can then position literature as participating in both producing and contesting hegemonic ideals of thinness. "Reading the Empire of Images" can be facilitated in numerous ways, although arguably the most transformative approach would involve students choosing the objects of study and collectively analysing the images.

An integral aspect of investigating how the thinness ideal works with students is discussing how 'fat' is a cultural phobia. For Butler, the intelligible subject's movement in processes of gender identification is driven in two directions – both towards an ideal, and away from the abjected and "its status for the subject as a threatening spectre."[167] If the ideal is thinness, than the threatening spectre in Western culture is surely fatness. Bordo reports that "when 500 people were asked what they feared most in the world, 190 replied, 'Getting fat.'"[168] She muses that "the fear 'getting fat' – is far more bizarre than the anorectic's misperceptions of her body image, or the bulimic's compulsive vomiting."[169] Such a morbid fear of fat can be read as the phobic abjection of *obesity*, which can impel all manner and severity of avoidance behaviour, from moderate dieting to extreme bingeing and purging. What Bordo calls a bizarre fear seems less pathological if we consider Butler's assertion that the abject is already "'inside' the subject."[170] Fat is literally an organic layer of substance below the surface of the skin, which has been constructed as a kind of enemy within – a view that Helen Malson points out is "evident in the jingoistic phrases used by the diet industry such as 'fight the flab,' 'burning off' calories or fat, and 'fatbuster' diets."[171] Presenting students with such information directly in concert with further media analysis of depictions of fat bodies can help draw out the associations with failed gender expectations, replicated endlessly by those who produce and consume these ideals. The investments that celebrity media and diet and fashion industries have in reproducing such associations with fat are evident and well-documented.[172] The further questions for students involved in analysing the problems of eating disorders, thinness ideals, and fat phobia concern assessing personal and social impact and imagining resistance to the content and consequences of the empire of images.

"But everyone knows that": Engaging Minimizing Claims

After these media images have been decoded, the work of interrogating their societal impact begins. However, even when students can perceive media as the transmitter of norms and values, they often strongly resist, dismiss, or minimize the influence of media on their self-concepts, actions, desires, and relationships. Bordo relates how "students accuse [her] of a kind of paranoia about the significance of these [media] representations as carriers and reproducers of culture. After all, they insist, these are just images, not 'real life'; any fool knows that advertisers manipulate reality in the service of selling their products."[173] Perhaps a variation on claims to individual choice discussed in chapter 2, this form of student resistance seems to reject any suggestion of being influenced or acting unconsciously. Considering the possible reasons for this form of student resistance is important when formulating problem-posing approaches to teaching depictions of eating disorders: if teachers are to create the conditions for breaking down Us/Them dichotomies in order to discern how hegemonic narratives circulate in Western culture, students must be prompted to reflect on the similarities and differences between their own experiences and those they classify as Other. If shared cultural conditions are examined rather than only individual difference, those deemed Other are not as easily cast in a pathological light. By countering minimizing claims with statistics that track "the current spread of diet and exercise mania across racial and ethnic groups, [and] the explosion of technologies aimed at bodily 'correction' and 'enhancement,'"[174] Bordo employs a more traditional pedagogical technique of engaging student resistance through presenting factual data. And yet, this approach may be limited in its ability to transform students' world views. This seems a more prescriptive pedagogical style, which "*prescribes* what we should think and do based on a predetermined 'right' analysis,"[175] when a revelatory approach, "a more open-ended synthetic approach based on the revelations – undetermined and uncertain – that we experience together"[176] is potentially more transformative.

I offer three ways to engage with minimizing claims, which I have found particularly generative in disrupting classroom dynamics in which students retreat to passivity or advance in hostility because they feel they are being asked to accept identity- or world view-threatening material on the authority of the teacher or statistics. The first approach shifts students' analysis away from media towards other aspects of their social worlds by using exercises from Kate Bornstein's *My Gender*

Workbook. By way of an example, I present Bornstein's illustration of what she calls the "The Gender/Identity/Power Pyramid"[177] for students to analyse. Those individuals that populate the apex of the pyramid are typically white, male, heterosexual, able-bodied, and "tall, trim, and reasonably muscled."[178] By asking students to perceive individual characteristics in terms of broader visibility, representation, and authority (represented by the rest of the pyramid), teachers can move beyond media analysis to ask how the thinness ideals and fat phobia impact social relations of power, privilege, and oppression. In other words, a crucial shift from understanding thinness as not just valued but rewarded with social, economic, and moral capital becomes more possible when students are prompted to ask why power can look so uniform or disproportionate. Ultimately, this process should clarify the concept of thin privilege, which refers to the unearned benefits that being aligned with thinness norms accrues. Like other forms of privilege (e.g. heterosexual, white, settler, gender, age, ability), people who benefit from being thin "are usually unaware of (the effects of) their privileged position."[179] Teachers can employ a variation of Peggy McIntosh's "unpacking the invisible backpack" exercise[180] in order to trace such advantages of being thin, which include expectations that doctors will not immediately assume diabetes as the likely cause of your ailment, that airlines will not charge you more for a seat, that you can find your clothing size and preferred style in local stores, and that people will not assume you are lazy and unhealthy based on your size.[181]

While introducing students to thin privilege is vital to facilitating revelatory analyses of the social impact of hegemonic and subversive eating disorder narratives, the transformative potential of such work is arguably more acute when students are encouraged to evaluate how thinness ideals and fat phobia impact their immediate lives. Experiential learning strategies like journaling and visual art provide opportunities for students to trace the interpersonal transmission of embodied values and assess how we hold ourselves, and perhaps others, to particular standards and according to particular assumptions – or what one student of mine called "quiet biases." Guided journaling assignments might ask students to apply course readings to their experience and comment on how, why, and with what effect course readings and discussion are emotionally and intellectually challenging. Another technique designed to help students conceptualize how they think of their identities in relation to their social world is through a visual art collection. At the beginning of the course, students are asked to visually represent their impression of how dominant values affect them. Throughout the course, in response to each course reading, they draw, paint, or design a picture that interprets how narratives depict the relationship between normative values and individual identity. The final stage of the assignment includes a written comparative analysis of the images, which must also employ the theoretical concepts introduced throughout the course.

An action-oriented variation on this assignment would prompt students to intervene in public discourses about representations of women and eating disorders. For example, teachers can assign a discourse analysis piece that asks students to analyse depictions of anorexia and bulimia in popular media. However, instead of submitting a formal paper, students are first prompted to do research on the currents of relevant popular cultural criticism in the blogosphere and other media. The final submission will take the form of a blog post that critiques depictions of thinness, fatness, and eating disorders media (e.g. newspaper, blogs, newscast, television show, celebrity magazines) that rely on or perpetuate stereotypes, explain why those stereotypes are problematic, and reference other popular cultural theorists and bloggers.

"The problem is too big": Engaging Student Futility

While a typical response to critiques of cultural and systemic influences is to minimize their effects on enlightened individuals, the opposite response is also common. Students who comprehend the ubiquity of ideological, cultural, and structural matrices of privilege and oppression also and understandably conclude that resistance is futile and minimizing individual harm through adaptation is the realistic course of action. This is a particular kind of denial of oppression, even if articulated as recognition, because it assumes that bearable, sustainable adaptation is possible, and it also risks prescribing to others that they can and should 'get used to it.'[182] Undoubtedly, teachers have encountered this reaction in many pedagogical contexts, so my offerings here are specific to resisting and transforming structural forms of oppression that find cultural expression through making size indicative of worth. The main ways I have engaged this response to systemic critique is to provide an initial map of existing strategies for social change, involve students in evaluating their efficacy, and encourage them to create their own models for transformation.

Feminist theorists pose several strategies for eating disorder prevention, the central proposals for which fall into two main categories. The first calls for resignifications in the empire of images, which involves producing more realistic and empowering representations of women; the second seeks to build strategies for individual resistance to the internalization of hegemonic images of women. In the first instance, Susan Bordo calls for "a transformation similar to what has been going on in the world of children's movies and books, which have normalized racial diversity"[183] to include bodily diversity. While an exciting and crucial aspect of cultural resistance, it is a strategy that teachers will have to frame as one possibility, rather than *the* answer. Such resignification practices alone cannot address the circuitries of power and oppression that police women's bodies. Having students trace those circuitries through the novels and their own lives is an important point of departure towards expanding notions of eating disorder prevention. Abigail Bray and Claire Colbrook denounce as dangerously limited the suggestions that "only representation can cure ... [and that] only a realistic, nonrepressive and less regulative form of representation will allow women to see themselves as autonomous subjects."[184] Such representational transformations must be accompanied by socioeconomic and medical transformations that denaturalize the associations between thinness, fatness, functionality, and accessibility, as well as register their contributing roles and limitations. As Kaslik's and Patterson's novels compellingly demonstrate, subjects arrive at moments of cultural consumption already in the grip of material and ideological forces of consumerism and individualism, which intimately affect their practices of self-formation.

Feminist critiques also argue that eating disorder prevention can occur at the level of individual resistance. For example, through analysing case studies on adolescent body image issues, Tolman and Debold contend that women can "negotiate a variety of relationships with this image of the desirable woman ... ranging from a complete rejection of themselves to a complete rejection of the image."[185] While students are typically drawn to this exercise, teachers should remain vigilant to problematize the assumptions undergirding this approach when asking students to evaluate existing forms of resistance. Researchers do not explain what conditions make individual resistance possible, nor how such conditions can be created for variously positioned subjects. Moreover, in addition to accessibility, an equally important issue surrounding this individualized formulation of resistance is the location of empowerment. Tolman and Debold posit that "the knowledge that girls and women hold in their bodies is a source of power that the image of the desirable women obscures";[186] and that women need to retrieve such pre-existing knowledge of their inherent power. The importance of conceiving the self as *deserving* of empowerment holds; however, it is vital to address how empowerment can and must occur *in practice*, within fully contextualized systemic conditions. Fundamental systemic inequalities risk going unaddressed when power and knowledge are reified as universal internal qualities that can somehow be released by a revolution of mind or be attained solely through representational modelling. As economically oriented subjects, characters in all of the novels studied in this book are empowered and disempowered within economic frameworks. Kaslik and Patterson create female protagonists who insightfully understand the possibilities and limitations of their respective socioeconomic domains. But such knowledge alone does not allow them to alter their methods of adaptation. These discussions focus on cultural transformations rather than also contemplating the necessity for broader systemic transformations in imagining how to prevent eating disorders.

The pressing question remains for students and teachers alike: how can the analysis of socioeconomics offered by *Skinny* and *Consumption* be mobilized towards resistance in concert with representational and individualistic strategies? The most striking feature shared by these novels in terms of their systemic critique is the way capitalism is depicted not as the norm or already installed mode of socioeconomic relations, but as a stage in the family history of the characters. *Skinny*'s immigration narrative positions Western capitalism as preferable to Eastern European communism, but its short-term promises have long-term, damaging consequences for Giselle as a result of Thomas's investment in its patriarchal and class hierarchies. *Consumption*'s assimilation narrative traces the deliberate and swift changes from a nomadic social dynamic to an industrial capitalist society, which estranges individuals from land, family, and self and installs consumer-based relations as the limits of social belonging. And yet, the critiques of capitalism forwarded by each novel vis-à-vis Giselle's and Marie's anorexic responses do not constitute calls to return to pre-capitalist societies. Ideas of nostalgic return to traditional Inuit life in an environmentally devastated North or to a communist past purged of its corruption are foreclosed by the ways in which each novel foregrounds capitalist processes as dismantling that which came before by virtue of the pervasive material and ideological reach of these processes. If there is a solution to eating disorders, it will have to be developed through transforming systemic relations of power and oppression that make thinness and fatness conditions of worth, and the body the site of empowerment.

One action-oriented approach to mobilizing the critiques offered by *Skinny* and *Consumption* is asking students to develop intervention and prevention plans in concert with or reaction to existing strategies. Teachers thus involve students in tackling the pervasive scope of normative narratives and social hierarchies that insidiously affect us in ways that emphasize the necessity of collective and multiple sites of resistance. The novels studied in this book represent treatment as an imposition, while conveying the lack of alternatives to heal those suffering from addiction and eating disorders – a fact which considerably shapes premises for moving forward outside of the pathology paradigm. *Skinny* and *Consumption* suggest that CBT treatment is relied on by the families of the anorexic characters because they do not know an alternative. However, crucial to this circuitry of diagnosis and treatment is the anorexic's silence. Giselle repeats the treatment language of her doctors and support group but never articulates her dis-ease within those contexts. Similarly, Marie says nothing during the hospital scenes in part because the terms of the dietician's narrative about anorexia have little relation to her experience of malaise. Underlying these representations of treatment as silencing or undervaluing the words of the anorexic protagonists is the assumption that the women needn't be consulted about the cause of their disease. This portrayal aligns with the DSM-IV's characterization of anorexics as "unreliable historians"[187] because they "lack insight into, or have considerable denial of, the problem."[188] However, until the protagonists come under the medicalizing gazes of their families and psychiatric agents, their insights into their problems are quite clear. By directing students towards these narrative tensions, teachers can ask what might have been done differently or what conditions need to be in place (or dismantled) to alleviate each protagonist's suffering. Their problems in the medical sense are physical, but in the broader context of each narrative, Giselle and Marie's problems are psychosocial with physical symptomology. And this is the perhaps humble but fundamentally paradigm-shifting intervention of Kaslik and Patterson's novels, which can be productively mobilized in the classroom: their narratives privilege the voices and internality of their anorexic protagonists to simultaneously foreground their reliability and demonstrate the erasure of their insights. Therefore, a necessary component of sustainable eating disorder treatment should include those who suffer or have suffered from such dis-ease in the development of community-based and -directed forms of prevention, which must also be pursued within decolonizing, non-hierarchal frameworks.

Whether responding with minimizing claims or futility, if students are willing to accept that the media transmits gendered, classed, and racialized ideals, then transforming this awareness into "meaningful or usable knowledge"[189] must involve course work that begins with questioning the notion of an autonomous space beyond the reach of hegemonic narratives and the ideologies embedded in them. Literary depictions of eating disorders testify otherwise.

Chapter Four

Dismantling the Myth of the "Drunken Indian" through Beatrice Culleton Mosionier's *In Search of April Raintree* and Eden Robinson's *Monkey Beach*

"And people around the Welfare office ... always had plenty to say about lazy, drunk Indians; attitudes were so ugly that if you weren't careful you could get into a fist fight with the Welfare person you'd have to see to register for assistance."

– Yvonne Johnson[1]

Haida/Tsimpsian scholar Marcia Crosby writes that, until she began to analyse Canada's policies of assimilation, "it seemed ... that the world was a binary system. First there were white people and then there was the Indian stereotype: The Drunken, Lazy, Dirty or Promiscuous Indian."[2] The "Drunken Indian" stereotype circulates freely in contemporary Canadian media, popular culture, and politics, and brings with it a long history of expression in scientific, anthropological, literary, and sociological discourses. The opening section of this chapter will describe the genealogy and persistence of the stereotype, consider its impact on the social, political, and medical treatment of Indigenous peoples in Canada, and examine how it is being employed, challenged, and at times replicated by Indigenous writers. The stakes of such analytical work are keenly political. Images and narratives of the "Drunken Indian" "turn oppressed peoples into objects, to be held in contempt, or to be saved from their fates by more civilized beings."[3] Through analysing two canonical Indigenous novels that engage with the myth of the "Drunken Indian" and exploring ways to teach critical interrogation of that myth, I seek to articulate the mainstream Canadian cultural reliance on a stereotype that distills complex socioeconomic issues into a racialized – and politically expedient – trait, and the corrosive influence of the myth among Indigenous people. My analysis adds to the body of criticism on stereotypes about Indigenous people by examining the ways in which logics of capitalism interlock with logics of settler colonialism and heteropatriarchy to construct this myth. Critics largely and quite rightly account for the tenacity of stereotypical images as a legacy of colonialism, which "amounts to racial prejudice and creates widespread discrimination."[4] However, Beatrice Culleton Mosionier's (Métis) *In Search of April Raintree* and Eden Robinson's (Haisla-Heiltsuk) *Monkey Beach* suggest there is a present-day economic, as well as ongoing colonial, context to both the stereotype and the realities of substance use in Indigenous communities that must be addressed. Anishinaabe journalist Wab Kinew describes this context: "The big thing that separates us here isn't the alcohol; it's the poverty. Because when a non-Native person passes out, they do it at a curling club or at a Nickelback concert. When a Native person does, they do it on the street, which is shameful – but oh so comfortable."[5] Just as naming the interests of colonial power is crucial in advancing decolonizing struggles, so too is it vital to name the settler capitalist interests that are (comfortably) served by the cultural and political perpetuation of the "Drunken Indian" stereotype.

Mosionier and Robinson's novels each contribute critical insights into the project of dismantling the myth of the "Drunken Indian." Like characters discussed in chapters 1 and 2, the Indigenous protagonists in *In Search of April Raintree* and *Monkey Beach* contend with the affective consequences of living in what Marx calls a "coerced" and "*forced labor*" economy.[6] Yet, because the forced transition to this mode of production is a relatively recent process within Indigenous histories – one that appears in the fiction as violently and insidiously imposed, rather than always already installed – it has not become fully naturalized. My analysis of non-Indigenous narratives of addiction could only interrogate depictions of habitual substance use under constant conditions of capital in the absence of experience and/or knowledge of viable alternatives. None of the texts gestures towards other ways of living, even as each undermines the naturalization of capitalism by exposing the contradictions and injustices of its internal logics. However, Lisamarie in *Monkey Beach* is haunted by memories of a recent past in which labour was land-based, familial, and communal, rooted in knowledge of natural and spiritual elements, and not solely a means of satisfying "the need to maintain physical existence."[7] So, as addiction appears as a response to alienating conditions of capitalism, the content and stakes of this analysis must also critique the complicity of Canadian capitalism in the ongoing colonization of Indigenous peoples and territories. Ultimately, experiences of alienation, which are strongly correlated with alcoholism in the examined novels, are tied to systemic obstacles to pursuing alternative forms of economic, social, and cultural development. Consequently, social suffering in these two canonical novels is depicted as engendered not only by historical trauma emergent from the dismantling of Indigenous lifeways connecting kinship, land, and spirituality, but also by the ideological and material conditions of capital.[8] In fact, these novels betray how the material conditions of late capitalism exacerbate colonial trauma and continue to serve the interests of settler colonialism.

While Robinson's novel contextualizes addiction within material and historical influences of colonial capitalism, Mosionier's *In Search of April Raintree* attends to the effects of the myth of the "Drunken Indian" on Indigenous peoples, as well as its political purchase in upholding logics of settler state capitalism. By engaging with the historically contested meaning of drinking among Métis people, Mosionier's novel strategically employs a metonymic figure for the myth of the "Drunken Indian." The novel refigures this stereotype as an ideological and material force of assimilation within circuitries of settler capitalism. By evoking the specter of the "the drunken Indian on Main Street,"[9] Mosionier's work makes visible the ways in which the image reinforces colonial notions of Indigenous peoples as both inherently inferior and a vanishing race – notions which differently but directly shape the Raintree sisters' aspirations and processes of self-formation, as well as their treatment of other Indigenous peoples. April evokes the image of the "gutter-creature"[10] as justification for repudiating her heritage. Her sister Cheryl, however, comes to internalize the image as destiny when the realities of addiction and suicide in her family collide with and undermine her efforts to "change the image of the native people."[11]

Robinson's *Monkey Beach* also contextualizes habitual drinking in Indigenous communities as a response to assimilation and alienation; it does so by employing cartographic imagery, generational juxtaposition, and a first-person point of view that negotiates a double vision between spectral and spiritless worlds. The novel emphasizes the incremental and seemingly innocuous advancement of logics of capital within the Haisla community of Kitimaat, British Columbia, their relation to the protagonist's experience of alienation, and the discordant external responses to her pain that are aligned with the very forces that inform her social suffering. Lisamarie's drinking is refigured as a practice of social belonging and a periodic response to the alienating experiences of seeing spirits that others cannot. Through interrogating each author's anti-capitalist creative interventions in representations of Indigenous addiction, I seek to expand existing frameworks for analysing Indigenous literatures in Canada – frameworks which tend to focus on acculturation and cultural dispossession. Such analysis unpacks the complicity of capitalist ideologies in the ongoing colonization of Indigenous peoples and thereby opens up potentially decolonizing critical tools and pedagogical strategies.

The final section of this chapter will consider the urgent, transformative role that education can and must play in mobilizing such analyses in the classroom. By equipping students with the critical tools necessary to perceive and challenge derogatory depictions of Indigenous peoples they encounter every day, teachers encourage students to be active, critical, and creative participants in cultural and political life. But in order to do so, students and teachers alike must be challenged through a variety of pedagogical methods to recognize the broader settler colonial, capitalist, and patriarchal relations of inequality in which they are themselves embedded on both sides of the classroom door. Only then will the subversive, resistant, and resurgence work of Indigenous artists – as well as the corrosive stereotypical depictions of Indigenous peoples – be approached with a critically informed sense of accountability. As Barbara Applebaum insists, "the type of responsibility that emerges when one recognizes that one is always part of the system of power and privilege"[12] does not always have to lead to paralytic settler guilt or defensive claims of innocence. Instead, when students become aware of their compelled participation in cultural hegemony, they can be encouraged to rethink complicity not as an individual failing or inescapable fact, but rather a social location from which they can mobilize their privilege and become part of a broader alliance against colonial, economic, and gendered violence.

Hegemonic Depictions of Indigenous People and Alcohol

The Oklahoma Indian Times reported in July 1999 that "Native American youth say ... that they see themselves characterized [in the media] as 'poor,' 'drunk,' 'living on reservations,' 'selling fireworks,' and 'fighting over land.'"[13] Similarly, in 2013, an Attawapiskat First Nation's teacher reported that Indigenous "children were very shaken up when they read the long string of abusive [online] comments that demeaned them as 'lazy Indians,' 'losers,' [and] 'gasoline sniffers.'"[14] Widespread media images of Indigenous peoples as drunk and poor consistently reproduce a causal link whereby drunkenness becomes synonymous with laziness and moral degeneracy. Clearly, such portrayals directly impact the emotional realities of Indigenous youth. The stereotype also costs lives. In 2008, forty-five-year-old Brian Sinclair, a homeless, Aboriginal man, died in a Winnipeg hospital waiting room after being ignored by staff for thirty-four hours, some of whom reported that they thought he was drunk. His family's lawyer argues that Sinclair's death was caused by "negative stereotyping … that led to numerous assumptions being made … [and] caused medical staff, who had the responsibility to intervene and provide Mr. Sinclair with the care he needed, not to do so."[15] By depicting Indigenous peoples as lazy, indulgent, and dependent – economically and chemically – the stereotype symbolizes a betrayal of capitalist ideals of hard work, self-control, and autonomy. As such, the settler capitalist myth of the "Drunken Indian" directly impacts the physical and emotional health of Indigenous peoples.

The myth of the "Drunken Indian" also undermines the legitimacy of Indigenous calls for self-determination and nation-to-nation relations by casting Indigenous peoples as unworthy and irresponsible. In a public example from 2008, a representative of the Canadian government inadvertently but brazenly voiced her belief that the majority of Indigenous peoples are indecorous alcoholics. Darlene Lannigan, aide to then Transport Minister Lawrence Cannon, patronizingly explained to an Algonquin protester, Norman Matchewan, that he could only enter Cannon's campaign office,

> if you behave, and you're sober, and there's no problems, and if you don't do a sit-down and whatever, I don't care. One of them showed up the other day and was drinking … I'm not calling you an alcoholic, it's just to say you're in a federal office. If you're coming in to negotiate, I expect, there's decorum that has to be respected.[16]

Matchewan is only identified in the news piece as a protester from Barriere Lake who came to deliver the demands of that community, the full details of which are left opaque in the article. In the ongoing dispute, the Algonquins of Barriere Lake demand that the Ontario government comply with the Trilateral Agreement, "a landmark resource co-management agreement signed in 1991."[17] Based on its implicit recognition that the Algonquin Nation never signed treaties relinquishing land and resource rights to the Canadian government, the agreement compels the government to consult with the Algonquins of Barriere Lake and share profits stemming from any resource extraction initiatives in the region. Lannigan's racist deployment of a ready cultural stereotype belies an anxiety of authority that seeks to undermine legitimate resistance to practices of settler state capitalism. In other words, by asserting the default assumption that all Indigenous peoples are alcoholics, an identity that already bears popular stigma, Lannigan obfuscates the Algonquin Nation's valid and legal land claims through the evocation of a stereotype that "characterize[es] Indigenous peoples as unmodern and dysfunctional."[18] As Hugh Brody argues, "The Middle Class Idea of the Indian" not only rehearses myths of "relative uncleanliness, lack of reliability in work, drunkenness, and violence," but it frames those traits as "expression[s] of Indian failure in their non-middle class habits and attitudes."[19] The "Drunken Indian" epithet becomes, then, an insidious colonial manoeuvre that frames Indigenous peoples as a hostile but containable threat to the values and material claims of propertied classes.

Through the Lannigan example, it is evident that such values are echoed in public sentiment. Although we cannot take online commenters[20] of the CTV news clip as wholly representative of the majority opinion, eighty per cent of them wondered where the insult lay. Hardly anyone mentioned the details of the Barriere Lake protest; instead the common refrain was, "let's get to the important issues of the election."[21] Far from an isolated example, the tenor of the comments is, according to NDP MP Charlie Angus, endemic of a broader "relentless pattern of malevolent attacks that would be considered inexcusable if they were used against other social, ethnic or religious minorities." Citing online responses to the 2013 floods in Attawapiskat and Kashechewan that included, "I guess the gasoline, drugs and alcohol made them stupid," and "I hope their cigarettes doesn't [sic] get wet … [o]r their oxycontin," Angus argues that these "dehumanizing caricatures" serve to derail conversations away from addressing systemic and political struggle, including "chronic infrastructure underfunding, third class education and the inability to share in economic development."[22] Such ubiquitous (and incensed) assurance that nothing is wrong with insinuating that all Indigenous peoples are alcoholics substantiates Crosby's claim that "the fictive stereotypical Indian … is still perceived as real by many people because of the enormous body of texts and images that support that notion."[23]

The pressing questions become, then, how and why has the cultural fiction that all 'Indians' are alcoholic become and remained so entrenched? And how can the stereotype be exposed and cut off at its roots? An extensive body of medical, historical, and literary work explores the geneses, types, and implications of cultural representations of Indigenous figures. The biological determinism informing the myth of the "Drunken Indian" stems from a long history of scientific work that attempts to prove that "Aboriginal peoples metabolize alcohol differently,"[24] a view which is rooted in "a very European, class-based conceptualization"[25] of what constitutes appropriate behaviours of intoxication. Furthermore, James B. Waldram shows that such racist and classist essentialism "parallels a kind of cultural essentialism ... a view in which the 'primitive,' either Arcadian or Barbarian, naturally succumbs to the demands of the inner savage when inebriated."[26] This belief found expression through eighteenth-century medical discourse, which constructed drunkenness as a defining aspect of "the Indian character," along with "'uncleanness' and 'idleness.'"[27] Although such essentialism has lost its scientific and anthropological legitimacy, traces of these theories linger – with clear political implications – in the contemporary popular imagination, as is clear from the Lannigan example.

Literary representations of Indigenous figures also have a long history of reproducing similarly derogatory portrayals of Indigenous peoples. Mary Lu MacDonald argues that representations of First Nations in nineteenth-century Canadian literature became more negative as contact between European settlers and Indigenous peoples decreased: "In the 1840s ... Indians were frequently depicted as ... either drunk or nostalgic for a long-gone heroic age when described in present time."[28] The figure of Cheryl Raintree's father in Mosionier's novel is portrayed, at least partially, in such a melancholy light. As Cherokee writer and critic Thomas King argued in 1987, "the dissipated savage"[29] can be seen as one of *the* three images of Indigenous literary figures in non-Indigenous writing, all characterized by savagery.

Two of the most canonical accounts of European settlement in Canada express such associations between Indigenous peoples and drinking that endure – but are increasingly challenged – today. In her novelized memoir, *Roughing it in the Bush,* Susanna Moodie claims that the "worst traits"[30] of the "genuine Indian"[31] are "those which he has in common with the wild animals of the forest ... [which] the pernicious effects of strong drink, have greatly tended to inflame and debase."[32] Alcohol is figured here as a triggering substance that provokes an already inherently brute nature into grosser acts of degradation. Similarly, in Frances Brooke's novel *The History of Emily Montague*, Col. Rivers observes the "Hurons" he encounters as curiously "patient of cold and heat, of hunger and thirst, even beyond all belief when necessity urges ... yet indulging themselves in their feasts even to the most brutal degree of intemperance."[33] Unlike Moodie's animalistic, naturalized depiction of the "Drunken Indian," Brooke's is more aligned with the view of willful – though still brute – abandon. While Moodie and Brooke produce more threatening versions of the stereotype, Terry Goldie explores the exploitation of the "drunken ignoble savage" image as a "vehicle for humour"[34] in settler literatures. The First Nations man in Judith Thompson's play, *The Crackwalker*, fulfills such a role, providing comic relief that trades on his incoherent inebriation. Underlying these literary depictions of the "Drunken Indian" stereotype is a broader discourse that constructs Indigenous peoples as inherently primitive, and whether noble or savage, tragic, threatening, or an amusing diversion, the figure of the "Drunken Indian" belongs to a dying past as progress marches inevitably on. And crucially, these images are imagined as neither capable nor deserving of self-determination.

The frameworks that contemporary cultural critics have developed to expose the fallacies of the myth of the "Drunken Indian" fall on either side of a paradigmatic sociological debate. According to Waldram, the "cultural continuity/integration paradigm" contends that "alcohol is best understood within the context of pre-contact cultural formations and post-contact learned behaviors."[35] However, more influential is the "disorganization paradigm," which states that "rapid sociological change, especially ... resulting from increased contact with more *cosmopolitan* Western influences, led to increasing rates of mental illness."[36] To whatever degree this existing critical work exposes the fallacies of the myth, the terms of analysis largely fail to interrogate how the stereotype functions in concert with the acculturative pressures of capitalism. While the "acculturative stress" theory also addresses the "physical and cultural genocide"[37] that occurred (and occurs) as a result of colonization, the focus on acculturation implies that the primary struggles of Indigenous peoples are cultural, while obviating the complex effects of capitalism. This suggestion is reinforced and refined by the description of Western influences as "cosmopolitan," a term that evokes images of genteel, worldly, upper class (and classy) influences confronting less cultured, more provincial peoples.

Literary criticism similarly tends to prioritize the acculturation paradigm in its analyses of addiction and is thereby limited in its capacity to address social suffering in Indigenous fiction. By using acculturation to describe the struggles faced by fictional Indigenous characters, literary critics fall short of doing the analytical work necessary to unpack the ways in which capitalism shapes those characters' experiences of choice, self-worth, and vulnerability. NunatuKavut critic Kristina Fagan identifies the cause of this theoretical limitation as the "critical division of culture from politics."[38] She argues that while "Canadian critics of Aboriginal literature have tended to look through the lenses of culture and colonialism," they do not address "concrete political issues of law, land ownership, and governance" – issues that accompany the recognition that "Aboriginal peoples are 'Nations,' not just 'cultures.'"[39] The novels examined in this chapter challenge the settler capitalist myth of the "Drunken Indian" in ways that reframe addiction as a habitual response to interlocking systems of economic, colonial, and gender-based oppression, rather than a pathological and racialized trait of Indigenous peoples. By reading these interests as "interlocking systems [that] need one another,"[40] I trace the crucial interventions made by these novels to expand similar work pursued by existing cultural and literary criticism, primarily because they depict socioeconomics as inextricably bound to cultural factors in the development and treatment of addiction.

"Bums. Boozers. Gutter-creatures": Internalizing, Wielding, and Deconstructing the "Native Image" in Beatrice Culleton Mosionier's *In Search of April Raintree*

The title character of *In Search of April Raintree* essentializes drinking as an intrinsic characteristic of Métis people. The stereotype is internalized by both April and her sister Cheryl through different reactions to similar forms of economic, physical, and cultural violence. Consequently, one sister starts drinking and eventually commits suicide, at least partially because she cannot interpret the extreme drinking of her father outside the deterministic framework instiled in her through dominant discourse. Prompted by Cheryl's death, April symbolically identifies alcohol as the root of Métis peoples' problems in a gesture that reaffirms the idea that Indigenous peoples are physiologically susceptible to alcoholism, thereby perpetually dodging the role that systemic socioeconomic violence plays in producing, assessing, and disciplining drinking behaviours. While the narrative foregrounds the assimilative power of the myth of the "Drunken Indian," it does not challenge the logic of this power; rather, the novel ultimately – and dangerously – affirms the myth as an inconvenient truth. This feature of the text is another consequence of what several critics[41] have noted as the novel's distinctive tension between depicting how each sister has internalized colonial beliefs about Métis people, and falling short of adequately problematizing those beliefs in ways that invite readers to do the same. Métis critic Aubrey Jean Hanson notes that April is "in many ways the primary voice of racism in the novel," which leaves readers "struggling to maintain a vigilant and critical decolonizing analysis of April's perspective."[42] My analysis of the myth of the "Drunken Indian" in Mosionier's novel is an attempt to maintain such critical vigilance to identify stereotypes and their internalization within the novel through a decolonizing lens.

With the exception of Hanson, the considerable body of criticism on *In Search of April Raintree* was generated in the 1990s and early 2000s, so I situate my analysis as an update to criticism on the novel. Such existing criticism falls into three overlapping categories of analytic concern: ideological, narrative, and sociological.[43] These discussions among critics often focus on interpreting the meaning of two central events in the novel: Cheryl's suicide and April's epiphanic acceptance of her Métis identity. While diversely explained, each event is read by most critics as intimately shaped by the impact of "the drunken Indian on Main Street"[44] stereotype on the characters' lives – indeed, it is the image common to both the "gutter-creatures"[45] and figures of the "'native girl' syndrome"[46] with which the sisters continually contend. However, while the stereotype certainly has racialized dimensions, criticism in all categories has not fully unpacked its class meanings. The stereotype is also shaped insidiously by a capitalist logic that serves specific socioeconomic functions in the narrative. What I seek to add to the existing criticism of the novel, which focuses primarily on institutionalized racism and the ongoing pressures of acculturation, is an analysis of mechanisms of economic violence – mechanisms that disproportionately affect racialized people and are facilitated fundamentally by capitalism. When critics read Cheryl's suicide and April's epiphany through lenses that leave the class struggles of Indigenous people insufficiently examined, such struggles risk being implicitly naturalized. Similarly, while both April and Cheryl express awareness of the socioeconomic dimensions of their struggles, they focus primarily on what it means to accept or deny a Métis identity, an identity into which poverty and addiction are subsumed as essentialized components in the novel.

In "The Limits of Sisterhood," Heather Zwicker (1999) argues that the ultimate incommensurability between April and Cheryl is rooted in "historical, material, and discursive conditions of systemic racism … [which] actively *produce* the relationship between the two sisters."[47] Certainly, the novel foregrounds the processes by which the sisters differently understand and identify with the history and popular perceptions of Métis people, as well as how they are differently identified as Métis. These processes have economic consequences in the novel, which Zwicker does not examine as closely. As such, the historical, material, and discursive conditions of systemic poverty also actively produce the relationships in the novel. By examining Cheryl's relationship with April and Nancy as it is inflected by class, my discussion explores the material challenges to "chang[ing] the image of the native people,"[48] a problem to which April and Cheryl repeatedly return and which is central to the moment of April's epiphany. It follows that the epiphany must be understood in relation to April's initial 'choice' to be (or attempt to pass as) 'white' because "being a half-breed meant being poor … and having to drink."[49] The scene in which April expresses her rage at the destruction addiction has wrought on "[her] people"[50] by smashing a whiskey bottle is debated in terms of whether or not it signifies acceptance of her Métis identity. The stakes of this debate inform the ways in which the final scene is read: critics ask if April's removal of Cheryl's son from Nancy's home constitutes her ultimate reclamation of Métis identity. This debate can be expanded by pointing out that April never has an epiphanic moment of recognizing her class privilege and reevaluating her previous classist assumptions; I will explore how her class privilege appears to intervene in the final scene. Throughout the novel, April's rejection of her Métis identity reflects internalized racism and colonialism, which plays out as a desire for financial and class stability. Believing that "being Métis means [she's] one of the have-nots,"[51] April vows "to become rich"[52] and concludes that the Children's Aid Society facilitates her desire for class mobility.[53] How then do we understand her revolution of mind when she begins her solidarity work by removing a Métis child from a Métis family home?

The goal of this analysis is not to construct hierarchies of marginalization or to subordinate colonial analysis to class analysis; rather, I consider the limitations of literary criticism focused primarily through one system of oppression and articulated through language that risks eliding the presence, specificity, and collusion of other systems of oppression. For example, Zwicker argues that "April's renunciation of history and community in the drive to be a self-made woman in white society marks her as a quintessentially liberal subject."[54] While her actions can indeed be characterized as liberal in terms of how they reflect an individualized notion of self-determination, April's choices are very clearly delineated by her experiences of social and economic mobility. She perceives that these barriers rise and fall depending on whether or not she is identified as Métis or willingly claims or renounces her Métis identity. Criticism that overlooks the class narrative that is encoded along the divergent trajectories of each sister's life does not register the ways the novel portrays April's pursuit of assimilation as economically driven. Sharon Smulders (2006) identifies state violence against the women and children in the novel as "ageism, sexism, and racism,"[55] without also identifying the violence of poverty that interlocks with those systems. Similarly, Anishinaabe writer Kateri Akiwenzie-Damm (1993) argues that Mosionier's novel stages a struggle against "the vestiges of imperialist thought which still cling to the edges of our minds,"[56] a reading that echoes Cheryl's call for reeducation and dispelling institutionalized racist lies. Yet, the present and evolving socioeconomic machinery in the novel that supports the vestiges of imperialism and colonialism (i.e., economic expansion, productive citizenry) must also be analysed. Mosionier frames April's pivotal decision to pursue economic "freedom"[57] as inextricably bound to her repudiation of Métis identity. When April concludes that "white superiority had conquered in the end,"[58] readers must think through how white superiority, or supremacy, also involves economic and political, as well as racial, power and privilege – which is to say, April comes to understand white power is economically leveraged. This chapter pursues an analysis of the capitalist logics of assimilation because *In Search of April Raintree* makes clear that Canadian dominant culture must be named as capitalist, as well as white and patriarchal. I do so by tracing the ways in which class and colonial assimilation inform articulations of alcohol consumption among Métis characters in the novel.

The opening pages of the novel establish a connection between poverty and addiction among Indigenous peoples that foreshadows April's behaviour for the rest of the novel. Explaining how her "mixed blood"[59] parents moved the family from a small northern Manitoba town to

Winnipeg because her father contracted tuberculosis, April declares, "and of course, we were always on welfare."[60] Told in retrospect, the early childhood recollections contain traces of April's adult belief in the inevitability of her parents' poverty because of their racialized status. Sensitive to her father's fluctuating shame and desperation about their poverty, she recalls that "after the welfare cheque days, came the medicine days";[61] and despite the domestic chaos that those days brought, April's sympathy holds when she insists, "I felt so sorry for them and ... was real glad I wasn't sick."[62] April's guileless voice in the opening pages constructs a double view of her parents: superimposed on her picture of them as chronically ill, periodically happy, and inconsistently concerned with the safety of their children, are the reader's knowing translations that 'medicine' actually means alcohol, that the 'peeing' man is actually masturbating,[63] and that her father isn't sleeping on the kitchen floor, he's passed out while his wife has sex with another man in the next room.[64] The gaps in the child's picture are easily filled with the images of the stereotypical "Drunken Indian" discussed earlier – images that depict the parents as deceitful, social welfare abusers, who are sexually immoral. April's naive perspective is portrayed as understandable childish ignorance rather than a sympathetic view of the Raintrees' actions. It is only after April is confronted with other people's explanatory models for her parents' behaviour that she seeks to disavow her heritage and try to pass as white.

The galvanizing shift in April's perspective occurs with her foster family at the DeRosier's farm. Accepting Mrs. DeRosier's accusation that April's parents were "too busy boozing it up to even come visit [her],"[65] Mrs. DeRosier's children mock April by mimicking her parents' drunkenness. April's subsequent realization that she "couldn't run away from *the truth*"[66] raises a crucial question. Why is the revelation articulated as "truth" within the novel? This moment is pivotal to understanding April's self-identification through the rejection of a constructed and abjected Other. While the literary criticism focuses on April's repudiation of her Métis identity, the passage following the discovery makes clear that she repudiates something else first: "So. That's why you never got any better. Liars! That's what you are! All those promises of getting well. All those lies about taking medicine. Liars! ... You never intended to get better. You never cared about us."[67] These lines are curious; at no time prior to this moment in the novel does April express any knowledge of alcoholism, but these immediate and vehement accusations that her parents never loved her because they cannot if they are alcoholics reveal an intertextual reality that assumes 'one truth' of alcoholism – a truth that is produced for April by CAS officials and confirmed by the DeRosier children's performance – that if someone is an alcoholic they cannot love another person.

Hoy points out that April "ultimately treats identity as verb not noun, as action not condition."[68] This observation also requires the caveat that her parents appear to her as irredeemable "gutter-creatures"[69] – nouns – who will not change because of April's belief in their moral and physiological disease. This belief is upheld by the quotation "you never intended to get better." As explored in the introductory chapter, a key assumption of the Alcoholics Anonymous script is that the alcoholic's self-awareness and intentionality are presumed to be compromised. Because they "acted and sounded just like [her] parents and their friends,"[70] the DeRosier kids' mimicry both confirms 'the truth' of her parents' drunken behaviour and inadvertently suggests to April that it is possible for her to avoid being identified as "part Indian," unlike "Poor Cheryl," whose brown skin precludes such "disguise."[71] By reasoning that her appearance could insulate her from detection, April belies her internalization and reproduction of the biological racialization of the 'disease' of alcoholism.

April's reaction to her parents' alcoholism does not take into consideration their complex and unresolved personal experience and its application to an entire population of people; however, April's reaction also characterizes that of social welfare policy. As Smulders argues, "while the conjunction of 'welfare cheque days' and 'medicine days' hints at the complex social forces that … overdetermine the girls' removal," the social workers decide to "apprehend [the] children rather than to support families through other forms of intervention."[72] Such absolutism belies an institutionalization of two intertwined stereotypes: that neither poor people nor alcoholics are capable of raising children. The implications for the children vary, of course. Perhaps their material and emotional circumstances do improve, but in the process, April internalizes the ideologies of oppression that have affected families intergenerationally, ideologies which infuse such state intervention: that Métis, alcoholic, and poor people are weak and dependent. April learns that these qualities are, first, interconnected, and second, morally degenerate and deserving of punitive response. The ironies of this lesson are tragic though. Under circumstances of relative powerlessness – she is economically dependent, segregated from other children, exploited for her labour, prohibited from communicating with her sister, and falsely accused of humiliating sexual acts – April at once recognizes the external forces of her oppression and seeks to achieve power within those systems by emulating the privileged. Such recognition and striving are exemplified through her pursuit of white privilege via economic means and her final act of removing her Métis nephew from a nurturing Métis community. It is important to highlight the circuitry through which such striving is made to appear desirable and necessary.

In a mirror scene to her later epiphany, April examines her light skin and decides she can pass as a tanned white person. Her decision has multiple dimensions. There is certainly a rejection of what she has internalized as a marker of physiological degeneracy, but the most gripping aspects of her racial concealment appear to be informed by class aspirations, which are made possible by white supremacy. As she explains,

> When I grew up, I wouldn't be poor; I'd be rich. Being a half-breed meant being poor and dirty. It meant being weak and having to drink. It meant being ugly and stupid. It meant living off white people. And giving your children to white people to look after. It meant having to take all the crap white people gave. Well, I wasn't going to live like a half-breed. When I got free of this place, when I got free from being a foster child, then I would live just like a real white person.[73]

This passage articulates April's internalization of a dominant discourse that frames Indigenous peoples as physically and morally squalid and grotesque, as well as a drain on state resources – this is the discourse that determines Mrs. DeRosier's treatment of April. A critical contradiction at the centre of April's world view is also evident in this passage: she expresses an awareness of how disenfranchisement has left Métis people vulnerable to "all the crap white people g[i]ve"; however, while she views drinking as disease, April persistently believes that Métis people can and do choose to drink and thus to "give" their kids away. That choice is, for April, the ultimate arbiter of success and failure, beyond any systemic influences. Moreover, the passage foregrounds April's belief that whiteness produces independence, wealth, responsible child rearing, cleanliness, and beauty *because* being Métis produces its opposites. And so, April's vow to "live just like a real white person" implicitly expresses a desire to give rather than take "all the crap white people g[i]ve."

April's decision to try passing as white also challenges Smulder's contention that "Mosionier emphasizes how the child welfare system socializes indigenous people to choose dependency."[74] April's experience in foster care generates a desire to be personally autonomous, which she believes is attainable as she "start[s] working and making money."[75] And indeed, such goals lead to forms of employment, marriage, and divorce that bring her significant capital and class power, especially relative to Cheryl. From this class position, April's relationship to "the imagery of the stereotypical Drunken Indian" represents what Duran calls the instrumental factor in "attun[ing] Western collective consciousness to the notion of a North America awaiting the civilizing and rationalizing mission of European settlement."[76] Throughout her relationship with Cheryl, April is positioned in ways that echo the colonial stance towards Indigenous peoples – with government in the role of beleaguered caretaker mirroring Irlbacher-Fox's characterization of the Canadian state's policies towards and treatment of Indigenous peoples. April expresses this anxiety when ruminating over how to spend her divorce settlement money in relation to her decision to live with Cheryl. In examining her options as a landlord, she anticipates that Cheryl will insist on taking "native boarders" and worries that she will "end up letting people stay for free all the time."[77] Her anxiety belies a fear of being taken advantage of by others. In this formulation, April peremptorily views Cheryl's anticipated actions as supporting dysfunction rather than part of a collective struggle for survival.

Cheryl's relationship to the "Drunken Indian" stereotype, on the other hand, seems more critical, political, and complicated than April's, perhaps because she was raised by more political parents who supported her early decolonizing approach to education. Meanwhile, April becomes something of an experiential empiricist. First, she reasons that she cannot be Métis because she does not have any of the stereotypical qualities of that identity, which speaks to how she has come to internalize the racialized aspects of the stereotype. And second, because she only ever sees Métis people on Skid Row, she equates the image with reality, leading her to definitively conclude that "making a better way of life for native people, giving them a better image"[78] is not possible, which again illustrates the insidious nature of the stereotype. The image is 'the truth' for April. Cheryl, however, is taught as a child that the "Native Image" is a deliberately constructed fiction that serves the nation-building efforts of the Canadian colonial state. Placed in the care of a Métis woman and a white man, Cheryl is taught to be proud of her heritage,[79] which influences how she sees and interprets the world around her. Cheryl learns to contextualize and challenge the colonial history she is taught at school.

This difference between the sisters' upbringings shapes the development and dramatic resolution of the tension between the three images of the "Drunken Indian" represented in the novel. The Métis figures seen through April's eyes are absolute, willful, and inveterate alcoholics; the Métis figures seen through a young Cheryl's eyes are "easy victims" to the "disease of alcoholism"[80] imposed by white settlers; and the Métis figures seen through an older Cheryl's eyes are individuals who are neither defined by nor condemned to die because of their drinking. The novel actually works to emphasize the inadequacy of explaining the marginalization of Indigenous peoples as a result of addiction by problematizing the first two views in contrast to the third. The CAS workers, the DeRosier family, and April believe in the former, insisting that drinking precludes the ability to be responsible for oneself and others. The characters Mark DeSoto and Henry Raintree resemble this stereotype.

Cheryl, however, struggles to make sense of the differences she perceives between the second and third views of alcoholism. As she explains to April about her friend Nancy,

> [She] does drink and does other things that you would never dream of doing. But she also holds a steady job, and she's been at the minimum wage for a long time. They use her and she knows it. And she gets depressed about it. But with her education and the way things are, she knows she doesn't have many choices ... Okay, she doesn't have much, maybe she never will have much, but what she's got she shares with her family. And she's not an exception.[81]

Instead of distilling Nancy's drinking into an identity, as symptomatic of another diseased 'gutter creature,' Cheryl bluntly – almost defiantly – notes that Nancy drinks, but she also works hard for very little money. Identifying drinking as just one of the many things April would not do, Cheryl highlights how Nancy's actions are situated on a continuum of negotiation; drinking, working hard, experiencing depression, and sharing with others are all framed as responses to a lack of economic choices. The unpatronizing and pragmatic empathy with which Cheryl figures Nancy as one of a multitude of people living in similar contexts is starkly contrasted to the explanations April gives for the condition of Métis people: "The Indian people allowed themselves to be treated like children."[82] Cheryl does not explain Nancy's drinking as a reaction to the suffering she has experienced; in fact, she does not defend her drinking at all. Rather, she emphasizes Nancy's exclusion from middle-class white Canada as a function of how a sexist and racist economy works. She locates Nancy's behaviour within a capitalist economy, in which race and gender can determine the limits of social reproduction. April responds that she "didn't know that,"[83] which might be unsurprising given how she separates herself from any Indigenous communities of mutual support. It is Cheryl who lives with Nancy and regularly interacts with other women at the Friendship Center who share similar experiences. Furthermore, Cheryl is part of a mutual support network that is populated perhaps by 'alcoholics,' but characterized by respect and trust. As she tells April later on, "[Cheryl] never made us feel like we owed her, you know? ... [She] made me laugh ... She did a lot for other girls, too. She had these big plans ... Then she quit."[84] Until Cheryl's moment of disillusionment, she seems to have developed a more nuanced, less essentializing, systemic view of alcoholism than she expressed as a younger woman. I argue that this second view informs Cheryl's suicide, as well as troubles a reading of April's epiphany as a decolonizing gesture.

As evident from her reaction to meeting her father, Cheryl's strategy of deconstructing the "native image"[85] is rooted in, as Damm points out, a romanticization of Métis people and their history that becomes just as unattainable and "unrealistic as April's negative perception of them as 'gutter creatures.'"[86] As we learn from her journals after her suicide, finding out 'the truth' about her parents – especially her father – has as profound an effect on Cheryl as it does on April. She laments that, *"in the olden days, he would have been a warrior if he had been all Indian. I had made something out of him that he wasn't, never was."*[87] However, this is not just an expression of disillusionment. This crucial passage reverses without subverting Moodie's view of the "genuine Indian"[88] who is inherently susceptible to dissipation. Evoking the idea of blood quantum as the basis of being *"all Indian,"*[89] Cheryl's lament implies that the "genuine Indian"[90] is inherently immune, rather than predisposed, to the desire for or pernicious effects of alcohol. The formulation belies her internalization of a dangerous claim of biological determinism that figures present-day Indigenous people as a dying race.

Cheryl's crisis also seems informed by other factors. As April wonders, "that meeting with Dad, maybe it destroyed her self-image. Funny, though, since she had seen that side of native life before."[91] Ironically, despite Cheryl's ability to contextualize and understand the lives she encounters every day, she cannot do it when it comes to her own family. On one level, the novel seems to suggest that an image, stereotype, or even social problem cannot be deconstructed if you look for evidence of change in individual, one-on-one encounters. The damage has been done, and the solutions are not easily achieved through revolutions of individual minds. But in addition to a methodological tragedy, Cheryl's tragedy can also be read as ideological. Her description of meeting Henry belies an unearthed foreboding that alcoholism is inevitable and unstoppable – "*the worst disease, for which there is no immunity*"[92]:

> *I stand quietly, hiding the horror which is boiling inside of me. I hadn't known what to expect. But it wasn't this, this bent, wasted human form in front of me. My father! I am horrified and repulsed ... by the surrounding decay; by the hopelessness. The cancer from the houses I've been to has spread into this house, too. To destroy.*[93]

In later conversations with her sister, she will 'admit' that April was right, that her parents were "Bums. Boozers. Gutter-creatures,"[94] echoing and bitterly accepting the words April uses, with all their implied meaning. However, in the initial moment of recognition, Cheryl accepts a different truth than April does as a child and adult. Certainly, it is a truth "no less misleading than April's similar callow conclusion as a youngster,"[95] but it reconfirms a different aspect of the "Drunken Indian" stereotype: that it is a physiological, cancerous epidemic, in which the "Drunken Indian" becomes further 'evidence' supporting the myth of a dying culture. As Zwicker argues, "the personal is deeply political in Cheryl's formulation of identity politics"[96]; and the opposite is true as well – the political is deeply personal. Because she identifies so closely with her father and struggles to both support individual people and change the system that shapes their circumstances and behaviour, Cheryl is shamed by her discovery, shamed by her father, and implicitly shamed by what he has let himself become. As she writes in her journal: "Gratefully, I swallow some beer. Disgust, hatred, shame...yes, for the first time in my life, I feel shame. How do I describe the feeling? I swallow more beer."[97] This passage seems unproblematically to equate Cheryl's drinking with the revelation that her father is an alcoholic. Compellingly, it also conveys how the personal, political, historical, and economic complexities of her experience are unspeakable, thereby configuring her drinking as both numbing strategy and avoidance. Despite a long history of naming colonialism as a significant obstacle to Indigenous healing, Cheryl's automatic response to overwhelming emotions suggests that self-medication appears understandable when experiential and material reality eclipses the capacity for critical analysis.

The narrative structure also leaves the reason for her deterioration a mystery. We do not understand why she retreats from her activism. Nor are we initially aware of the circumstances surrounding her hospitalization, which her journal later reveals to be the result of being assaulted by a john. But when the journal finally explains her reaction to meeting her father, it is the effect not the content of the revelation upon which April focuses. The discovery of her father's alcoholism then becomes the answer, the understandable reason, for her self-destruction, according to April.

Critical readings of Cheryl's suicide also seem to accept the discovery as a justified reason for her extreme behaviour. Michael Creal (1999), for example, describes Cheryl's "discovery that [her father] was a hopeless and pathetic drunk … [as] shattering for Cheryl and eventually led Cheryl herself into a life of alcoholism and prostitution."[98] To accept this trajectory does not illuminate the circuitous connections between the two events, while it risks reproducing the stigma of addiction in general and the myth of the "Drunken Indian" in particular. Perceived as hopeless and pathetic by Cheryl, her father is given room to speak[99] and contextualize his present circumstances, even if such historicization may be emotionally inadequate for Cheryl. Such a reading seems to echo April's reading of Cheryl's diary, which perhaps accounts for a largely unproblematized critical interpretation of April's epiphany as an acceptance of her Métis heritage. This acceptance is based on a troubling reliance on the belief by both April and most critics of this novel that the fundamental problem facing Indigenous communities is alcoholism. I argue that this narrative works to reveal the dangerous inadequacies of explaining the material inequities of Indigenous peoples as a result of addiction. It does this through the development and climax of April's understanding of alcoholism, as well as through consistently emphasizing her individualized notions of liberation.

The articulation of April's prejudice begins with abstract proclamations about the inherent degeneracy of all Métis people and erodes further into reactions to her parents' and Cheryl's drinking that border on the absurd. Her initial claims that her parents abandoned her "all for a bottle of booze"[100] ascribe full, malicious intent to the Raintrees, without questioning the legitimacy of CAS's authority to remove April and Cheryl from their home. Her subsequent anxiety that Cheryl has "come down with a drinking problem"[101] also expresses April's internalized understanding of alcoholism as a physiological disease, which carries racialized dimensions given her childhood view of her sister as racially predisposed to alcoholism. Her epiphanic moment of accepting her Métis identity is complicated because it is predicated on the contextually inadequate blaming of alcohol for all problems facing Indigenous peoples, rather than a pride in her Nation, history, and culture. The scene in which April smashes Cheryl's empty whiskey bottle follows Cheryl's funeral and occurs before April reads Cheryl's diary. Without recognizing the systemic issues that Cheryl articulates and both sisters experience, albeit differently, April's "frenzied rage at how alcohol had torn"[102] apart the lives of her family and people appears as not only simplistic, but rather dismissive of the complexities of Métis people's lived realities in its displacement of systemic and historical issues onto a single decontextualized factor (or symptom). It is on this narrow foundation that April is understood by critics to have accepted her identity.

Hoy describes April's subsequent epiphany as evidence of a "mobilization of the relations, historic and present, in which she finds herself. She begins to deploy positively connections she has hitherto resisted, especially when she claims, 'MY PEOPLE, OUR PEOPLE.'"[103] Such mobilization appears mainly conceptual, however. Despite the significance of the moment as a starting point, the 'community' April chooses is confined to her affluent, white partner (with all his questionable political ethics) and her Métis nephew. In light of Zwicker's astute argument that the major tension in the novel is the incommensurability between April's "deeply liberal"[104] feminism and Cheryl's "uncompromising … insist[ence] that mainstream society come to terms with her indigeneity,"[105] April's claim, while profoundly moving and no doubt "redemptive within the text,"[106] seems like a continuation of the liberal paternalism she has internalized: registering Henry as wholly "innocent,"[107] she frames herself as his saviour. And while Hoy argues that the final scene "enacts a political affiliation, an involvement with others in the hopeful shaping of the future,"[108] the details of April's reflections suggest otherwise. April relates: "Nancy began explaining but I stopped her. I told her I understood everything … for Henry Lee and me, there would be a tomorrow … I would strive for it. For my sister and her son. For my parents. For my people."[109] The abstract articulation of her commitment is significant: April will strive for a better tomorrow in the name of her relatives and more generally all Métis people, yet unfortunately she refuses dialogue with a person who could provide vital insight into the practical challenges of attaining such a goal, believing that she understands "everything." Her adoption of Henry is certainly understandable as a way of keeping familial kinship ties close. Yet, it is important to trace the ways in which the colonial beliefs April has internalized are still at play in this pivotal decision. Perhaps the scope of her understanding has expanded to view Indigenous peoples in the light that Cheryl does in her early essays, as "easy victims"[110] who need saving through a 'striving' with which April has little experience in a community-based sense. The final scene effectively places her in a position of unquestioned class- and capital-based authority similar to that of the CAS officials who removed April and Cheryl from their parents earlier in the novel.

Margery Fee argues that the "novel [is] about the forcible construction of Native as Other,"[111] by focusing on the ways in which a Native stereotype is constructed to become the dominant psychological reality for the characters, as well as the lens through which meaning is made of what is seen. The narrative figures the construction and interpretation of image as pivotal to understanding the ways in which self-identification is negatively constructed. The novel is also about the forcible assimilation and acculturation of Métis people into a capital-based economy through coerced striving for class privilege. The choices presented to April and Cheryl – and their negotiation of them – foreground a tension between pro/claiming Métis heritage and involvement in Métis community, and securing economic stability. April associates being Métis with being one of the "have-nots"[112] and therefore strives for upper-class white privilege. Eager to be among the "rich girls" who go to "academies,"[113] she studies décor and fashion magazines[114] so that "when fortune kissed [her] with wealth, [she]'d be well prepared."[115] While she quickly becomes disillusioned with the superficial and ambitious hypocrisy of the rich family she marries into and recognizes that she too "criticized the native people,"[116] April continues to insulate herself from interacting with other Métis people or taking on "native boarders"[117] as a means of perceived financial survival. Conversely, Cheryl is taught pride in her heritage, is encouraged to speak her beliefs, and remains committed to mutually supportive Indigenous communities, none of which constitute economically secure or physically safe choices in the novel. That is not to suggest that Métis pride and beliefs are inherently "unsafe" and economically damaging. However, I argue that Mosionier renders the context of claiming proud Métis identity and nationhood "dangerous" because expressions of such pride can be punitively disciplined (whether through violence or through restraint from workplace mobility).

Mosionier's narrative critically interrogates this deeply conflicted framework of choice by juxtaposing the sisters' trajectories based on their repudiations and reclamations of indigeneity. The effect is that survival is depicted as contingent on ideological investment in striving for a promised, possible future, which requires acceptance of individualist and colonial values of self-determination within the Canadian state economy. Such values are emphasized through the reproduction and racialization of the lens through which Indigenous addiction is viewed in Western culture: as evidence of laziness, indulgence, and moral and physiological (yet willful) disease; as negative motivation for Indigenous peoples to pursue class-based success; and as a means of undermining broader public support for Indigenous rights to self-determination. Mosionier's novel positions the "Drunken Indian" myth as central to plot and characterization in ways that expose these insidious consequences. Eden Robinson's *Monkey Beach* invites an interrogation of the "Drunken Indian" myth for different reasons than *In Search of April Raintree*. Rather than an explicit narrative force, the myth is undermined through historical contextualization of habitual substance use.

'There's a treatment centre where the residential school used to be': From Colonial to Capitalist Confinements in Eden Robinson's *Monkey Beach*

Monkey Beach refigures addiction as social suffering by portraying chronic drinking and drug use as common, adaptive habits of characters who have endured residential schooling, lateral violence, cultural dispossession, and poverty. The novel also situates sobriety as more likely for those characters who have attained relative privilege by adjusting to colonial and capitalist transformations imposed on their shared community. The latter group of characters rejects the legitimacy of Indigenous spirituality and resistance through reiterations of an individualistic and secular ethos. This ideological pressure forms the thematic and narrative structure in which substance abuse emerges as a means of both social belonging and personal pain management. Within this clearly delineated character schema, the protagonist, Lisamarie Hill, is positioned as having to negotiate her parents' assimilative expectations against the reality and responsibility of her spiritual visions. As prophet and warrior, Lisamarie loses the remaining members of her community who were invested in fostering her gifts. Following these losses, she begins drinking "as a way to escape"[118] the lonely responsibility demanded by her visions. As when *Heave*'s Serrie embraces sobriety, Lisamarie does so by enthusiastically immersing herself in the narrative of individual salvation through work. And also like Serrie, the original reasons for her pain do not evaporate; the novel ends with Lisamarie seeking to reunite with those who share her spiritual visions in "The Land of the Dead"[119] after experiencing another tragic consequence of past colonial violence. Lisamarie's drinking is refigured as social suffering insofar as her drinking has an adaptive function. I will conclude by addressing the sacrificial logic of Robinson's narrative and its uneasy relation to the settler capitalist myth of the "Vanishing Indian."

Like *In Search of April Raintree*, Robinson's novel significantly revises the "Drunken Indian" stereotype. In contrast to each of the texts examined in this study, however, it is not drinking that is primarily treated as individual pathology – it is the perceived refusal, signified by habitual inebriation, to accept the supposed inevitabilities of a naturalized colonial and capitalist future. *Monkey Beach* foregrounds legacies of both residential schooling and corporate incursions into Haisla territory as reiterating values of secularity and individualism in ways that shape Lisamarie's emotional and spiritual health. In this way, her habitual drinking functions to mute her knowledge not only that life can be otherwise, but also that it is already richer and more spiritually meaningful. Her failure (or inability) to conceal her spiritual visions is perceived by her family as a mental health issue – precisely because her gift has become decontextualized from kinship and tribal relations. Through its portrayal of drinking as a consequence of the traumas of acculturation, *Monkey Beach* re-signifies addiction as exposing the limits of full participation in a colonial and capitalist economy precisely because of the cultural violence on which such systems are predicated. By mobilizing Indigenous and Marxist theory, I demonstrate how Marxist analytical tools can be deployed in a decolonizing analysis of Indigenous depictions of addiction. Establishing the compatibility between these two anti-capitalist modes of analysis assists in understanding what the imposition of a capitalist mode of production means for Indigenous governance, subsistence, and cultural practices, which arise from a fundamentally antithetical view of the human than that implied under capitalism.

Presupposing that "man's physical and spiritual life is linked to nature mean[ing] simply that nature is linked to itself, for man is a part of nature,"[120] Marx argues that humanity's pre- or non-capitalist state is one of species being, or a state of relationship to the rest of humanity and the natural world that is not separate or individually driven. I do not use Marx's theory to suggest that Indigenous peoples are inherently closer to nature or more spiritual than non-Indigenous peoples. Rather, I emphasize the compatibility between Marx's view of a non-capitalist state of being and an element common to many Indigenous world views that sees the relationship among humans, land, nature, the spiritual realm, and ancestors as continuous and interdependent. Justice, for instance, describes Indigenous kinship relations in ways that particularize, necessarily, the abstraction of Marx's theory: "Indigenous nationhood is ... an understanding of a common social interdependence within the community, the tribal web of kinship rights and responsibilities that link the People, the land, and the cosmos together in an ongoing and dynamic system of mutually affecting relationships."[121] Through this critical lens, I seek to articulate the major tension in *Monkey Beach* between Lisamarie's knowledge and memories of past kinship relations – relations characterized by interdependence and shared spirituality – and her fragmented familial and social relations in the present, which are shaped by the increasing pressures of acculturation into an individualizing economy. I address the evidence and implications of such compelled transition primarily through examining the state of the oolichan fishing industry, the imagined futures of the Haisla youth, and the depictions of psychiatric interventions in Robinson's novel.

This framework also seeks to expand literary analysis of *Monkey Beach* to address the complex representational critiques of capitalism developed by Robinson, an approach that contributes to unpacking the novel's decolonizing possibilities. The majority of existing criticism on the novel examines its depictions of past colonial trauma and contemporary cultural tensions and subversions. For example, by reading *Monkey Beach* as a "distinctly Aboriginal reformulation of the Canadian Gothic,"[122] Jennifer Andrews argues persuasively that the novel contests and subverts a literary tradition in which "Natives are marginalized, romanticized, or entirely absent ... creating a space for Native cultural revitalization."[123] Following Andrews, Jodey Castricano interprets the Gothic or "supernatural" elements of the text as contesting dominant cultural norms of secularity and rationality by "confront[ing] the reader ... with the possibility of a spirit world and asks that we at least reflect upon the ontological, epistemological, and spiritual consequences of Western culture's materialist drive that has attempted to eradicate 'superstition or 'mysticism' in the name of psychology."[124] Similarly, Richard Lane asserts that "in reworking the Canadian Gothic via her use of trickster writing,"[125] Robinson contests hegemonic gender norms that reveal the complexities of "mediating between (at least) two cultures (Haisla and Western, commodity culture)."[126] Focusing instead on the cultural identity politics surrounding Robinson's novel, Kit Dobson grapples with what he perceives as the novel's "anxiety about how it will be recognized as either a representative 'Native' text or as a more universal/Western novel aimed at a mainstream audience."[127] Yet, these analyses seem to exemplify Kristina Fagan's concern that Canadian criticism of Indigenous literatures "look through the lenses of culture and colonialism,"[128] while eliding examination of "concrete political issues of law, land ownership, and governance," issues that accompany the recognition that "Aboriginal peoples are 'Nations,' not just 'cultures.'"[129] My reading of *Monkey Beach* focuses on the ways in which Robinson constructs colonial violence as paving the way for capitalist expansion. Such expansion compels dependence on and complicity in the perpetuation of capitalist modes of production and ideological values that are, as Glen Coulthard (Yellowknives Dene) so astutely puts it, "structurally committed to maintain ... ongoing state access to the land and resources that contradictorily provide the material and spiritual sustenance of Indigenous societies on the one hand, and the foundation of colonial state-formation, settlement, and capitalist development on the other."[130]

Robinson emphasizes the colonial and corporate appropriation of Haisla territory in the North Coast region of British Columbia by employing cartographic imagery This develops a circuitry among the corporate transformation of Kitimat and Kitimaat Village,[131] the dismantling of interdependent kinship practices, and the habitual drinking of Haisla youth. Industrial capitalism, symbolized by the history and continuing presence of the Alcan aluminum smelter in Kitimat, is the mechanism that sustains and perpetuates the legacies of colonization and residential schooling, while simultaneously creating new forms of social suffering. Robinson builds this path-clearing function of colonialism into the narrative through the sequencing of historical events that opens the novel. Following her description of colonial settlement in the area, Lisamarie explains that, "when Alcan Aluminum moved into the area in the 1950s, it built a 'city of the future' *for its workers*."[132] This industrialized form of settlement is predicated on the belief that the company is entitled to move into Haisla territory, as well as build an entire city to house its workers. The possessive pronoun also implies that its workers will be comprised of both settler managers and inhabitants of Kitimat, whose community will be transformed into a host for the plant and delineate the boundaries of economic belonging in the area.

Significantly, this corporate incursion was not an isolated decision of one company but rather a state-driven project. According to Alcan BC Operations, "Alcan was invited by the B.C. government to investigate the establishment of an aluminum industry in the northwest"[133] in the 1940s, and by the 1950s, Alcan and the BC government came to an agreement over the necessary land and water rights. Echoing the ways in which missionaries established villages to house their converts,[134] Alcan transformed the Kitimaat region to house its workers and to produce aluminum. According to the official BC tourism website in 2013, "today, Rio Tinto Alcan, Eurocan Pulp and Paper and the construction of the Enbridge oil pipeline make up the economic engine that fuels the economy in this area."[135] Over the course of one generation, then, a narrative informed by government, tourism, and industry has discursively positioned progress in the region as indispensable, resulting from a process of intrusion and transformation of the land and people. Alcan provided steady work for Lisamarie's dad,[136] which was preferable to tenuous self-employment or band council work. Figuring itself as the future of Kitimat (and by extension, Kitimaat) in the novel, Alcan relegates its pre-existing residents to the past or the decaying present. Fostering an image of "a 'dying people'"[137] in the public imaginary, this narrative of progress has been instrumental in reproducing the colonial argument that Indigenous peoples are holding on to an obsolete past. This sentiment has an underlying capitalist logic: Indigenous peoples pose a threat to the Canadian state because they remind settlers of their broken treaty obligations. Indigenous movements like Idle No More, Grassy Narrows, and the Unist'ot'en Camp actively continue to resist resource extraction and corporate expansion into Indigenous territories[138] because, as Thomas King reminds us, "land has always been a defining element of Aboriginal culture. Land contains the languages, the stories, and the histories of a people. It provides water, air, shelter, and food. Land participates in the ceremonies and the songs. And land is home."[139] Corporations and the Canadian state, however, are capitalist enterprises; as King puts it, "for non-Natives, land is primarily a commodity, something that has value for what you can take from it or what you can get for it."[140] As Ella Soper explains, despite "[Alcan's] attempts to naturalize its presence in British Columbia with the slogan, 'Aluminum, an element of B.C.' … Robinson's criticism of the smelter … is nonetheless palpable."[141] Indeed, Robinson's criticism constitutes a denaturalization of the state-initiated capitalist settlement in Kitimat and transformations of Kitimaat Village.

The material and social intergenerational effects of Alcan's presence form the context in which Lisamarie's drinking becomes refigured as adaptation or psychic survival. Traditional fishing practices – and the kinship relations associated with them – are disrupted by the labour demands of the Alcan factory. While Soper argues that "Robinson implicates colonial violence for the imminent collapse of the oolichan industry,"[142] the details of Lisamarie's memories of her family's trips during her childhood to catch oolichan incite another reading. As Lisamarie explains, not only have resources become severely compromised from pollution "by all the industry in town [… but] you have to pay for gas, and you need a decent boat and have to be able to spend a few weeks out there if you want to make grease. If you have a job, it's hard to get enough time off work."[143] She traces the practical sequence of events that are interrupted by the imposed dependence on labour to make a living. These utilitarian considerations thus become an ironic confirmation of Ma-ma-oo's advice to her granddaughter Lisamarie that "old ways don't matter much now. Just hold you back."[144]

The individualism and secularity expressed by Lisamarie's parents, Al and Gladys, reinforces through generational juxtaposition the social consequences of a fundamental shift from traditional forms of subsistence and kinship relations to a capitalist mode of production and family arrangements. Marx argues that the process of forcing estranged labour onto humans "changes for [them] the *life of the species* into a means of individual life … It makes individual life in its abstract form the purpose of the life of the species."[145] Gladys, in particular, is portrayed as deliberately disavowing the spiritual gifts of her youth that had connected her to the community, and instead rehearsing to her children the promises of individual achievement within a capital-based economy. Ma-ma-oo reveals to Lisamarie that Gladys had "the gift" for "predictions,"[146] but she has either forgotten or chosen to ignore how to "see things."[147] Rather than act as a guide to her daughter, Gladys refuses to validate Lisamarie's connection to the spirit world, consistently disciplining her daughter to re-produce capitalist norms according to logic of individualism and secularity. In the novel's opening scene, Gladys responds to her daughter's curiosity about what the crows were trying to tell her by saying, "clearly a sign, Lisa ... that you need Prozac."[148] The terms of this refusal are significant because Lisamarie is refigured as mentally unstable for trying to communicate with a world unrecognized by mainstream society. Although expressed as innocuous sarcasm, this reinterpretation is far from benign when it leads to Lisamarie being sent for psychiatric assessment. Gladys also insists that Lisamarie pursue what constitutes both monetary and class success according to capitalist values. Rejecting her simple desire to make "good money"[149] by working a blue-collar job, Gladys instead argues that she "could be a doctor or lawyer or whatever [she] wanted."[150] The irony is clear: Lisamarie's "idea of being free"[151] means relief from having to constantly strive for material stability, while Gladys's is more attuned to the social dimensions of class; a white-collar professional job garners more capital *and* class privilege. Significantly, Gladys seems to believe in the promise of unfettered possibility and choice.

Robinson highlights the intergenerational psychological and economic impacts of capitalist ideology within contemporary Indigenous communities through her representation of the ways in which the industry in the town also shapes the dreams expressed (or not) among Indigenous youth in the novel. The juxtaposition between Gladys's generation and Lisamarie's constitutes the second way in which *Monkey Beach* portrays industrial capitalism as a mechanism that sustains and perpetuates the legacy of colonization and residential schooling. The intergenerational consequences of early colonial incursions are symbolized through a clear character schema. Every character in the novel who struggles with addiction (except Lisamarie) is a survivor of residential schooling. Of four Hill siblings, Lisamarie's Uncle Mick and Aunt Trudy were sent to residential school.[152] They are the ones that also struggle with alcoholism, while Lisamarie's father Al and his sister Kate do not. The intergenerational impacts and lateral violence wrought by the system are also established in a number of other ways. For example, days before his disappearance, Jimmy learns that his girlfriend, Karaoke, was raped by her uncle Josh, a local fisherman, who also suffered from sexual abuse at residential school.[153] This discovery prompts Jimmy to take a job on Josh's boat, where he kills Josh and accidentally drowns in the process. Robinson further suggests that Josh's nephew and Lisamarie's close friend Pooch may have also been abused by Josh.[154]

However, the legacy of residential schooling is not the whole story of *Monkey Beach*, nor is it the whole story of settler state tactics of acquisition and assimilation against Indigenous communities and peoples in North America. Roland Chrisjohn (Onyota'a:ka of the Haudenausaunee), Sherri Young, and Michael Maraun caution against focusing too closely on addressing individual experiences of residential schooling as the basis for Indigenous health and liberation. They argue that the schools "were only one of the tactics deployed to bring about the 'normalization' of Aboriginal Peoples,"[155] and warn that state-funded (even if not entirely state-run) treatment centres are invested in ensuring Indigenous and non-Indigenous people alike assimilate, or self-reform, to meet the demands of living in a capital-based economy. While *Monkey Beach* explores the intergenerational legacies of residential schooling, it also reveals the limitations of an analysis of residential schooling as a historical cause that eclipses more systematic understandings of the myriad present-day factors that continue to inform and compel self-harming behaviours. The intersections between the past and present forces of acculturation in the novel are well illustrated in Sam McKegney's description of the absent presence of residential schooling as "a hidden weapon, a deadhead lying beneath the water's surface."[156] Arguing that "the reality of residential schooling abuse remains, for Lisa-Marie [sic], cryptic and elusive," McKegney also implies that a pervasive complex of contemporary forces works to maintain a silencing surface tension.[157]

The deadheads of traumatic memories are often forcibly submerged in the novel by the grinding requirements of economic survival, which work in Robinson's novel to impede healing, prompt aggressive pursuits of inebriation, and offer a single uniform vision of survival. Lisamarie, Tab, Pooch, and Frank all voice similar dreams for the future, which are characterized by individual notions of self and predicated on escape from Kitimaat and separation from family. Lisamarie wants to quit school and work in the cannery[158] because "the idea of being free" appeals to her;[159] Tab declares she will "work in the cannery ... and save all [her] money ... Then [she's] going buy a house";[160] Pooch commits to a "'work in the potlines and buy a truck' plan";[161] and Frank simply intends to "[get] the hell out of [Kitimaat]."[162] Despite their own financial problems, their parents directly and indirectly encourage these goals.

The thematic link between the young people's goals and their drinking is illuminated by Judith Butler's theory of performativity. The novel seems to exaggerate the dreams of Lisamarie and her friends in a way that frames their efforts to achieve them as the "incessant and *panicked* imitation of its own naturalized idealization."[163] Perhaps we could read such hyperbole as a dramatization of the "point[s] of weakness"[164] that occur when such norms are forcibly rehearsed. By the end of the novel, Pooch has committed suicide; Tab is living in Vancouver, estranged from her family; and Lisamarie is deciding whether or not to return from the Land of the Dead. While Frank does find employment working on the Kemano II project,[165] it is work unwittingly implicated in the further environmental degradation and social deterioration of Haisla territory.

Unlike the struggles of the other youth in the novel, however, Lisamarie's has an added spiritual dimension, which results from her negotiation of dual – validated and invalidated – visions of what she experiences as reality. As Lane points out, the narrative presents "the notion that connecting with spirit worlds can be a normative behaviour"[166] through the continual repetition of such encounters. Reading her as a trickster figure, Lane argues that Lisamarie transcends gender constructs in ways that demonstrate that

> notions of normative behavior are constantly produced by society, and constantly need to be re-addressed; if a society comes into conflict with another set of "norms," say via colonization, then it may be trickster's talk to show the way back to previous modes of behaviour prior to the "originary" set of norms. Note that the constant re-production of norms is also a point of weakness.[167]

As discussed above, the narrative describes Haisla pre-capitalist subsistence and spiritual practices as non-capitalist forms of social reproduction, which can be read as an "'originary' set of norms." Therefore, we can see that Lisamarie is taught through interactions with her mother and grandmother that another set of norms must be practiced in order to survive. Even though Ma-ma-oo still shows Lisamarie the "old ways,"[168] she believes they have little practical application in contemporary Kitimaat. However, Lisamarie has little control over the appearances of the "the little man,"[169] nor does she seem willing to or capable of resisting communication with the crows or the b'gwus. It is Lisamarie's double-visioned position between these ideological relations to her lived reality that incite her parents to send her to therapy and lead later to her drinking.

In the world of the novel, then, industry and psychiatry are elements of the same circuitry governed by compatible ideologies of individualism and secularity. The industry in town shapes the dreams, or sense of possibility, expressed by the Haisla community by reiterating capitalist values of individual survival or achievement and refusing the existence of a spirit world. Lisamarie is not sent to a psychiatrist because of perceived addiction, even though she regularly drinks with her friends. Rather, her parents react to her emotional withdrawal, insomnia, and seeing of ghosts by taking her to the hospital "to find out what was wrong."[170] When no physical causes are found, her mother makes a psychiatric appointment. The therapist, Ms. Jenkins, does all but draw a map for Lisamarie outlining the limits of normalcy. After goading her into falsely admitting that she sees ghosts "for attention,"[171] Ms. Jenkins assures Lisamarie she will be "back to normal in no time"[172] – 'normal' defined as denying the extra-rational elements of the universe. It is important to note that, at this point, the reader knows that Lisamarie has been raped by Cheese, that it is the one-year anniversary of Mick's death, and that she is struggling with how to communicate with spirits and the responsibility such correspondence involves. But the articulation of these issues is not fostered in the therapeutic setting.

Castricano interprets the encounter as exhibiting "Ms. Jenkins's blindness to the spiritual implications of Lisa's experience," as well as her determination to impose "her worldview on that experience."[173] This claim supports the argument that "Western culture's materialist drive has attempted to eradicate 'superstition' … in the name of psychology,"[174] yet the more punitive aspects of the "worldview"[175] being imposed require further examination. The hegemonic secularity underpinning Ms. Jenkins's outright dismissal of the existence of ghosts is certainly evident. However, requiring more analysis is the significance of "the thing," with "no flesh, just tight, thin skin over bones," that Lisamarie sees clinging to Ms. Jenkins, "whispering in her ear."[176] Lisamarie overhears the creature taunting Ms. Jenkins about her partner's fidelity; it also feeds on Lisamarie while Ms. Jenkins prompts her to deny that she sees ghosts. Crucially, it is the thing that tells Lisamarie what it "knew Ms. Jenkins wanted to hear."[177] In effect, it actually saves her from being pathologized by Ms. Jenkins's world view. The scene's subversive possibility lies in its destabilization of psychiatric authority. But, of course, the underlying threat in the scene is that Lisamarie must capitulate to survive. Following this experience, Lisamarie announces to her parents her plans to quit school and work at the cannery.[178] I argue that the narrative establishes a continuum between familial intervention and treatment in ways that suggest psychiatric treatment functions to reshape a particular kind of subject, according to a secular ideology that reframes spirituality or spiritual awareness as mental illness.

The assimilative logic of Lisamarie's psychiatric experience has far-reaching consequences, which eventually lead to her drinking as well as shape the tenor of her sobriety. After therapy, she continues to have visions but tries to ignore them. Regardless of the accuracy of her belief, she blames herself for Ma-ma-oo's death because, as she reasons, "if I had listened to my gift instead of ignoring it, I could have saved her."[179] Her guilt captures the novel's broader thematic concerns with the danger of repressing the spiritual realm, not simply because Lisamarie could have prevented her grandmother's death, but rather, because her guilt arises from feeling compelled to renounce her gifts given the threat they pose to her social and economic survival. It is this combination of guilt and desire for community that leads her to Vancouver, where "for the first time in [her] life," she feels "cool, if only because [she] bought the booze. What had started out as a way to escape turn[s] out to be a ticket to popularity."[180] The specific escape she seeks can only be inferred by the sequence of events. Her guilt regarding Ma-ma-oo's death is grounded in her fraught relationship with her visions. In order to avoid seeing them, she stays drunk or high, only seeing ghosts "when [she's] sober."[181] She spends two years living on trust-fund cheques until Tab's ghost appears to her one morning to say that her recklessness is a threat to others and that her chosen community does not care about her. Evidently ready to listen to ghosts who remind her of her family connections, Lisamarie returns to Kitimaat to get sober.

Throwing herself into schoolwork "with an enthusiasm [she] usually reserved for partying,"[182] Lisamarie finds an alternative way to suppress her guilt and her gifts. The parallel between studying and partying suggests that the underlying motivation for such zealousness is escape. She reasons that "it's hard to philosophize about how crappy life is when you're trying to finish a zillion things at once ... When I started to feel sad, I'd head back inside and hit the books."[183] This period is characterized by her attempts to fulfil her family's expectations, figured as a reprieve from her sadness and its broader spiritual significance. However, the Vancouver scenes are not portrayed as an entirely negative experience. Lisamarie describes it as "a blur. A smudge. Two years erased, down the toilet, blotto."[184] While this indicates that it was largely a waste of time, money, and her body, the ironic double meaning of "smudge" also suggests that the two years might have been a cleansing – "a smudge" to prepare her body for healing and a return to a participatory role in her family. And yet, Jimmy's disappearance disrupts Lisamarie's newfound contentment. His disappearance symbolizes the resilience of colonial violence, which is also facilitated by contemporary confines of class and gender inequalities. Jimmy dies while killing Josh, whose abuse of Karaoke and Pooch is represented as a repetition of past abuse – "the cyclical extension of violence seemingly initiated through residential school abuse."[185]

The novel ends as it begins with cartographic imagery, which seems to reinforce its portrayal of a Haisla nation fractured, dispersed, and contained by persistent forms of colonial and economic violence. The final chapter, entitled "The Land of the Dead," separates out from the quotidian realm a spiritual world, in which Lisamarie is reunited with Ma-ma-oo and Mick, who signify both tradition and resistance, respectively. There, it seems, Lisamarie finds connection with a sense of "Indigenous nationhood ... a common social interdependence within the community, the tribal web of kinship rights and responsibilities that link the People, the land, and the cosmos together."[186] While Ma-ma-oo tells her to "go back,"[187] Lisamarie's choice is left ambiguous. Yet it is certain that going back means leaving behind the community that would support her growth into a visionary and warrior who sees "magical things"[188] and shares the responsibility to help "Fuck the Oppressors."[189] By returning to her family, who instead support her pursuits of individual achievement and financial security, Lisamarie risks re-immersion in circumstances that engender her spiritual alienation. In the Land of the Living, Lisamarie's habits of drinking, drug use, and enthusiastic studying in a non-Indigenous education system are all framed as methods of repressing her "dangerous gift."[190] If readers are to assume she will choose to return to that world, they are given little indication that the ideological and material circuitries of her social suffering have been positively transformed.

The indeterminate ending of *Monkey Beach* seems to hinge on Lisamarie's ability to choose between assimilation and death (literally, but also through the persistent insensibility of inebriation). While sustaining the novel's central critique of the unlivable choice faced by Lisamarie's generation of Haisla youth, the ending also risks re-inscribing the "Vanishing Indian" myth. A kinship-founded Haisla nationhood characterized by spiritual knowledge (Ma-ma-oo) and political resistance (Uncle

Mick) becomes accessible only in the Land of the Dead. The characters who imagine themselves as part of "an ongoing and dynamic system of mutually affecting relationships"[191] have all died, except for Lisamarie. The final image of the novel – Lisamarie coming to consciousness on Monkey Beach – implies that she will pursue a middle ground between the Land of the Dead and the world she sees in dreams, which is "whole, with no clear-cuts, no pollution, no boats, no cars, no planes."[192] As she wakes on the shore of the Land of the Dead, she hears the b'gwus[193] "close, very close," but also "in the distance ... the sound of a speedboat."[194] Both seem to provide her with solace. The b'gwus' howling signifies the enduring, if invisible, presence of "magical things" that profoundly comfort her,[195] while the boat perhaps suggests rescue – or at least an equally enduring presence to that of the b'gwus. And yet, the underlying source of Lisamarie's struggle throughout the novel has been negotiating the spiritual within an increasingly colonized and individualized context. Until the concluding moment, it has clearly framed this negotiation as untenable. Survival – economic, emotional, and physical – for all the characters risks dependency on assimilation and renunciation of the spiritual.

Within this climate of constraint, addiction in Robinson's novel comes to signify what Métis critic Jo-Ann Episkenew calls "a form of self-medicating to temporarily ease the despair of personal and political powerlessness."[196] Because habitual drinking and drug use are portrayed in *Monkey Beach* as ongoing consequences of colonial and capitalist acculturation, it stands to reason that the interconnected grip of both systems should be taken into consideration in the prevention and treatment of addictions. Fagan's argument that narrowly focusing on Indigenous cultural issues serves to obfuscate ongoing issues of land rights, and the fact that "a foreign justice system has been imposed on Aboriginal nations"[197] applies to reading addiction and its treatment in *Monkey Beach*. During Aunt Trudy's last party before admitting herself to an eight-week rehabilitation program, someone exclaims, "Alberni? Really? There's a treatment centre where the residential school used to be?"[198] The image of a treatment facility literally replacing a residential school decades later is potent in several ways. It signifies for Trudy a direct trajectory from residential school to rehab, which suggests that the trauma of residential schooling has led to her drinking and that the treatment centre is an attempt to ameliorate the symptoms of that trauma. Both facilities are also figured as places of state-run cultural separation, confinement, and discipline. Trudy must leave her community for eight weeks; the imposition of treatment seems inevitable given the absence in the novel of any tribal-based healing options. And given that the only other representation of psychiatric discourse in *Monkey Beach* highlights its coercive and regulatory logic, the Alberni treatment centre symbolizes an extension of colonial and capitalist acculturation. By explicitly identifying drinking as a consequence of the traumas of acculturation, *Monkey Beach* re-signifies addiction as exposing the limits of full participation in a colonial and capitalist economy, precisely because of the cultural, economic, and spiritual violence on which such systems are predicated.

Monkey Beach differs from *Heave, Skinny,* and *Consumption* in its method of refiguring addiction as a collective rather than individual iteration of social suffering. Although I focus primarily on the context of Lisamarie's drinking, Robinson develops a clear schema that depicts characters with histories of residential schooling and lateral violence as habitual substance users, who are resistant to or unable to meet the individualistic and secular demands of the sober characters. While my analysis supports the claim that *Monkey Beach* portrays drinking as a method of personal pain management in response to forces of colonial and capitalist alienation, it risks implying that addiction is a symptom of incomplete assimilation. The novel does leave room for such an interpretation given both the stark contrast between characters based on their user status, and the absence of any characters who have suffered personal violence but do not use alcohol or drugs. The novel's ending seems to relegate to the Land of the Dead the possibility for Indigenous nationhood, resistance, and resurgence. So too does *Monkey Beach* risk rehearsing the myth of the "Vanishing Indian" on a structural level by "consign[ing] to dysfunction"[199] those characters who cannot or will not adapt to the ideological and material demands of an increasingly industrialized and secular economy. However, rather than dismiss the novel's significant destabilization of individualizing concepts of addiction, both *Monkey Beach* and *In Search of April Raintree* condition an awareness of the influences of colonial and capitalist forces on habitual substance use, which requires an attendant critical resistance to viewing those influences as deterministic. While these texts are problematic, they are still significantly subversive, even as they risk reproducing uncomfortable stereotypes of inevitability and addiction vis-à-vis political trauma. The final section of this chapter considers ways to mobilize rather than elide these contradictions in the classroom.

Undoing Indigenous Stereotypes in the Classroom

When taken up in the classroom, literary depictions of addiction among Indigenous people provoke questions about the construction and influence of stereotypes, the politics of representation and cultural consumption, and the impact of historical events on the present and future. This section will offer an introductory discovery exercise to facilitate such generative questions, as well as address two particularly common forms of student resistance to recognizing contemporary forms of colonization and Indigenous decolonization efforts. Justice argues that Indigenous writers "challenge both Natives and non-Natives to surrender stereotypes, committing ourselves instead to untangling colonialism from our minds, spirits, and bodies."[200] As educators, we are tasked with re-presenting Indigenous literatures in ways that show how such untangling, or decolonization, involves identifying and dismantling racist stereotypes in their most insidious forms. We may individually denounce stereotypes, but any commitment to decolonization must also include recognition of how and why they are reproduced and a vigilant commitment to contesting them. Through their depictions of habitual alcohol and drug use as emotionally adaptive responses to conditions of colonial capitalism, *Monkey Beach* and *In Search of April Raintree* certainly contest the myth of the "Drunken Indian." But recognizing that the authors' depictions of addiction experienced by Indigenous characters represents a counter-hegemonic discourse is not a straightforward endeavour in the classroom. As a settler teacher, I am also mindful of the ongoing work I need to do to inform myself of how my education and experiences as a non-Indigenous person inform my pedagogy. Resources that have been instructive in this regard include Anishinaabe-Kwe scholar Sheila Cote-Meek's *Colonized Classrooms: Racism, Trauma and Resistance in Post-Secondary Education*, Quechua writer Sandy Grande's *Red Pedagogy: Native American Social and Political Thought*, and Paulette Regan's *Unsettling the Settler Within*.

The concept of adaptation assumes a dynamic between individual and influential context, or in Butler's terms, between improvising behaviours and scenes of constraint.[201] Yet, we cannot assume that students will recognize historical and contemporary colonialism, economic barriers, and generational trauma as politicized, instrumental contexts. Students arrive in the classroom already shaped by dominant cultural beliefs and differently engaged in critical self-reflection and social critique. As Justice discovered in his university teaching, "culturalism – a conceptual model of timeless cultural stasis over adaptive and dynamic political nationhood – had shaped (perhaps distorted?) [his] students' understanding of Aboriginal peoples and issues long before they'd even entered the classroom."[202] How, then, can educators pose Indigenous stereotypes as a problem – a problem in which settlers in particular are implicated, and which has interpersonal as well as broadly social consequences – in order to unsettle and encourage students to recognize Indigenous issues and nationhood in literature and society, engage in critical self-reflection, and ideally, pursue transformative social engagement?

Involving students in the problem of stereotyping must first prompt the identification of stereotypes in our daily social and media interactions in order to establish the existence of dominant discourses and the real impact they have on the lived realities of Indigenous peoples. In order to identify and deconstruct stereotypes, students must also be provided with the critical tools to resist complicity and acceptance of such stereotypes. As Martin J. Cannon (Six Nations of Grand River) argues, a transformative pedagogical approach to teaching Indigenous literatures must prompt students to "think about the construction of the Other, and their own investment in that construction."[203] This means discovering students' own participation in cultural hegemony, and their responsibility to be critical in their consumption of culture. To this end, an opening exercise should involve identifying and analysing Indigenous stereotypes. While an approach similar to the ones described in chapters 2 and 3 could be cautiously employed, I hesitate to recommend having students write poems or lists that make claims about Indigenous peoples. Instead, by immediately presenting students with a comprehensive list of stereotypes compiled from Indigenous sources, educators avoid potential student arguments that stereotypes do not exist. Teachers can then facilitate class discussion that seeks to identify from where these depictions or impressions come, what definitions of addiction they imply, and how such depictions might affect the lived reality of Indigenous people in general, as well as those who use substances habitually.

Rob Schmidt's website *Blue Corn Comics* explores Native Americans in popular culture. A significant portion of the website's content seeks to tackle stereotypes. "The Harm of Native Stereotyping: Facts and Evidence,"[204] is a comprehensive resource for the discovery exercise described above. It provides a crucial counterpoint to dominant stereotypes because it explains in detail how such stereotypes are individually and collectively harmful to Indigenous peoples. By mapping the sources of knowledge from which depictions of Indigenous addiction emerge, students can begin to recognize patterns and discrepancies. They can then see the need to develop critical tools capable of tracing thematic patterns and political meaning of dominant narratives, as well as discern the meaning and stakes of subversive narratives of addiction. This opening exercise situates individual reflection within an atmosphere of collective inquiry, a dynamic which can be a touchstone for educators to return to when students personalize or become defensive about the social implications of stereotypes in which they may be invested. By being able to reference the pervasiveness of certain (mis) conceptions, educators can frame the response as collective and collaborative, rather than entirely personal. In terms of its applicability in a literature classroom, this opening exercise also (re)positions students to distinguish stereotypes as themes or tropes in the literature to be critically recognized and analysed.

Engaging Student Resistance

By starting from "the framework that everybody is a potential ally,"[205] this opening exercise can situate students as active, critical consumers of culture, invite them into a collective struggle for meaning, and begin to clarify the stakes of such work. From this foundation of collective inquiry and within a problem-focused framework, students can begin to critically approach literary depictions of substance use among Indigenous people in their aesthetic, social, and political contexts. Yet, students currently express several common forms of resistance to the premises of critical thinking about colonialism, oppression, and Indigenous nationhood. Because identifying and dismantling stereotypes requires an examination of the historical and present-day socioeconomic positions of those about whom the stereotypes are constructed, and because such dismantling requires the formation of a critical lens capable of assessing who is telling such stories and to what effect, teaching critical consciousness means talking about power. It also means tracing how power works as a set of direct and indirect relationships in which we are personally implicated from relative positions of privilege and oppression and as cultural producers and consumers. Educators should expect resistance to this process.

Similar to those explored in chapters 2 and 3, arguments that minimize oppression and assert the ultimate autonomy of all individuals are particularly strong when teaching Indigenous literature. Students frequently resist the suggestion that certain media images and narratives are 'political' or have real-world implications. They reason that they are not so gullible as to 'buy in' to racial and gendered stereotypes. Similarly, a few students in my classes have even characterized the politics of representation as 'borderline conspiracy theory' because, steeped in the intentional fallacy, they find it unbelievable that dominant narratives are premeditated and coordinated so pervasively. Students can also struggle with the notion of colonial narratives as a twenty-first century reality and doubt that historical injustices are still playing out in contemporary politics. And finally, even if they provisionally accept that stereotypes shore up unequal power relations and have material implications, when it comes to addiction, students frequently assert that individuals always have choice and that the ultimate onus is on the individual to withstand and overcome material constraints. Certainly, facilitating the "Addiction is" exercise discussed in chapter 2 could productively problematize these assumptions about addiction in general. In relation to addiction among Indigenous peoples, pushing students to reconsider the idea that high rates of addiction are due to a lack of willpower, students will no longer have fodder for their generalizations. Evidently, these rebuttals emerge from deeply personal, as well as political, contexts, and so critical pedagogical practices must be informed by and tailored towards students' various emotional, moral, social, and material investments in resisting the development of critical consciousness. Two distinct expressions of resistance to this process that have been identified by Razack, which I will consider in relation to teaching Indigenous literature, are rights thinking and essentialism.

Rights Thinking and the Denial of Historical Influence

The critiques imbedded in subversive literary depictions of addiction among Indigenous peoples rely on the recognition that past and ongoing forms of colonial oppression have a direct impact on the emotional, spiritual, and physical wellbeing of Indigenous peoples. Given the pervasive dehistoricizing force of neoliberal policies and thinking, the pedagogical task of analysing the history and effects of the "Drunken Indian" myth becomes acutely challenging. Razack identifies the source of denials of historical influence as rights thinking, which is "based on the liberal notion that we are all individuals who contract with one another to live in a society where each of us would have the maximum in personal freedom. Starting from this premise, there then are no marginalized people and no historical relations of power."[206] This form of individualism has consequences for undoing stereotypes about Indigenous peoples in the classroom: students' perceive empowerment as an inherent possession that can be exerted by will and hard work, or suppressed through disease or a weak will; historical influence becomes invisible and irrelevant; and relations of power and oppression, "privilege and penalty,"[207] are denied.

If students resist tracing continuities between historical and contemporary power relations, educators are faced with a rather daunting challenge. It can be tempting to opt for a lecture-style approach, which certainly has its advantages in that students are presented with a clear analysis that they can consider and question. Yet, this approach risks establishing a dynamic that positions teachers as authoritative messenger of an individual 'perspective' or 'belief.' This leaves students both unengaged in deeper questions of their individual complicity and agency in a historicized present, as well as operating under the assumption that teachers are trying to convince them of a new truth. Teaching history backwards is one way high school history teachers have approached this problem. It begins from the premise that current events arise from a sequence of historical events, and aligns with Friere's concept of problem-posing pedagogy because it involves students in interrogating events in their social world in ways that are meaningful to them.

In an Indigenous literature class, students could be asked to build a list of current events that involve Indigenous peoples and issues. If, for example, students raised the issue of calls for a national inquiry into missing and murdered Aboriginal women in Canada, the first task for teachers would be to identify what students already know about the issue. Illuminating inconsistencies and links between such responses will then guide teachers to ask why people think Indigenous women are particularly exposed to violence and why Stephen Harper's Conservative government opposed an inquiry in 2014. These lines of inquiry necessarily pull on the strings of colonial history. When appropriate, to assess whether students are willing to begin analysing Indigenous issues through a historicized lens, ask students to consider what is lost when colonization is situated as something that occurred in the past.

Rights thinking and the denial of historical influence are forms of student resistance that express skewed, essentialized notions of empowerment, which ultimately situate individual choice as more powerful than systemic relations of power. Fundamental to this form of resistance is investment in Us/Them dichotomies. The starting place from which many critical pedagogy theorists (see hooks, Razack, Spivak) engage with this form of resistance is identifying and challenging mechanisms of marginalization, or those cultural, political, and geographic forces that divide Us from Them and facilitate dehumanization of Them by Us. Within such patterns of Us versus Them thinking, Indigenous peoples have two choices: they can either seek success through assimilation or choose marginalization by resisting assimilation. For example, in his work with privileged learners, Cannon works to break down such dichotomies between Indigenous and non-Indigenous peoples by reframing identity-making processes.[208] Through posing a series of questions that seek to elucidate the ways in which non-Indigenous identity and privilege depends on the maintenance of "certainty about Indigenous difference,"[209] Cannon offers a framework within which to challenge divisions between Us/Them. These questions include asking students to find out on whose land they live, learn, and work;[210] to identify "their varying exclusions, so that an invested and shared sense of commitment and thinking about action might be realized";[211] and to examine how environmental sustainability is a shared problem between Indigenous and non-Indigenous peoples.[212] Through prompting students to articulate shared and contingent relations of power and oppression, Cannon seeks to illuminate opportunities for alliance that proceed from dismantling binary understandings of the Other. One of the objectives in a literature or cultural studies classroom is to eventually situate the stereotype of the "Drunken Indian" as an example of Othering, as a feature of colonial narratives that relies on dehumanizing stereotypes to delegitimize Indigenous claims to sovereignty and self-determination, and thus clear the way for Indigenous art to create new ways of knowing.

Essentialism

Razack identifies recognizing the essentializing of women as a significant aspect of addressing denials of oppression. Exploring "the perils of both essentialism and non-essentialism,"[213] Razack echoes Martha Minow's conclusion that "when difference is thought to reside in the person rather than in the social context, we are able to ignore our role in producing it."[214] When attempting to dismantle the myth of the "Drunken Indian," essentialism is a minefield that must be tread upon carefully. For example, teachers logically cite the high rates of addiction among Indigenous peoples as proof of a systemic problem. But students often want to interpret such rates as endemic of a pathological attachment to what they perceive as a dying culture. Countering this claim with strategic essentialism – that is, that all Indigenous peoples share a central form and experience of oppression rather than an innate inferiority – does the crucial work of "emphasizing cultural values and practices, [which] is an important oppositional strategy."[215] However, this position risks promoting systemic determinism as well as reinforcing biological essentialism by implying that, as a racialized group, Indigenous peoples react uniformly to systemic oppression. Two approaches to engaging student resistance rooted in essentialist assumptions include tracing complicity and mobilizing Indigenous explanatory models of addiction.

Extending Razack's response to the problematic essentializing of women, an approach to dismantling the "Drunken Indian" myth should involve "tracing complicity" by the "mapping of relations among"[216] Indigenous and non-Indigenous peoples along multiple, interlocking axes of privilege and oppression. As with the problem of rights thinking, essentialism concludes with the notion of fundamental difference and autonomous existence. But because privilege relies on oppression, teachers must work to provoke students to make connections where they mainly see divisions. Andrea Smith suggests in teaching about racism that "it is easier to talk about capitalism first. When everyone begins to see that they are not part of the five percent, it gives them the investment to start addressing the other privileges. They realize that addressing issues of class entails their own liberation too."[217] Numerous critical pedagogy theorists provide excellent resources for undoing privilege in the classroom (see Applebaum, Razack, Spivak, Cannon, and hooks, for example). But one rather exemplary exercise specific to recognizing privilege in relation to Indigenous addiction would be to map through close reading the ways in which the Raintree sisters are implicated in each other's class, race, and gender privilege. As outlined in the textual analysis earlier in this chapter, April's class privilege involves investing in and leveraging the racialized myth of the "gutter creatures" against Cheryl. As such, the construction of stereotypes as a function of relations of power may become the focus of analysis, rather than Cheryl's innate disease.

Essentialist claims that ultimately reproduce the myth of the "Drunken Indian" can also be challenged through presenting students with – or assigning a research project that tasks students with identifying – Indigenous understandings of habitual substance use and pathways to healing. Episkenew frames addiction as one form of "postcolonial traumatic stress response"[218] that demands healing models that name colonialism as the sickness.[219] By asking students to take seriously Episkenew's argument that "most settlers deny that their society is built on a sick foundation and, therefore, deny that it requires a cure,"[220] teachers challenge students to evaluate how this view of addiction challenges essentialist views, as well as interrogate investments in refusing or dismissing Indigenous knowledge. Sto:Lo writer Lee Maracle suggests that habitual drinking occurs in what she calls "a state of madness,"[221] which is outside family and community. In her view, people end up "quarantined" from one another via a "very Euro tradition."[222] She relates that her family found "re-entry to wholeness," or sobriety, in part through story and positive rituals,[223] which means that "colonization has to be addressed. And then dis-integration has to be addressed and then restoration of family has to be addressed."[224] Maracle's visual conceptualization of addiction depicts the "whole person" at the centre of several rings of concentric circles, the outer ring of which is the site of madness.[225] Students can be encouraged to creatively engage with this view of the individual as inextricably tied to context, family, social support, and systemic forces to create their own depictions of intersections among sickness, suffering, healing, and health.

Episkenew and Maracle counter essentialism by tying substance use to colonial trauma and fragmentation of family. While similar in their critiques of colonialism, they offer distinct views that may be interpreted by students as personal views. The Aboriginal Healing Foundation's 2007 report "Addictive Behaviours among Aboriginal People in Canada" provides an expansive analysis of addiction and healing strategies. The AHF explains that "knowledge of the collective experience of Aboriginal people, especially related to the legacy of residential school abuse and its intergenerational impacts, has become a cornerstone of the Aboriginal healing movement."[226] Following a detailed explanation of how the colonization of Canada by Euro-North Americans – *The Indian Act* – forced relocation and confinement to reservations, and how residential schooling constituted "aggressive assimilation" and "cultural genocide,"[227] the report explicitly connects these historical events to the epidemics of addiction, suicide, and violence that plague many Indigenous communities. The bulk of the report outlines changes made to state-run treatment centres guided by the AHF's recommendations.

Developed from contributions by "eighteen key informants," as well as Elders of the Ottawa community and "keepers of [traditional cultural teachings] in Inuit, Métis, and First Nation communities across Canada,"[228] these recommendations are unanimous: only through a full understanding of colonization and how its various technologies continue to affect the emotional, spiritual, mental, and physical well-being of Indigenous peoples in Canada can healing begin and effectively disrupt cycles of violence and self-destruction. The AHF model for Indigenous healing can be mobilized to demonstrate how de-essentializing views of addiction foster tangible healing initiatives and have been recognized by the state.[229]

Taiaiake Alfred (Mohawk) explains that "young people, those who have not yet learned to accommodate to the fact that they are expected to accept their lesser status quietly, are especially hard hit by defeatism and alienation ... Suicide, alcohol and drug abuse, cultural confusion, sexual violence ... they suffer these scourges worse than anyone else."[230] These expectations are communicated through structural and cultural forms of oppression. Stigmatizing depictions of addiction in general and of addiction among Indigenous peoples specifically participate in such harmful messaging. This chapter argues that challenging addiction through reading and teaching *In Search of April Raintree* and *Monkey Beach* involves recognizing how hegemonic narratives reproduce the myth of the "Drunken Indian," interrogating how this myth shores up settler colonial interests, acknowledging its devastating effects on Indigenous peoples, developing critical tools to examine how depictions of addiction may be subverting such stereotypes, and mobilizing such narratives within a broader decolonizing movement. Towards these ends, educators not only need to share analyses around why students resist critical thinking in relation to Indigenous literature, but we must also share approaches to transforming denial of oppression into recognition and recognition into action.

Because the classroom is not a vacuum and learning is not a time-limited process, students will take their experiences of critically analysing stereotypes of Indigenous peoples within a decolonizing framework into their lives in ways that cannot be predicted. Whatever the specific activities pursued to mobilize course content into social action, the question of what constitutes decolonizing action-oriented pedagogy must be guided by a clear understanding of positionality. So often, wanting to 'make a difference' in marginalized communities can look like telling marginalized communities what is best for them. Involving guest speakers and assigning extracurricular community or cultural activities are two common ways of challenging students to engage with a course by interacting with people they may perceive as directly impacted by their views. For example, teachers can invite Indigenous artists to share their creative and political philosophies with students, and assign each student to ask a question based on problems posed in previous class discussions. While teachers can certainly suggest ways to apply a critical awareness of the "Drunken Indian" myth outside the classroom, it is integral to facilitate discussion among students that asks them what they think such action should look like, and frame an analysis of each suggestion within an understanding of solidarity. South Asian activist and writer Harsha Walia explains that,

> One of the basic principles of Indigenous solidarity organizing is the notion of taking leadership. According to this principle, non-natives must be accountable and responsive to the experiences, voices, needs and political perspectives of Indigenous people themselves...Specifically, this translates to taking initiative for self-education about the specific histories of the lands we reside upon, organizing support with the clear consent and guidance of an Indigenous community or group, building long-term relationships of accountability and never assuming or taking for granted the personal and political trust that non-natives may earn from Indigenous peoples over time.[231]

Leadership is the key concept here. Because the myth of the "Drunken Indian" is leveraged to delegitimize Indigenous people's and nation's ability and right to self-determination, action-oriented pedagogy must proceed from the premise that Indigenous communities know what they need to heal and thrive. Making space to talk about what this means for students outside the classroom is crucial action-oriented pedagogy.

Beyond the Classroom: From Innocence to Accountability

"If our imaginations do not work, then neoliberal ideology does not have to dictate what we do; rather it infects us like a virus and we speak the old, oppressive story as though we believe it and it alone, without recognizing that it lies at the root of our privations. It is not censorship; it is a much more insidious and subtle form of social control."

Larissa Lai[1]

I conclude *Challenging Addiction* by briefly returning to the question that animates this book: how can literature incite social change? After several years of researching discourses of addiction, mapping its representation in popular culture, examining its meaning in my personal life and in the lives of friends and family who often had a lot to say about the subject, teaching addiction narratives in university classrooms, and most recently, facilitating community-based harm reduction workshops with people who use drugs and alcohol, this question is just as urgent now as it was when I began writing this book in 2007.

Stereotypes about addiction permeate our social, cultural, and political realms. The term itself is so laden with a mixture of scorn, judgment, pity, fear, and resignation that it is difficult to interrogate its history, meaning, and effects without reproducing those same stereotypes. As this book has examined, such stereotypes are often internalized, which makes their use in justifying the interests of capitalism, settler colonialism, and patriarchy even more insidious. This book has examined the ways in which select Canadian fiction variously works to refigure addiction as social suffering rather than individual pathology or immoral indulgence. By implicating logics of capitalism, patriarchy, and settler colonialism in the development and treatment of habitual behaviours marked as pathological, *Heave, lullabies for little criminals, Skinny, Consumption, In Search of April Raintree,* and *Monkey Beach* challenge stigmatizing views of addicts and anorexics that essentialize adaptive behaviours as physical, psychological, and/or moral disease and often justify disciplinary interventions. I have also argued that teaching literary depictions of addiction requires setting the conceptual stage for students to perceive and interrogate the systemic critiques that the novels offer. By examining the common forms of student resistance that such critiques can spark, I engage with Sherene Razack's call to understand denials of oppression as attempts to position oneself as innocent in the face of forms of inequality. Given that "as long as we see ourselves as not implicated in relations of power, as innocent, we cannot begin to walk the path of social justice and to thread our way through the complexities of power relations,"[2] challenging or undoing addiction in the classroom by teaching social suffering means tracing relations of complicity and accountability in order to pursue collaborative, sustainable, and transformative pathways towards structural equality and justice.

So, can literature incite social change? I think so, but only with collective effort, intention, and accountability at all points along the continuum of artistic creation and reception – from fostering critical reflection on how language and power intersect, nurturing the radical imagination, strengthening independent publishing and distribution networks, teaching literature as participating in creating or exploding deeply held cultural assumptions, pointing to the need for and examples of struggles for social justice, and positioning ourselves as accountable learners, producers, critics, and teachers of literature, which necessarily involves forging connections between classroom learning and social action. In his 2015 dissertation, "Literature and Social Change: Writing, Criticism and Teaching in Neoliberal Canada," Greg Shupak examines "the political and economic conditions influencing the actual and potential uses of literary texts by authors, scholars, and teachers,"[3] locates "literary activism in the spheres of literary authorship, production and reception, and ... consider[s] how writers, critics, and teachers have sought to foster opposition to transnational neoliberalism." I structure my concluding remarks about future possibilities for writers, literary critics, and teachers to challenge stereotypes about addiction and the systemic relations of power that produce and enforce them within Shupak's discussion of literary activism. I do so in order to leave readers with more tools to inform their creative, critical, and pedagogical practices specifically as they engage with the problem of addiction-as-identity.

Fiction writers are instrumental in how drug and alcohol use is understood in the cultural imaginary. *Challenging Addiction* deliberately focuses on the cultural meaning of each author's depictions of addiction and rarely evokes the authors' stated intentions behind their works. I chose this approach not merely to avoid the intentional fallacy, but also to privilege the narrative and social effects of the novels in order to point out how they function as counterhegemonic narratives. Moreover, as I note in chapter 3, while Ibi Kaslik set out to challenge a view of anorexics as sexless perfectionists, her novel quite vividly reproduces a pathologizing image of the protagonist. Also, in the absence or denial of public claims to initiate social change, we cannot assume that authors are uninformed or uncaring about systemic issues. Christy Ann Conlin, for example, wrote a report called "The System Sucks: A Discussion of Homeless Youth in Halifax" (1993) for the Nova Scotia Public Research Group, but does not connect her artistic production to social justice publically.

Yet, if we are to consider further how literature can incite social change, authors must be actively part of this project. Many contemporary authors explicitly situate their writing within broader struggles for social justice – and against capitalism, white supremacy, colonialism, and heteropatriarchy – including Dionne Brand, Lee Maracle, Joseph Boyden, Larissa Lai, Leanne Simpson, and Zoe Whittall, to name a few. What would it mean to write fiction that deliberately challenges stereotypes of addiction, that writes *with* rather than *about* marginalized communities and people who are often vilified and criminalized for their use of drugs and alcohol? How do fiction writers negotiate artistic freedom and aesthetic play against an awareness of the pernicious effects of stereotypes? Conlin and O'Neill seem to approach this issue by casting their protagonists in a sympathetic light. By contextualizing drug and alcohol use as mitigation of socially inflicted pain, the authors' approach to challenging stereotypes largely depends on a sympathetic reader. Yet I am curious about what fiction could look like that responds to Rinaldo Walcott's call to authors to write "in a fashion that requires more action and less sentiment."[4] While readers may indeed sympathize with the experiences of Baby (*lullabies for little criminals*) and Serrie (*Heave*), the novels do not offer alternative ways, like harm reduction services, that each protagonist could have found support for their struggles that is informed by the systemic analysis each novel fosters. Consequently, readers are not left with a clearer sense of how to channel their sympathy and increased awareness about the connections between substance use and systemic inequalities.

Literary critics, then, are also instrumental in pushing into the mainstream media narratives that challenge systems of power and oppression. We must also participate in the production of counterhegemonic meaning through our interpretive practices. Shupak identifies several strategies that literary critics employ to contest neoliberalism:

> those that inform the public about specific details of political issues misrepresented in mainstream news media; those that familiarize readers with resistance and its underlying logic; those that evaluate texts at least in part for whether they are in any sense useful to social movements; those that stimulate the radical imagination by exploring utopian moments that can often be found in even the most straightforwardly realist literary works; those that read texts within a larger political system so as to generate critique of that entire system or its central features; and those that cite in literary scholarship the experiences and analyses of activists who are not professional intellectuals so as to enable these experiences and analyses to earn the social status of knowledge.[5]

Many of these strategies of literary activism are evidenced throughout this book by the critical conversations about each novel and most explicitly by critics who connect their interpretive practices to broader struggles for decolonization. In speaking to other Indigenous literary critics, Cherokee writer Daniel Heath Justice asks, "if … our literatures assert a consciousness of land and ancestry, of community and kinship ties, of traditions and ceremonies, of survival and presence outside of colonialist death narratives, shouldn't our criticism attempt to do the same?"[6]

As a settler scholar, one of my responsibilities is to interrogate such death narratives that I understand as upholding the unearned privileges I have accrued as a settler, one of which is the myth of the "Drunken Indian." I have attempted to provide one possible methodology to connect depictions of this stereotype to political discourse that seeks to justify settler land occupation, resource extraction, and removing Indigenous children from Indigenous communities of care. This approach has required positioning my textual analysis in relation to colonial systems that silence or obscure this knowledge, confronting the stereotypes I have internalized, and seeking out resources developed by Indigenous people and communities that articulate both the realities of drug and alcohol use, and philosophies and practices of Indigenous-led healing initiatives. Literary critics who identify as activists or agents for social change must take seriously the role that stereotypes about addiction play in upholding settler colonialism, as well as capitalism and patriarchy. We must learn more about the stereotypes, seek out research and personal accounts produced by criminalized communities, write criticism that points out discrepancies between literary depictions of people who use drugs and alcohol, and connect the stakes of such depictions to systemic inequalities.

As we do this in our criticism, we can also take this knowledge into classrooms to work with students to question 'common sense' assumptions about addiction. Each chapter in this book has offered specific strategies to break down resistance and transform critical analysis of addiction discourses into social action. But as I conclude this book, I see the work ahead for teachers, writers, students, and literary critics to ask how can we all accountably participate in ensuring literature is part of movements for social change.

I close by echoing Helen Keane in saying that my intention is not to "diminish the experiences of the many people who have struggled with compulsive behaviours and have found relief and happiness using the language and tools of addiction and recovery";[7] nor do I wish to deny the altruistic intentions of addiction treatment professionals. Rather, I wish to emphasize two unavoidable and significant realities: countless people do not find relief from – or even recognition of – their suffering through dominant treatment models; and the incidence of addiction is not decreasing. As an illustration of these factors, as well as of the implications of largely myopic addiction discourses, I borrow Anthony Weston's invocation of Irving Zola's parable:

> I am standing by the shore of a swiftly flowing river and I hear the cry of a drowning man. So I jump in the river, pull him to shore, and apply artificial respiration. Just when he begins to breathe, there is another cry for help. So I jump in the river, reach him, pull him to shore … [and then] another cry for help. So back into the river again, reaching, pulling, applying, breathing, and then another yell. Again and again, without end, goes the sequence. I am so busy jumping in, pulling them to shore, applying artificial respiration, that I have no time to see who the hell is upstream pushing them all in.[8]

There are several ways to methodologically mobilize this parable. Cree public health analyst Tanya Wasacase argues that "we ought not to forget a common intuition about this parable: though our hero may not be able to save everyone, at least he is able to save some people. Looking too far upstream may be just as problematic as focusing too far downstream."[9] Wasacase captures the quandary of the individual person confronting social suffering – and recognizing it as such. One's actions become laden with the question of individual and collective responsibility. Even if the drowning are pulled out of the water (or out of poverty or addiction, as the phrases are colloquially used), the paths to and locations of drowning still exist where others can become ensnared. Our immediate response as individuals is to figure out where to direct our efforts. The power of the parable builds if we also imagine hundreds, thousands, or millions of people standing not only on the shores watching or rescuing, but standing knee-deep in the water – as well as blindfolded or wide-eyed pushing others in upstream. To intervene effectively, whether as literary critic, teacher, daughter, sister, partner, friend, or community organizer, requires both a self-awareness of one's place within this circuitry of social suffering, as well as a commitment to offering such actions as one among and accountable to countless others.

Notes

Introduction

1 Lynn Coady, "Wireless" in *Hellgoing* (Toronto: House of Anansi Press, 2013), 13.
2 Khalfa, Introduction in *History of Madness*, by Michel Foucault. Ed. Jean Khalfa, trans. Jonathan Murphy and Jean Khalfa. (London: Routledge, 2009), *xv*. The comparison between madness and addiction extends Foucault's critique of power systems that transform behaviours into pathologized, stable identities.
3 Glen Sean Coulthard defines settler colonialism as "a relationship characterized by a particular form of *domination*; that is, it is a relationship where power – in this case, interrelated discursive and nondiscursive facets of economic, gendered, racial, and state power – has been structured into a relatively secure or sedimented set of hierarchal social relations that continue to facilitate the *dispossession* of Indigenous peoples of their lands and self-determining authority." *Red Skin, White Masks: Rejecting the Colonial Politics of Recognition* (Minneapolis: University of Minnesota Press, 2014), 6–7.
4 Sherene Razack, *Looking White People in the Eye: Race, Gender, and Culture in Courtrooms and Classrooms* (Toronto: University of Toronto Press, 1998), 12.
5 Arthur Kleinman, Veena Das, and Margaret Lock, eds., *Social Suffering* (Berkeley: University of California Press, 1997), *ix*.
6 See Stephanie Irlbacher-Fox's analysis of Bourdieu et al, Das, Kleinman, Wilkinson, and Farmer in *Finding Dahshaa: Self-Government, Social Suffering, and Aboriginal Policy in Canada* (Vancouver: UBC Press, 2009), 28–9.
7 Kleinman et al, *Social Suffering, ix*.
8 Christy Ann Conlin, *Heave* (Toronto: Doubleday, 2002), 8.

9 Heather O'Neill, *lullabies for little criminals* (Toronto: Harper, 2006), 195.
10 Ibid., 287.
11 Kevin Patterson, *Consumption* (Toronto: Vintage Canada, 2007), 282.
12 Ibi Kaslik, *Skinny* (Toronto: HarperCollins, 2005), 51.
13 Beatrice Culleton Mosionier, *In Search of April Raintree*, ed. Cheryl Suzack (Winnipeg: Portage & Main Press, 1999), 198.
14 Eden Robinson, *Monkey Beach* (Toronto: Alfred A. Knopf, 2000), 296.
15 Kate Bezanson and Meg Luxton define social reproduction as the "processes involved in maintaining and reproducing people, specifically the labouring populations, and their labour power on a daily generational basis" (3). Such reproduction includes providing for the necessities of life (i.e. food, shelter, healthcare, clothing, safety), but also the "transmission of knowledge, social values … and the construction of individual and collective identities," *Social Reproduction: Feminist Political Economy Challenges Neo-Liberalism* (Montreal, QC: McGill-Queen's University Press, 2006), 3. The corporeal and psychosocial dimensions of social reproduction echo Althusser's theory of ideological production: not only must workers be physically sustained for labour, they must also be socialized to consciously participate in the perpetuation of ethics of production, accumulation, and consumption.
16 Eve Kosofsky Sedgwick, "Epidemics of the Will," *Tendencies* (London: Taylor & Francis e-library, 2004), 142.
17 Irlbacher-Fox, *Finding Dahshaa*, 28.
18 Patterson, *Consumption*, 333.
19 Kaslik, *Skinny*, 221.
20 "Epidemics of the Will," *Tendencies*, 143.
21 Ibid., 144.
22 Ibid., 143–4.
23 Bela Szabados and Kenneth G. Probert, eds. *Writing Addiction: Towards a Poetics of Desire and its Other* (Regina: Canadian Plains Research Center, 2004), 3.
24 Ibid., 4–5.
25 Ibid., 2.
26 Ibid., 3.
27 Lorna Crozier and Patrick Lane, eds. *Addicted: Notes from the Belly of the Beast* (Vancouver: Greystone Books, 2001), xiii.
28 Ibid.
29 Ibid.
30 Jeff Shantz, *Against All Authority: Anarchism and the Literary Imagination* (Charlottesville, VA: Imprint Academic, 2011), 41.

31 Ibid., 43.
32 Conlin, *Heave*, 37, 129.
33 Roxanne Rimstead, *Remnants of Nation: On Poverty Narratives by Women* (Toronto: University of Toronto Press, 2001), 5.
34 Helen Malson and Maree Burns, eds., "Not Just 'A White Girl's Thing': The Changing Face of Food and Body Image Problems," *Critical Feminist Approaches to Eating Dis/Orders* (London: Routledge, 2009), 51.
35 Mosionier, *In Search of April Raintree*, 180.
36 Alan Hunt defines moral regulation as a set of discursive and political practices whereby "some social agents problematise some aspect of the conduct, values, or culture of others on moral grounds and seek to impose regulation upon them," *Governing Morals: A Social History of Moral Regulation* (Cambridge: Cambridge University Press, 1999), ix.
37 Judith Butler, *Undoing Gender* (New York: Routledge, 2004), 1.
38 Irlbacher-Fox, *Finding Dahshaa*, 30.
39 Ibid.
40 Felix Guattari, "Socially Significant Drugs," *High Culture: Reflections on Addiction and Modernity*, eds. Anna Alexander and Mark S. Roberts (Albany, NY: SUNY University Press, 2003), 202.
41 Peter Ferentzy explains that the "enlightenment-born distinction between will and desire" produced the potential for "a self divided against itself," which seems a key discursive move that elides recognizing the many dynamics between self and society. "Foucault and Addiction," *Telos* 125 (2002), 171.
42 Razack, *Looking White People in the Eye*, 10.
43 Paulo Freire, *Pedagogy of the Oppressed*, trans. Myra Bergman Ramos (New York: Continuum, 2007), 104.
44 Ibid.
45 This line is the refrain from Rush's song, "Subdivisions," written by Neil Peart, Alex Lifeson, and Geddy Lee, in *Signals* (Mercury Records, 1982).
46 The CBC Canada Reads 2014 competition sought to determine which among five novels was the "One Novel to Change our Nation," accessed 19 February 2016, http://www.cbc.ca/player/Shows/Shows/Canada+Reads/ID/2440911767/.
47 Kimberly A. Nance, *Can Literature Provoke Social Change?: Trauma Narrative and Social Action in Latin American Testimonio* (Nashville: Vanderbilt University Press, 2006), 34.
48 I refer here to Gerald Graff's influential essay "Other Voices, Other Rooms: Organizing and Teaching the Humanities Conflict" (in *New*

Literary History 21, no. 4 (1990): 817–39), which calls on teachers to share with students the academic debates surrounding a particular issue or text, so they might become active participants within, rather than outsiders to, the academic community. Jeffrey Wallen provides an incisive critique of the exclusive and exclusionary politics of Graff's model in *Close Encounters: Literary Politics and Public Culture* (Minneapolis: University of Minnesota Press, 1998).

49 Simon During, "Introduction," *The Cultural Studies Reader*, 2nd edition, ed. Simon During (London: Routledge, 1999), 25.

50 Ibid.

51 "From a Language to a Theory of Resistance: Critical Pedagogy, the Limits of 'Framing,' and Social Change," *Educational Theory*, 64, no. 4 (2014), 372.

52 Ibid.

53 Ibid.

54 For examples, see *Utopian Pedagogy: Radical Experiments against Neoliberal Globalization* (Coté, Day, and de Peuter, eds.); *Retooling the Humanities: The Culture of Research in Canadian Universities* (Coleman and Kamboureli, eds.); *Neoliberalism's War on Higher Education* (Henry A. Giroux); *Critical Pedagogy and Teacher Education in the Neoliberal Era: Small Openings* (Groenke and Hatch, eds); and *Private Learning, Public Needs: The Neoliberal Assault on Democratic Education* (Weiner).

55 For examples, see *Cultural and Pedagogical Inquiry*; *Cultural Studies ↔ Critical Methodologies*; *Radical Teacher*; *The Review of Education, Pedagogy, and Critical Studies*; and *Upping the Anti: A Journal of Theory and Action*.

56 "Deconstructing Privilege When Students Resist," in *Deconstructing Privilege: Teaching and Learning as Allies in the Classroom*, ed. Kim A. Case (New York: Routledge, 2013), 34.

57 Freire, *Pedagogy of the Oppressed*, 109.

58 Ibid.

59 Antonio Gramsci, *Selections from the Prison Notebooks*, eds. and trans. Quintin Hoare and Geoffrey Nowell Smith (New York: International Publishers, 1971), 326–7.

60 bell hooks, *Teaching to Transgress: Education as the Practice of Freedom* (New York: Routledge, 1994), 28.

61 Gramsci, *Selections from the Prison Notebooks*, 324.

62 Marcelo Diversi and Claudio Moreira, "Real World: Classrooms as Decolonizing Sites Against Neoliberal Narratives of the Other," *Cultural Studies ↔ Critical Methodologies* 13.6 (2013), 473.

63 Razack, *Looking White People in the Eye*, 8.

64 Rebecca Tarlau, "From a Language to a Theory of Resistance: Critical Pedagogy, the Limits of 'Framing,' and Social Change," in *Educational Theory* 64, no. 4 (2014), 370.
65 Rimstead, *Remnants of Nation*, 269.
66 Razack, *Looking White People in the Eye*, 16–17.
67 hooks, *Teaching to Transgress*, 12.
68 Ibid., 8.
69 Chris Dixon identifies three distinctive features of anti-oppression: "an understanding of power relations as fundamentally intertwined," "a commitment to confronting the ways in which people replicate power relations," and "a focus on transforming systems of domination in broader society" (*Another Politics: Talking Across Today's Transformative Movements*, Oakland: University of California Press, 2014, 73–4). I have used four specific guidelines in my own teaching: critique ideas not people; move beyond feeling guilty to examining our responsibilities; personalize knowledge, rather than generalize knowledge by using "I" statements; and treat everyone as an individual rather than a representative of any specific group. For reference, see Lisa Fithian's "Anti-Oppression Principles and Practices," *Organizing for Power, Organizing for Change*, accessed 19 February 2016, https://docs.google.com/document/d/1TnaLJXy6WSkJ-MQv4BlMhRXM1cc-4wBqNcgrD4W-VZQ/edit.
70 Baldev et al, "Being Leaders for Socially Just Education: Engaging New Politics of Possibility," *Cultural Studies ↔ Critical Methodologies* 13, no. 6 (2013), 495.
71 Michael D. Giardina and Norman K. Denzin, "Confronting Neoliberalism: Toward a Militant Pedagogy of Empowered Citizenship," *Cultural Studies ↔ Critical Methodologies* 13, no. 6 (2013), 449.
72 Freire, *Pedagogy of the Oppressed*, 87.
73 Ibid., 99.
74 Ibid.
75 Andrea Smith, "The Problem with 'Privilege,'" *Andrea366*, 14 August 2013, accessed 19 February 2016, https://andrea366.wordpress.com/2013/08/14/the-problem-with-privilege-by-andrea-smith/.
76 "A Systems Approach to Substance Use in Canada: Recommendations for a National Treatment Strategy." Ottawa: National Framework for Action to Reduce the Harms Associated with Alcohol and Other Drugs and Substances in Canada, 2008. 2.
77 On 26 September 2011, the Supreme Court of Canada ruled that, "Insite saves lives. Its benefits have been proven. There has been no discernible

negative impact on the public safety and health objectives of Canada during its eight years in operation." (See CBC News, "Vancouver's Insite drug injection clinic will stay open," 30 September 2011, accessed 19 February 2016, http://www.cbc.ca/news/canada/british-columbia/vancouver-s-insite-drug-injection-clinic-will-stay-open-1.1005044.)

78 "Substance Abuse in Corrections: FAQs," (Ottawa: CCSA, 2004), 2.

79 "What Happens After Sentencing," *Correctional Service Canada*, 5 March 2015, accessed 19 February 2016, http://www.csc-scc.gc.ca/vids/htm/whas-eng.shtml.

80 "Substance Abuse in Corrections: FAQs," (Ottawa: CCSA, 2004), 5.

81 Ibid., 2.

82 *In the Realm of Hungry Ghosts: Close Encounters with Addiction* (Toronto: Knopf, 2008), 284.

83 Angela Davis, *Are Prisons Obsolete?* (New York: Seven Stories Press, 2003), 16.

84 Beck and Beck-Gernsheim, chapter 1.

85 Rimstead, *Remnants of Nation*, 41.

1. Ideological Tropes of Contemporary Addiction Narratives

1 Review of Lauren B. Davis's *The Empty Room*, (Toronto: HarperCollins, 2013, Kindle Edition), 237.

2 Winehouse's 2006 hit song. Winehouse died of alcohol poisoning in 2011.

3 Anne Mullens, "Addicted or Afflicted?: Should Your Tax Dollars Buy Drugs for Abusers?" *Reader's Digest* (August 2008).

4 CBC News, "PM Wants Mandatory Sentences for 'Serious' Drug Crimes," 4 October 2007, accessed 19 February 2016, http://www.cbc.ca/news/canada/pm-wants-mandatory-sentences-for-serious-drug-crimes-1.647115.

5 Helen Keane, *What's Wrong with Addiction?* (Carlton South: Melbourne University Press, 2002), 1.

6 Oxford Dictionaries permits the use of "they" as a singular pronoun when the gender of the noun to which it refers is ambiguous. I opt not to linguistically reproduce 'he' or 'she' as the only possibilities for gender identification. See "'He or she' versus 'they,'" accessed 19 February 2016, http://www.oxforddictionaries.com/words/he-or-she-versus-they.

7 Ferentzy, "Foucault and Addiction," 171.

8 Ibid., 172.

9 "Origins: 1935," *Alcoholics Anonymous*, accessed 19 February 2016, http://www.aa.org/pages/en_US/aa-timeline.

10 "Origins," *Alcoholics Anonymous*, accessed 19 February 2016, http://www.aa.org/pages/en_US/aa-timeline.

11 "A.A. Fact File," *Alcoholics Anonymous*, 9. Accessed 19 February 2016, http://www.aa.org/assets/en_US/m-24_aafactfile.pdf.

12 Mariana Valverde, *Diseases of the Will: Alcohol and the Dilemmas of Freedom* (Cambridge: Cambridge University Press, 1998), 123.

13 Ibid.

14 Ibid., 29.

15 Sedgwick, "Epidemics of the Will," 143.

16 Valverde, *Diseases of the Will*, 28.

17 *Intervention*'s high ratings in Canada make strict national distinctions difficult given the pervasive presence of American-produced portrayals of addiction in Canadian culture.

18 Ferentzy, "Foucault and Addiction," 174.

19 Jason Kosovski and Douglas Smith, "Everybody Hurts: Addiction, Drama, and the Family in the Reality Television Show *Intervention*," in *Substance Use & Misuse* 46 (2011), 854. Their analysis refers to the US healthcare system. In-patient treatment in Canada is similarly very difficult to secure given the long wait times in public facilities and the expense of private facilities, which average between $5,000-$15,000 for stays ranging from 60–90 days.

20 Ibid., 855–6.

21 Jacques Derrida's proclamation that the addict seeks "pleasure in an experience without truth" is another variation on the theme of the deceitful addict (whether ignorantly or willfully). See "The Rhetoric of Drugs," in *High Culture: Reflections on Addiction and Modernity*, eds. Anna Alexander and Mark S. Roberts (Albany, NY: SUNY University Press, 2003), 26.

22 The rhetoric of the Big Book reinforces this portrayal: "Those who do not recover are people who cannot or will not completely give themselves to this simple program, usually men and women who are constitutionally incapable of being honest with themselves. There are such unfortunates. They are not at fault; they seem to have been born that way. They are naturally incapable of grasping and developing a manner of living which demands rigorous honesty … Our stories disclose in a general way what we used to be like, what happened, and what we are like now." See "How it Works," *The Big Book*, 4th ed., 58, accessed 19 February 2016, http://www.aa.org/pages/en_US/alcoholics-anonumous.

23 For classic examples, see Thomas De Quincey's *Confessions of an English Opium-Eater*; Edgar Allan Poe's "Ligeia;" Wilkie Collins' *Moonstone*;

F. Scott Fitzgerald's *The Great Gatsby*; Chuck Palahniuk's *Fight Club*; and Ann Marlowe's *How to Stop Time: Heroin from A to Z*.

24 In February 2011, Sheen proclaimed, "I was shackled and oppressed by the cult of AA for 22 years … It's vintage, outdated and stupid, and it's followed by stupid people. I hate them violently … I have a disease? Bullshit. I cured it right now with my mind." See "Charlie Sheen's Bizarre New Interview: Slams Alcoholics Anonymous, Says His Rate For Beating Addiction is 100%," *Radar Online.com*, February 2011, accessed 19 February 2016, http://radaronline.com/exclusives/2011/02/charlie-sheens-bizarre-new-interview-slams-alcoholic-anonymous-says-his-rate/.

25 In one of several moments that gesture towards this contextual view of addiction, Dr O'Hara tells Jackie, "how you manage the pain is a private matter." See "Years of Service," *Nurse Jackie: Season Two*, writers Liz Brixius and Linda Wallem, dir. Paul Feig (Alliance Films, 2011), 13:20.

26 Quoted in Nancy J. White, "Alcoholics Anonymous Has a Terrible Success Rate, Addiction Expert Finds," *The Toronto Star*, 28 March 2014, accessed 19 February 2016, http://www.thestar.com/life/2014/03/28/alcoholics_anonymous_has_a_terrible_success_rate_addiction_expert_finds.html. White also cites an AA study meant to defend their success rate: "for those who seriously work the program, the success rate is 75 per cent (that's 50 per cent achieving immediate reward and another 25 per cent who slip then recover). But here's an important caveat: Of all AA prospects, they say, about 20 to 40 per cent fall into that category of seriously trying the program."

27 Ibid.

28 Published on May 18, 2013, the fifth edition of the *DSM* combines the Substance Abuse and Substance Dependence categories under "Substance Use Disorder" and creates the new category "Addictive Disorders," which to date, includes only gambling disorder. The revisions reflect attempts to strengthen the specificity of diagnostic criteria, so that "whereas a diagnosis of substance abuse previously required only one symptom, mild substance use disorder in DSM-5 requires two to three symptoms from a list of 11." The revisions also eliminate the phrase "problems with law enforcement" because "cultural considerations … make the criteria difficult to apply internationally" (see "Substance-Related and Addictive Disorders," *American Psychiatric Association: DSM-5 Development*, accessed 19 February 2016, http://www.dsm5.org/Documents/Substance%20Use%20Disorder%20Fact%20Sheet.pdf.

However, all references to the *DSM* will be from the IV-TR edition given its contemporary relevance to the novels under study.

29 Michael B. First, ed., *Diagnostic and Statistical Manual of Mental Disorders (DSM-IV-TR™)*, 4th edition, *STATRef Online Electronic Medical Library.*

30 "War Over Addiction: Evaluating the DSM-V," *The Huffington Post*, 11 February 2010, accessed 19 February 2016, http://www.huffingtonpost.com/stanton-peele/war-over-addiction-evalua_b_456321.html.

31 First, *DSM-IV-TR.*

32 Michel Foucault, *The Birth of the Clinic* (London and New York: Routledge, 2008), 5.

33 Caroline J. Acker, "Stigma or Legitimation? A Historical Examination of the Social Potentials of Addiction Disease Models," in *Journal of Psychoactive Drugs*, 25, no. 3 (1993), 201.

34 Ibid.

35 Valverde, *Diseases of the Will*, 27.

36 Kouimtsidis Christos, Paul Davis, Martine Reynolds, Colin Drummond, and Nicholas Tarrier, *Cognitive-Behavioural Therapy in the Treatment of Addiction: A Treatment Planner for Clinicians* (West Sussex: John Wiley & Sons, 2007), 11.

37 Ibid., 8.

38 Ibid., 9.

39 Ibid.

40 Ibid., 10.

41 However, experts in the discipline seek to change this methodological failing. For example, Andrew Samuels argues that "where the public and the private, the political and the personal, intersect or even meld there is a special role for depth psychology in relation to political change and transformation," in *The Political Psyche* (New York: Routledge, 1993), 4.

42 Celia Kitzinger and Rachel Perkins, *Changing Our Minds: Lesbian Feminism and Psychology* (New York: New York University Press, 1993), 5–6.

43 Derrida, "The Rhetoric of Drugs," 37.

44 Ibid., 25.

45 Ibid., 21.

46 Ibid., 38–9.

47 Ibid., 28.

48 Felix Guattari, "Socially Significant Drugs," *High Culture: Reflections on Addiction and Modernity*, 202.

49 Ibid., 199.

50 Ibid., 204.

51 Ibid., 206. Note, however, the dangerous limitations of agency implied by the "*we*" who "will be able to alter the situation of drug addicts," suggesting that we, the critics, have more insight into "the situation of drug addicts" than those who use drugs.
52 Ibid., 203.
53 Jane Lilienfeld, Introduction in *The Languages of Addiction*, eds. Jane Lilienfeld and Jeffrey Oxford (New York: St. Martin's Press, 1999), xiv.
54 Conlin's novel is set in 1980s Annapolis Valley, NS, where, as David Creelman explains, in addition to considerable disruptions of the fishing, lumbering, farming sectors, "the failure of the industrial sector … result[ed] [in] persistent economic hardships" across Atlantic Canada. See *Setting in the East: Maritime Realist Fiction* (Montreal & Kingston: McGill-Queen's University Press, 2003), 11–13.
55 Rimstead, *Remnants of Nation*, 5.
56 Lilienfeld, *The Languages of Addiction*, xiv.
57 Roland Chrisjohn, Sherri Young, and Michael Maraun, *The Circle Game: Shadows and Substance in the Indian Residential School Experience in Canada* (Penticton, BC: Theytus, 1997), 106–7.
58 Ibid., 108.
59 Ibid., 115.
60 Ibid., 116.
61 Ibid., 119.
62 Ibid., 116.
63 Louis Althusser, "Ideology and Ideological State Apparatus," *Mapping Ideology*, ed. Slavoj Žižek (New York: Verso, 1994), 123.
64 Email to author, 14 September 2015.
65 Collins et al., eds. Marlatt et al, "Current Status, Historical Insights, and Basic Principles of Harm Reduction," *Harm Reduction: Pragmatic Strategies for Managing High-Risk Behaviors*, 2nd ed., (New York: The Guilford Press, 2012), 5.
66 Ibid., 6.
67 "The Evolution of the Four Pillars: Acknowledging the Harms of Drug Prohibition," *International Journal of Drug Policy*, 17 (2006): 125.
68 In *Postmodernism, or, the Cultural Logic of Late Capitalism* (Durham: Duke UP, 1991), Frederic Jameson defines late capitalism as emerging in the 1950s: "What 'late' generally conveys is … the sense that something has changed, that things are different, that we have gone through a transformation of the life world which is somehow decisive but incomparable with the older convulsions of modernization and industrialization, less perceptible and dramatic, somehow, but more permanent precisely because more thoroughgoing and all-pervasive" (xxi).

69 Berridge and Edwards, quoted in Sedgwick, "Epidemics of the Will," 142.
70 Sedgwick, "Epidemics of the Will," 142.
71 Isabelle Meuret, *Writing Size Zero: Figuring Anorexia in Contemporary World Literatures* (Brussels: P.I.E. Peter Lang, 2007), 52.
72 Ibid., 13.
73 Ibid.
74 Ibid., 266.
75 Ibid.
76 Ibid., 54–5.
77 In Meuret's words, she chose to study "*experiential texts*, that is primary sources written mostly by anorexics, either as first-person accounts, or in other literary formats" (14; original emphasis).
78 Frederic Jameson, *The Political Unconscious: Narrative as a Socially Symbolic Act* (Ithaca: Cornell University Press, 1981), 81.
79 Bela Szabados and Kenneth G. Probert, eds, *Writing Addiction: Towards a Poetics of Desire and its Other* (Regina: Canadian Plains Research Center, 2004), 4.
80 See, for examples, Jackson's "The Devil, The Doppelgänger, and the Confessions of James Hogg and Thomas De Quincey" (2001); Kopelson's "Radical Indulgence: Excess, Addiction, and Female Desire" (2006); Goldsmith's "Cigarettes, Tea, Cards, and Chloral: Addictive Habits and Consumer Culture in *The House of Mirth*" (2011); Wilson's "Dying for a Smoke: Freudian Addiction and the Joy of Consumption" (2002); Weinstone's "Welcome to the Pharmacy: Addiction, Transcendence, and Virtual Reality" (2002); Stalcup's "Trainspotting, High Fidelity, and the Diction of Addiction" (2008); and McClure's "The Word, Image, and Addiction: Language and the Junk Equation in William S. Burroughs's *Naked Lunch*" (1996).
81 William S. Burroughs, *Naked Lunch: The Restored Text*, eds. James Grauerholz and Barry Miles (New York: Grove Press, 2001), 205.
82 To eat the naked lunch in Burroughs's words means to strip away comforting or romantic illusions that cloak "obscene, barbaric and disgusting" truths (ibid., 205). It is the "frozen moment when everyone sees what is on the end of every fork" (ibid., 199). For the junkie, it means understanding the "total need" to which he or she is subjected (ibid., 201).
83 "Seclusion and Compulsion," *Canadian Literature* no. 186 (Autumn, 2005): 160–1. Accessed 19 February 2016, http://ezproxy.uwindsor.ca/login?url=http://search.proquest.com/docview/218781383?accountid=14789.
84 Burroughs, *Naked Lunch*, 201.
85 Ibid.

86 Ibid.
87 Allan Johnston, "Consumption, Addiction, Vision, Energy: Political Economies and Utopian Visions in the Writings of the Beat Generation." *College Literature* 32, no. 2 (2005): 103–26.
88 Lindsey Michael Banco, *Travel and Drugs in Twentieth-Century Literature* (New York: Routledge, 2010), 21.
89 Allan G. Borst, "Towards National Identity: Addiction, Subjectivity, and American Literary Culture," PhD diss. (University of Illinois, 2009), 235.
90 Ann Marlowe, *How to Stop Time: Heroin from A to Z* (New York: Anchor Books, 1999), 46.
91 Gordon Bowker, *Pursued by Furies: A Life of Malcolm Lowry* (Toronto: Random House of Canada, 1993), xviii.
92 Ibid.
93 Ibid., 458.
94 Ibid., xx.
95 Robert Morrison, *The English Opium Eater: A Biography of Thomas De Quincey*, (London: Weidenfeld & Nicholson, 2010), xvi.
96 Ibid., xv.
97 Ibid., xiv
98 For examples, see *Beautiful Losers* (Leonard Cohen, 1966), *The Edible Woman* (Margaret Atwood, 1969), *Thrasher … Skid Row Eskimo* (Anthony Apakark Thrasher, 1976), *The Crackwalker* (Judith Thompson, 1980), *Slash* (Jeannette Armstrong, 1985), *Nights Below Station Street* (David Adams Richards, 1988), *Keeper'n Me* (Richard Wagamese, 1994), *The Lesser Blessed* (Richard Van Camp, 1996), *Strange Heaven* (Lynn Coady, 1998), *Wise and Foolish Virgins* (Don Hannah, 1998), *Mouthing the Words* (Camilla Gibb, 1999), *Stolen Life* (Yvonne Johnson and Rudy Wiebe, 1999), *Flat* (Mark Macdonald, 2000), *Inside Out* (Evelyn Lau, 2001), *The Torn Skirt* (Rebecca Godfrey, 2001), *Daughters are Forever* (Lee Maracle, 2002), *Down to This* (Shaughnessy Bishop-Stall, 2004) *Three Day Road* (Joseph Boyden, 2005), *Blood Sports* (Eden Robinson, 2006), *With a Closed Fist* (Kathy Dobson, 2011), *The Empty Room* (Lauren B. Davis, 2013), and *Hellgoing* (Lynn Coady, 2013).
99 Creelman, *Setting in the East*, 18.
100 Gramsci, *Selections from the Prison Notebooks*, 326–7.
101 Creelman, *Setting in the East*, 18.
102 Introduction in *Octavia's Brood: Science Fiction Stories from Social Justice Movements*, adrienne maree brown and Walidah Imarisha, eds. (Oakland: AK Press, 2015), 4.
103 "Mapping the Margins: Intersectionality, Identity Politics, and Violence Against Women of Color," in *Standford Law Review* 43, no. 6 (1991), 1242.

104 Razack, *Looking White People in the Eye*, 12.
105 O'Neill, *lullabies*, 188.
106 Ibid., 187.
107 Conlin, *Heave*, 32.
108 Guattari, "Socially Significant Drugs," 203.
109 Jameson, *The Political Unconscious*, 85.
110 Ibid., 86.
111 Karl Marx, *Economic and Philosophic Manuscripts of 1844*. (New York: International Publishers, 1964), 111 (original emphasis).
112 Rimstead, *Remnants of Nation*, 92.

2. Christy Ann Conlin's *Heave* and Heather O'Neill's *lullabies for little criminals*

1 *Mouthing the Words*, (Toronto: Pedlar Press, 1999), 112.
2 "stigma," *OED Online.*
3 Margaret Atwood, *Payback: Debt and the Shadow Side of Wealth* (Toronto: Anansi, 2008), 116.
4 Ibid., 82.
5 All quotations in this section are taken from the record of November 4, 2008 proceedings in the Legislative Assembly of Ontario during Question Period. See "Official Records for 4 November 2008," Legislative Assembly of Ontario, accessed 19 February 2016, http://www.ontla.on.ca/web/house-proceedings/house_detail.do?Date=2008-11-04.
6 Ruth L. Smith contends that such associations become naturalized, unfolding within liberal humanist discourse that claims that access to citizenship and the market economy is free and equal, even as the constant incidence of unemployment and poverty immediately disproves such claims. In "Order and Disorder: The Naturalization of Poverty," *Cultural Critique* 14 (1989–90), 209–29.
7 Rimstead, *Remnants of Nation*, 45.
8 Conlin, *Heave*, 166.
9 Marx, *Manuscripts*, 72.
10 Pierre Bourdieu, *Distinction: A Social Critique of the Judgment of Taste*, trans. Richard Nice (Cambridge, MA: Harvard University Press, 1984), 175.
11 "Readers Will Root for this Heroine," *The Montreal Gazette*, 9 February 2002, K4.
12 "How To Be Good," *Canadian Literature* 185 (2005), 166.
13 "First Novels," *Books in Canada* 31, no. 4 (2002), 38.
14 Ibid., 39.

15 This statement is cited as the truth of alcoholism in the Foreword to the first edition of the Blue Book, xiii.
16 Ibid., xiii, original emphasis.
17 Michel Foucault, *The History of Sexuality: An Introduction*, vol 1, trans. Robert Hurley (New York: Vintage, 1990), 58.
18 Ibid., 59.
19 Ibid.
20 Carole Cain, "Personal Stories: Identity Acquisition and Self-Understanding in Alcoholics Anonymous," *Ethos* 19, no. 2 (1991), 220.
21 Ibid.
22 Ibid., 219.
23 Ibid., 225.
24 Ibid.
25 Conlin, *Heave*, 11 (original emphasis).
26 Ibid., 3.
27 Ibid., 6.
28 Ibid., 108, 296.
29 Ibid., 296.
30 Ibid., 307.
31 Ibid., 11.
32 Ibid., 38.
33 Robin Campbell, Introduction, in *Letters from a Stoic: Epistulae Morales Ad Lucilium*, by Lucius Annaeus Seneca, trans. Robin Campbell (Middlesex: Penguin Books, 1969), 174.
34 Ibid., 17.
35 Ibid., 16.
36 Conlin, *Heave*, 37.
37 Ibid., 129.
38 Ibid., 82.
39 Ibid.
40 Cain, "Personal Stories," 219.
41 G. Baker and P.M.S. Hacker, "The Grammar of Psychology: Wittgenstein's Bemerkungen über die Philosophie der Psychologie," *Language and Communication* 2 (1982), 229–30.
42 Conlin, *Heave*, 115.
43 Ibid., 117.
44 Ibid., 121.
45 Ibid., 155 (emphasis added).
46 Ibid., 166.
47 Ibid., 32.
48 Kinsella, "First Novels," 40.

49 Ibid., 38.
50 Conlin, *Heave*, 310.
51 Ibid., 311.
52 Ibid., 57.
53 Ibid., 53.
54 Ibid., 67.
55 Ibid., 311.
56 Ibid., 86.
57 Ibid.
58 Ibid.
59 Rimstead, *Remnants of Nation*, 36.
60 Ibid.
61 Conlin, *Heave*, 311.
62 Ibid., 86.
63 Ibid., 137.
64 Ibid., 228.
65 Acker, "Stigma or Legitimation?" 201.
66 *Heave*, 231.
67 Cain, "Personal Stories," 225.
68 Conlin, *Heave*, 185.
69 Ibid., 247.
70 Ibid., 243.
71 Marx, *Manuscripts*, 68.
72 Ibid., 70.
73 Marx, *The Marx-Engels Reader*. 2nd ed. Ed. Robert C. Tucker (New York: Norton, 1978), 349.
74 Ibid.
75 Conlin, *Heave*, 246.
76 Ibid., 272.
77 Ibid., 282.
78 Ibid., 304.
79 Jolene M. Sanders, "Women and the Twelve Steps of Alcoholics Anonymous: A Gendered Narrative," *Alcoholism Treatment Quarterly* 24, no. 3 (2006), 4.
80 Conlin, *Heave*, 280.
81 Ibid., 281.
82 Ibid., 303.
83 Ibid., 3.
84 When asked what the phrase meant to her, Conlin replied, "I have no idea of the historical origins of the expression 'tits to the wind.' I didn't know it was a nautical expression. I mean, it always brought to my mind

figureheads at the front of ships as many of them were barechested ladies. And it also brought mermaids to mind and I liked this imagery for the world of *Heave*. But its origins in *Heave* were from something that we drunken party girls used to say, this impassioned credo of how we would live our lives, tits to the wind baby, tits to the wind. I always liked it because it was so feminine and yet so brash, things we don't normally put together" (email correspondence with author, 17 May 2013).

85 Cain, "Personal Stories," 215.

86 *Alcoholics Anonymous: The Story of How Many Thousands of Men and Women Have Recovered from Alcoholism*, 4th ed. (New York: Anonymous World Services, 2001), xx.

87 Quoted in Judy Stoffman, "Lyrical Lullabies: Heather O'Neill's first novel, inspired by her hardscrabble childhood, draws raves," *Toronto Star*, 13 December 2006, D4.

88 Nancy Campbell, *Using Women: Gender, Drug Policy, and Social Justice* (New York: Routledge, 2000), 7.

89 Ibid.

90 Bourdieu, *Distinction*, 175.

91 Ibid.

92 O'Neill, *lullabies*, 95.

93 Ibid., 96.

94 Ibid., 220.

95 Ibid., 221.

96 Bourdieu, *Distinction*, 175.

97 "Montreal Underground," *Journal of Canadian Studies/Revue D'études Canadiennes*, 46, no. 3 (Fall 2012): 266.

98 O'Neill, *lullabies*, 187.

99 Bourdieu, *Distinction*, 175.

100 O'Neill, *lullabies*, 6.

101 Ibid., 1.

102 Ibid., 5.

103 Ibid., 6.

104 Ibid.

105 Ibid., 21.

106 Ibid.

107 Ibid.

108 Stephen C. Infantino, "Female Addiction and Sacrifice: Literary Tradition or User's Manual?" in *The Languages of Addiction*, eds. Jane Lilienfeld and Jeffrey Oxford (New York: St. Martin's Press, 1999), 93.

109 O'Neill, *lullabies*, 10.

110 Ibid., 12.
111 Ibid., 13.
112 Ibid., 17–18.
113 Ibid., 14.
114 Ibid., 4.
115 Ibid., 181.
116 Joan Sangster, *Girl Trouble: Female Delinquency in English Canada* (Toronto: Between the Lines, 2002), 4.
117 Campbell, *Using Women*, 6.
118 See "Housing Conditions that Serve as Risk Factors for Tuberculosis infection and disease," *Canadian Communicable Disease Report* 33 (2007), accessed 19 February 2016, http://www.phac-aspc.gc.ca/publicat/ccdr-rmtc/07pdf/acs33-09.pdf. According to the Public Health Agency of Canada, tuberculosis is strongly associated with poor housing conditions, a major marker of poverty. Unable to afford consistent or adequate central heating as an adult or as a child, Jules develops pernicious tuberculosis.
119 O'Neill, *lullabies*, 26.
120 Ibid., 28.
121 Ibid., 29.
122 Ibid.
123 Ibid., 27.
124 Ibid., 30.
125 Ibid., 45.
126 Ibid., 57.
127 Ibid., 70.
128 Ibid., 76.
129 Ibid., 71.
130 Ibid., 72.
131 Ibid., 71.
132 Ibid., 72.
133 Ibid.
134 Ibid., 86.
135 Ibid.
136 Ibid., 87.
137 Ibid., 92.
138 Ulrich Beck and Elisabeth Beck-Gernsheim, *Individualization: Institutionalized Individualism and its Social and Political Consequences* (London: SAGE Publications Ltd., 2002), 3.
139 O'Neill, *lullabies*, 100.
140 Ibid., 101.

141 Ibid., 100.
142 Ibid., 157.
143 Ibid.
144 Bourdieu, *Distinction*, 175.
145 O'Neill, *lullabies*, 161.
146 Ibid., 181.
147 Ibid., 167.
148 Ibid., 187.
149 Ibid., 286.
150 Infantino, "Female Addiction and Sacrifice," 99.
151 Bourdieu, *Distinction*, 175.
152 Atwood, *Payback*, 82.
153 O'Neill, *lullabies*, 187–8.
154 Ibid., 188.
155 Ibid., 203.
156 Ibid., 202.
157 Alan Hunt, "Moral Regulation and Making-up the New Person: Putting Gramsci to Work" in *Theoretical Criminology* 1, no. 3 (1997), 277.
158 Hunt, *Governing Morals*, 4.
159 Krista Ratcliffe, "A Rhetoric of Classroom Denial: Resisting Resistance to Alcohol Questions While Teaching Louise Erdrich' *Love Medicine*," in *The Languages of Addiction*, eds. Jane Lilienfeld and Jeffrey Oxford (New York: St. Martin's Press, 1999), 110.
160 This exercise occurred organically during a class I taught on *lullabies for little criminals* for a Canadian Literatures of Imprisonment course. In response to a classmate's comment that the novel depicted poverty as a form of confinement, another student recalled how Alice Munro's short story "The Beggar Maid" depicted poverty as exposure or a lack of protection from social inspection. This observation quickly led to us building together on the chalkboard other words or phrases to complete the phrase "Poverty is."
161 During the spring of 2014, Oberlin College and University of California, Santa Barbara, both passed motions that directed instructors to provide trigger warnings to their students. These events sparked debates among academics about how or if to provide trigger warnings that advise of potentially traumatizing or retraumatizing course content. While it is beyond the scope of this endnote to engage with the numerous issues raised by both sides of the debate, it is crucial to remember that the use of trigger warnings originated in community-based, anti-violence against women movements. Such warnings were employed in concert with other

healing strategies "designed to de-privatize and collective healing. They came out of the recognition that we are not unaffected by the political and intellectual work that we do" (see Andrea Smith's "Beyond the Pros and Cons of Trigger Warnings: Collectivizing Healing," *Andrea366*, 13 July 2014, accessed 19 February 2016, http://andrea366.wordpress.com/2014/07/13/beyond-the-pros-and-cons-of-trigger-warnings-collectivizing-healing/). It is unclear how these practices migrated into the academy. Perhaps social justice oriented instructors were providing trigger warnings to offer students the foreknowledge to prepare themselves for difficult material. Employed out of context and in a distinctly neoliberal framework, its roots in collective empowerment have become coopted or strained, if not entirely severed, and instead trigger warnings have become mired in concerns about liability, mental health concerns, and faculty responsibilities (see Freeman et al.'s "Trigger Warnings are Flawed," *Inside Higher Education*, 29 May 2014, accessed 26 October 2014, https://www.insidehighered.com/views/2014/05/29/essay-faculty-members-about-why-they-will-not-use-trigger-warnings). These matters are indeed pressing, as are the calls for "systematic, robust, and proactive institutional attention to such matters as sexual assault, racially motivated attacks, harassment, and other practices of violence on campus" (Freeman et al). Yet, what concerns me is that critical or transformative pedagogical practices rather inevitably incite emotional, as well as intellectual and creative, engagement that are not always post-traumatic responses. To acknowledge that students and teachers can experience uncomfortable, difficult feelings in the classroom as part of the learning process should involve a degree of transparency about how those emotional responses might be aroused, valued, and treated with respect by everyone in the classroom. Such debates should continue, but new terminology and reframing questions about the goals of education are necessary to break out of the pros and cons approach to trigger warnings.

162 Kristina Ratcliffe, "A Rhetoric of Classroom Denial," 119.

163 Razack, *Looking White People in the Eye*, 36.

164 Ibid, 47. This is Razack's summary reading of Uma Narayan's "Working Together Across Differences: Some Considerations on Emotions and Political Practice."

165 See Peggy McIntosh's "White Privilege: Unpacking the Invisible Knapsack," *Independent School* 49 (1990), 31–5.

166 hooks, *Teaching to Transgress*, 84.

167 Ibid.

168 Ibid., 83.
169 Ibid., 81.
170 Ibid., 84.
171 Chrisjohn et al, *The Circle Game*, 108.
172 Butler, *Undoing Gender*, 1.
173 Razack, *Looking White People in the Eye*, 34.

3. Ibi Kaslik's *Skinny* and Kevin Patterson's *Consumption*

1 *The Edible Woman* (London: A. Deutsch, 1969), 256.
2 Susan Bordo, "Not Just 'A White Girl's Thing:' The Changing Face of Food and Body Image Problems," in *Critical Feminist Approaches to Eating Dis/Orders*, eds. Helen Malson and Maree Burns (London: Routledge, 2009), 47.
3 Sue Saltmarsh, "Becoming Economic Subjects: Agency, Consumption and Popular Culture in Early Childhood." *Discourse: Studies in the Cultural Politics of Education* 30, no. 1 (2009), 50.
4 Judith Butler, *Undoing Gender*, 1.
5 Louis Althusser and Étienne Balibar, *Reading Capital*, trans. Ben Brewster (London: Verso, 1997), accessed 19 February 2016, https://www.marxists.org/reference/archive/althusser/1968/reading-capital/ch02.htm/.
6 Ibid.
7 Frederic Jameson, *The Political Unconscious*, 102.
8 "anorexia," *OED Online*.
9 The *DSM-IV-TR* was the standard North American tool for defining, identifying, and treating mental disorders until May 2013. Published 18 May 2013, the fifth edition of the *DSM* revised its diagnostic criteria to concentrate on "behaviours, like restricting calorie intake, and no longer includes the word 'refusal' in terms of weight maintenance since that implies intention on the part of the patient and can be difficult to assess" (see American Psychiatric Publishing, "Feeding and Eating Disorders," accessed 19 February 2016, http://www.dsm5.org/documents/eating%20disorders%20fact%20sheet.pdf). However, all references to the *DSM* will be from the IV-TR edition given its contemporary relevance to the novels under study.
10 *DSM-IV-TR* Section 307.1.
11 While the exact origin of this concept is difficult to locate, during the late 1970s and early 1980s, several influential studies were published, which documented and analysed the increasing cultural fixation on thin body types in women, including Garner et al.'s "Cultural expectations

of thinness in women," *Psychological Reports* (1980); Kim Chernin's *The Obsession: Reflections on the Tyranny of Slenderness* (1981); Garfinkel and Garner's *Anorexia Nervosa: A Multidimensional Perspective* (1982); and later, Naomi Wolf's *The Beauty Myth* (1990).

12 Susan Bordo, "Not Just 'a White Girl's Thing,'" 47.

13 Ibid.

14 Ibid., 48.

15 See Melora Koepke's interview with Kaslik, "Ibi Kaslik's *Skinny*: Spilling Some Pink," *Hour Community* 27 (May 2004), accessed 19 February 2016, http://hour.ca/2004/05/27/spilling-some-pink/.

16 The cultural abjection of fat bodies is explored in the pedagogy section below.

17 "anorexia," *OED Online*.

18 Insisting that "eating disorders cannot be explained at the level of individual pathology," Bray and Colbrook echo other cultural theorists in exploring sociocultural factors related to eating disorders, like ideals of thinness and self-control, which remain marginalized by or tangential to biomedical and methodologically individualistic explanatory models (see "The Haunted Flesh: Corporeal Feminism and the Politics of [Dis] Embodiment," *Signs* 24, no. 1 [1998], 35). Such critics situate anorexic behaviours among several forms of body and food crises in Western patriarchal and consumer culture. The methodological inclusion by cultural critics of forms of eating and body crises less visible than anorexia, such as bulimia and 'overeating,' is the second way in which institutionalized diagnostic and treatment models are destabilized. These critics cite the significant occurrence of such crises among racialized, poor, and queer women and, increasingly, men. Becky Thompson, for example, insists that gender is not the only predictor of eating disorders, arguing that a "cultural emphasis on thinness simply [is]n't the primary factor" See "Food, Bodies, and Growing Up Female: Childhood Lessons about Culture, Race, and Class," *Feminist Perspectives on Eating Disorders*, eds. Patricia Fallon, Melanie A. Katzman; and Susan C. Wooley (New York: Guilford Press, 1994), 363. These challenges have mobilized ongoing critiques of heteropatriarchal, racist, sexist, and classist biases shaping sociological, psychological, and biomedical discourse. See also Malson and Burns's *Critical Feminist Approaches to Eating Disorders* (2009), Dawn Atkins's *Looking Queer: Body Image and Identity in Lesbian, Bisexual, Gay, and Transgender Communities* (1998), and Fallon et al's *Feminist Perspectives on Eating Disorders* (1994).

19 Bordo, "Not Just 'A White Girl's Thing,'" 51.

20 Naomi Wolf, *The Beauty Myth* (Toronto: Vintage, 1990), 14 (original emphasis).
21 Susan Bordo, *Bodies* (New York: Picador, 2009), 128.
22 Ibid., 128–9.
23 Saltmarsh, "Becoming Economic Subjects," 48.
24 Ibid., 49.
25 According to Foucault, "technologies of the self … permit individuals to effect by their own means or with the help of others a certain number of operations on their own bodies and souls, thoughts, conduct, and way of being, so as to transform themselves in order to attain a certain state of happiness, purity, wisdom, perfection, or immortality." See *Technologies of the Self: A Seminar with Michel Foucault*, eds. Luther H. Martin, Huck Gutman, and Patrick H. Hutton (Amherst: University of Massachusetts Press, 1988), 18.
26 Kaslik, *Skinny*, 131–5.
27 Ibid., 132.
28 Ibid., 50.
29 Ibid.
30 Ibid.
31 Ibid., 227.
32 Ibid., 28.
33 Ibid., 51.
34 Ibid., 5.
35 Ibid., 99–100.
36 Ibid., 100.
37 Ibid., 99.
38 Ibid., 51.
39 For example, Bordo claims that anorexia exemplifies a "fear of loss of control over our future." See "Anorexia Nervosa: Psychopathology as the Crystallization of Culture," *Food and Culture: A Reader*, eds. Carole Counihan and Penny Van Esterik (New York: Routledge, 2008), 163.
40 Deborah L. Tolman and Elizabeth Debold, "Conflicts of Body and Image: Female Adolescents, Desire, and the No-body Body," *Feminist Perspectives on Eating Disorders*, eds. Patricia Fallon, Melanie A. Katzman, and Susan C. Wooley (New York: Guilford Press, 1994), 302.
41 Mebbie Bell, "Re/Forming the Anorexic 'Prisoner': Inpatient Medical Treatment as the Return to Panoptic Femininity," *Cultural Studies ↔ Critical Methodologies* 6.2 (2006), 297. Bell expands on Foucault's theory of the Panopticon. Foucault analyses the disciplinary effects of Jeremy Bentham's architectural description of the panopticon (circular) prison,

in which prisoners are always observed but cannot see their captors. Foucault argues in *Discipline and Punish* that this arrangement, which inspires self-discipline in prisoners, forms a "disciplinary society … that stretches from the enclosed disciplines, a sort of social 'quarantine', to an indefinitely generalizable mechanism of 'panopticism'" (216).

42 Kaslik, *Skinny*, 28.
43 Bell, 293.
44 Kaslik, *Skinny*, 28.
45 Paula Saukko, "A Critical Discussion of Normativity in Discourses on Eating Disorders," in *Critical Feminist Approaches to Eating Disorders*, eds. Helen Malson and Maree Burns (London: Routledge, 2009), 67–8.
46 Kaslik, *Skinny*, 69.
47 Ibid., 116.
48 Ibid., 70.
49 Ibid., 113.
50 Ibid., 62.
51 Ibid., 64.
52 Ibid.
53 Ibid., 169.
54 Ibid., 170.
55 Ibid.
56 Ibid.
57 Tolman and Debold, "Conflicts of Body and Image," 302.
58 Ibid.
59 Kaslik, *Skinny*, 30.
60 Ibid., 122.
61 Ibid.
62 Ibid., 123.
63 Ibid., 113.
64 Bell, "Re/Forming the Anorexic 'Prisoner,'" 297.
65 Ibid., 296–7.
66 Ibid., 296.
67 Kaslik, *Skinny*, 19.
68 Ibid., 5.
69 Ibid., 173.
70 Ibid., 16.
71 Ibid.
72 Ibid., 63.
73 Ibid., 17.
74 Ibid., 18.

75 Ibid. 20.
76 Saukko, "A Critical Discussion of Normativity in Discourses on Eating Disorders," 63.
77 Ibid., 50.
78 Ibid., 159.
79 Thompson, "Food, Bodies, and Growing Up Female: Childhood Lessons about Culture, Race, and Class," 363.
80 Bell, "Re/Forming the Anorexic 'Prisoner,'" 297.
81 Kaslik, *Skinny*, 22.
82 Ibid., 180.
83 Saltmarsh, "Becoming Economic Subjects," 49.
84 Ibid.
85 Ibid.
86 Bordo, "Not Just 'A White Girl's Thing,'" 51. .
87 Jameson, *The Political Unconscious*, 102.
88 Anne McClintock, "The Angel of Progress: Pitfalls of the Term 'Post-Colonialism,'" *Social Text* 31/32 (1992), 93.
89 Jo-Ann Episkenew, *Taking Back our Spirits: Indigenous Literature, Public Policy, and Healing* (Winnipeg: University of Manitoba Press, 2009), 5.
90 For the vast majority of this period, Rankin Inlet was in the Northwest Territories.
91 Patterson, *Consumption*, 8.
92 Ibid., 10.
93 Marx, *Reader*, 232.
94 Ibid., 230,
95 Patterson, *Consumption*, 267.
96 Ibid., 18.
97 Ibid.
98 Ibid., 21.
99 Ibid., 23.
100 Ibid.
101 Ibid., 29.
102 Ibid., 31.
103 Ibid.
104 Ibid., 53.
105 Ibid., 31.
106 Ibid., 35.
107 Ibid., 27.
108 Ibid., 26.
109 Ibid.

110 Sherrill E. Grace, *Canada and the Idea of North* (Montreal: McGill-Queen's UP, 2001), 33.
111 Ibid., 124.
112 See discussion of Burroughs' term in chapter 1.
113 Patterson, *Consumption*, 72.
114 Ibid., 74.
115 Marx, *Reader*, 230.
116 Robert G. Dunn, *Identifying Consumption: Subjects and Objects in Consumer Society* (Philadelphia: Temple University Press, 2008), 3.
117 Patterson, *Consumption*, 249.
118 Ibid.
119 Ibid.
120 Ibid., 61.
121 Ibid., 62.
122 Ibid., 64.
123 Ibid.
124 Ibid., 113.
125 Ibid.
126 Ibid.
127 Ibid., 138.
128 Ibid., 132.
129 Ibid., 135.
130 Ibid., 132.
131 Ibid., 130.
132 Ibid.
133 Ibid., 13.
134 Inuit Qaujimajatuqangit Task Force, quoted in Keavy Martin's *Stories in a New Skin: Approaches to Inuit Literature* (Winnipeg: University of Manitoba Press, 2012), 122.
135 Ibid.
136 Patterson, *Consumption*, 265.
137 Ibid., 239.
138 Ibid., 271, 276, 284.
139 Ibid., 277.
140 Ibid., 276.
141 Ibid.
142 The North West Company grocery and supply store has been established in Rankin Inlet since the late 1980s (see "The North West Store: History," *The North West Company*) and sells, albeit at notoriously high prices, the selection of goods found in any southern grocery store. Also, within

Consumption's storyline, the reader has already been made aware that Marie's family eats both "country food" and store-bought "fish sticks, toast, [and] beans" (Patterson, *Consumption*, 130).

143 Patterson, *Consumption*, 276.

144 Ibid.

145 This assumption also echoes Stephen Harper's claim (one year after his apology to former residents of residential schools, in which he cited assimilation as the main goal of the system) that Canada has "no history of colonialism." See Derrick O'Keefe, "Harper in denial at G20: Canada has 'no history of colonialism,'" *rabble.ca*, 28 September 2009, accessed 19 February 2016, http://rabble.ca/blogs/bloggers/derrick/2009/09/harper-denial-g20-canada-has-no-history-colonialism.

146 Chrisjohn et al., *The Circle Game*, 129.

147 Ibid.

148 Ibid., 129–30.

149 Louis Althusser and Étienne Balibar, *Reading Capital*, trans. Ben Brewster (London: Verso, 1997), accessed 19 February 2016, https://www.marxists.org/reference/archive/althusser/1968/reading-capital/ch02.htm/

150 Patterson, *Consumption*, 282.

151 Ibid., 113.

152 Ibid.

153 Ibid., 280.

154 Ibid., 282.

155 Ibid., 281.

156 Ibid., 282.

157 Quoted in Saltmarsh, "Becoming Economic Subjects," 48.

158 Patterson, *Consumption*, 274.

159 Ibid.

160 This is Félix Guattari's term, which is discussed in chapter 1.

161 Freire, *Pedagogy of the Oppressed*, 109.

162 The questions and challenges raised by the likelihood of personal disclosure and the importance of understanding how students may be emotionally activated, or triggered, by such discussions are discussed in chapter 2.

163 Released in 1979, 1987, 2000, and 2010, the series focuses exclusively on media representations of women.

164 High traffic examples of such online cultural critique and social activism include *Gawker*, *Jezebel*, *Crunk Feminist Collective*, *Bitch* magazine, *Shameless* magazine, *Feministing*, and *MediaGirl*.

165 See Shari L Dworkin et al, *Body Panic: Gender, Health, and the Selling of Fitness*.

166 Ibid., 1.

167 Judith Butler, *Bodies that Matter: On the Discursive Limits of 'Sex'* (New York: Routledge, 1993), 3.
168 Bordo, *Bodies*, 140.
169 Ibid., 140–1.
170 Butler, *Bodies that Matter*, 3.
171 Helen Malson, *The Thin Woman: Feminism, Post-Structuralism and the Social Psychology of Anorexia Nervosa* (New York: Routledge, 1998), 132.
172 See, for example, Susie Orbach's *Fat is a Feminist Issue* (1978); Susan Bordo's *Unbearable Weight: Feminism, Western Culture, and the Body* (1993); *Bodies Out of Bounds: Fatness and Transgression*, edited by Jana Evans Braziel and Kathleen LeBesco, eds. (2001); and Marisa Meltzer's compelling article, "Are Fat Suits the New Blackface?" *BITCHFest: Ten Years of Cultural Criticism from the pages of Bitch Magazine.*
173 Susan Bordo, *Unbearable Weight: Feminism, Western Culture, and the Body* (Berkeley: University of California Press, 1993), 103–4.
174 Ibid., 104.
175 I adapt the distinction between prescriptive and revelatory from Chris Dixon's critique of correct line politics in *Another Politics*, 61 (original emphasis).
176 Ibid.
177 Kate Bornstein, *My Gender Workbook* (New York: Routledge, 1998), 44.
178 Ibid., 43.
179 Noortje van Amsterdam, "Big Fat Inequalities, Thin Privilege: An Intersectional Perspective on 'Body Size,'" in *European Journal of Women's Studies* 20, no. 2 (May 2013), 11, accessed 24 October 2014.
180 See McIntosh, "White Privilege: Unpacking the Invisible Knapsack," *Independent School* 49 (1990): 31–5.
181 For a comprehensive list of thin privileges, see Shannon Ridgeway's "20+ Examples of Thin Privilege," in *Everyday Feminism*, 30 November 2012, accessed 19 February 2016, http://everydayfeminism.com/2012/11/20-examples-of-thin-privilege/.
182 This is the pervasive refrain in Conlin's *Heave*, which I analyse in chapter 2.
183 Bordo, "Not Just 'A White Girl's Thing,'" 55.
184 Bray and Colbrook, "The Haunted Flesh," *Signs* 24, no. 1 (1998), 35.
185 Tolman and Debold, "Conflicts of Body and Image: Female Adolescents, Desire, and the No-body Body," 310.
186 Ibid., 313.
187 *DSM-IV*, Section 307, 1.
188 Ibid.
189 Bordo, *Unbearable Weight*, 104.

4. Beatrice Culleton Mosionier's *In Search of April Raintree* and Eden Robinson's *Monkey Beach*

1 Rudy Wiebe and Yvonne Johnson, *Stolen Life: The Journey of a Cree Woman* (Toronto: Alfred A. Knopf, 1998), 86.

2 Marcia Crosby, "Construction of the Imaginary Indian," in *Vancouver Anthology*, ed. Stan Douglas (Vancouver: Talonbooks, 1991), 268.

3 Razack, *Looking White People in the Eye*, 3

4 Hugh Brody, *Indians on Skid Row* (Ottawa: Information Canada, 1971), 240.

5 "Strombo: Soap Box: Wab Kinew," January 10, 2012, *YouTube*, accessed 19 February 2016, https://www.youtube.com/watch?v=GlkuRCXdu5A.

6 Marx, *Manuscripts*, 111.

7 Ibid., 113.

8 I mobilize Marx's theory of capital as that which is produced and accrued through "the production of commodities" and "their circulation" (*Reader* 329), processes that necessitate a constant supply of "labour-power offered as commodity" (*Reader* 336). The concept of capital can be conceived within non-capitalist social formations in ways that do not require the exploitation of labour. But, according to Marx, within a capitalist mode of production, "capital can spring into life, only when the owner of the means of production and subsistence meets in the market with the free labourer selling his labour-power … Capital, therefore, announces from its first appearance a new epoch in the process of social production" (*Reader* 339). In a Canadian context, capitalism establishes the conditions for subsistence, for social reproduction, as requiring the selling of one's labour-power.

9 Mosionier, *In Search of April Raintree*, 154.

10 Ibid., 180.

11 Ibid., 105.

12 Barbara Applebaum, *Being White, Being Good: White Complicity, White Moral Responsibility, and Social Justice Pedagogy* (Maryland: Lexington Books, 2010), 183.

13 See Robert Schmidt, "The Harm of Native Stereotyping: Facts and Evidence," *Blue Corn Comics*, accessed 19 February 2016, http://www.bluecorncomics.com/stharm.htm.

14 See Charlie Angus, "Taking on the Trolls: Why the Online Race-Hatred Against First Nations?" *The Huffington Post*, 16 July 2013, accessed 19 February 2016, http://www.huffingtonpost.ca/charlie-angus/aboriginal-online-commenters-_b_3600686.html.

15 "Brian Sinclair Inquest Wraps with Lawyer Calling ER Death a Homicide," *CBC News*, 12 June 2014, accessed 19 February 2016, http://www.cbc.ca/news/canada/manitoba/brian-sinclair-inquest-wraps-with-lawyer-calling-er-death-a-homicide-1.2672810.

16 "Tories Sorry for Comments to Native Protester," *Caledonia Wake Up Call*, 18 September 2008, accessed 19 February 2016, http://www.caledoniawakeupcall.com/updates/080918ctv.html.

17 "Barriere Lake Legal Defense Fund," *Barriere Lake Solidarity*, 21 August 2011, accessed 19 February 2016, http://www.barrierelakesolidarity.org/2011_08_01_archive.html.

18 Irlbacher-Fox, *Finding Dahshaa*, 31. Irlbacher-Fox situates this claim within a broader analysis of what she calls the Canadian state's "dysfunction theodicy," which frames Indigenous suffering as "self-imposed" because of "cultural difference and poor lifestyle choices," while "simultaneously positioning the state as a source of redemption and healing" (ibid.).

19 Brody, *Indians on Skid Row*, 45.

20 The original story no longer appears on the CTV News website, and so these comments have been deleted. Only the article was reproduced on the Caledonia webpage.

21 Commenter name is "ellie." See note 20.

22 "Taking on the Trolls," *The Huffington Post*. See note 14. No pagination.

23 Crosby, "Construction of the Imaginary Indian," 271.

24 James B. Waldram, *Revenge of the Wendigo: The Construction of the Mind and Mental Health of North American Aboriginal Peoples* (Toronto: University of Toronto Press, 2004), 135.

25 Ibid., 136.

26 Ibid.

27 Bonnie Duran, "Indigenous versus Colonial Discourse: Alcohol and American Indian Identity," in *Dressing in Feathers: The Construction of the American Popular Culture*, eds. Elizabeth S. Bird (Boulder, CO: Westview, 1996), 114.

28 MacDonald, Mary Lu, "Red & White Men; Black, White, & Grey Hats: Literary attitudes to the interaction between European and Native Canadian in the first half of the nineteenth century," in *Native Writers and Canadian Writing*, ed. W.H. New (Vancouver: UBC Press, 1990), 94.

29 Thomas King, Introduction in *The Native in Literature*, eds. Thomas King, Cheryl Calver, and Helen Hoy (Winnipeg: ECW Press, 1987), 8.

30 Susanna Moodie, *Roughing it in the Bush* (Toronto: McClelland & Stewart, 1989), 287.

31 Ibid., 286.
32 Ibid., 387.
33 Frances Brooke, *The History of Emily Montague* (Toronto: McClelland & Stewart, 2005), 40.
34 Terry Goldie, *Fear and Temptation: The Image of the Indigene in Canadian, Australian, and New Zealand Literatures* (Kingston, ON: McGill-Queen's University Press, 1989), 98.
35 Waldram, *Revenge of the Wendigo*, 147.
36 Ibid., 143, emphasis added.
37 Ibid., 146.
38 Kristina Fagan, "Tewatatha:wi: Aboriginal Nationalism in Taiaike Alfred's 'Peace, Power, Righteousness: An Indigenous Manifesto,'" *American Indian Quarterly* 28, no. 1/2 (2004), 14.
39 Ibid., 12–13.
40 Razack, *Looking White People in the Eye*, 13.
41 See Fee, Horne, Lundgren, and Smulders.
42 "'Through White Man's Eyes': Beatrice Culleton Mosionier's *In Search of April Raintree* and Reading for Decolonization," *Studies in American Literatures* 24, no. 1 (Spring 2012), 27.
43 Ideological: The novel's portrayal of the ideological construction of, and resistance to, racist stereotypes about Indigenous peoples and how these processes shape social status; narrative: the novel's narrative strategies, particularly its partial use of a naïve child narrator and the dialectical production of meaning through the sisters' relationship; and sociological: the novel as social realism, as dramatizing the socioeconomic and psychological conditions of Indigenous peoples in Canada, especially in relation to the role of child protection and welfare.
44 Mosionier, *In Search of April Raintree*, 154.
45 Ibid., 105.
46 Ibid., 62, 105.
47 Heather Zwicker, "The Limits of Sisterhood," in *In Search of April Raintree*, by Beatrice Culleton Mosionier, ed. Cheryl Suzack (Winnipeg: Portage & Main Press, 1999), 331.
48 Mosionier, *In Search of April Raintree*, 105, 125.
49 Ibid., 47.
50 Ibid., 194.
51 Ibid., 101.
52 Ibid., 91.
53 Ibid., 92.
54 Zwicker, "The Limits of Sisterhood," 327.

55 Smulders, Sharon, "'A Double Assault': The Victimization of Aboriginal Women and Children in *In Search of April Raintree*," *Mosaic: A Journal for the Interdisciplinary Study of Literature* 39, no. 2 (2006), 6.
56 Damm, Kateri, "Dispelling and Telling: Speaking Native Realities in Maria Campbell's *Halfbreed* and Beatrice Culleton's *In Search of April Raintree*." *Looking at the Words of Our People: First Nations Analysis of Literature*, 113.
57 Mosionier, *In Search of April Raintree*, 89.
58 Ibid., 87.
59 Mosionier, *In Search of April Raintree*, 11.
60 Ibid.
61 Ibid.
62 Ibid., 15.
63 Ibid., 14.
64 Ibid.
65 Ibid., 44.
66 Ibid., 45 (emphasis added).
67 Ibid., 46.
68 Hoy, "Nothing but the Truth," 286.
69 Mosionier, *In Search of April Raintree*, 180.
70 Ibid., 45.
71 Ibid., 46.
72 Smulders, "A Double Assault," 5. Lee Maracle's *Daughters Are Forever* also vividly dramatizes the dominance of this practice. The protagonist, a CAS worker, reviews photographs from removal cases, and notes the ubiquitous presence of alcohol bottles.
73 Mosionier, *In Search of April Raintree*, 47.
74 Smulders, "A Double Assault," 7.
75 *April Raintree*, 85.
76 Bonnie Duran, "Indigenous versus Colonial Discourse: Alcohol and American Indian Identity," 113.
77 Mosionier, *In Search of April Raintree* 126.
78 Ibid., 125.
79 Ibid., 43.
80 Ibid., 155.
81 Ibid., 152.
82 Ibid., 155.
83 Ibid., 152.
84 Ibid., 191.
85 Ibid., 105.

86 Damm, "Dispelling and Telling," 96.
87 Mosionier, *In Search of April Raintree*, 198 (emphasis in original).
88 Moodie, *Roughing it in the Bush*, 286.
89 Mosionier, *In Search of April Raintree*, 198 (emphasis in original).
90 Moodie, *Roughing it in the Bush*, 286.
91 Mosionier, *In Search of April Raintree*, 201.
92 Ibid. 155 (emphasis in the original).
93 Ibid., 197–8 (emphasis in original).
94 Ibid., 180.
95 Hoy, "Nothing but the Truth," 278.
96 Zwicker, "The Limits of Sisterhood," 327.
97 Mosionier, *In Search of April Raintree*, 198.
98 Creal, Michael, "'What Constitutes a Meaningful Life?': Identity Quest(ion)s in *In Search of April Raintree*," in *In Search of April Raintree*, by Beatrice Culleton Mosionier, ed. Cheryl Suzack (Winnipeg: Portage & Main Press, 1999), 254.
99 After revealing that Cheryl's mother had committed suicide, Henry Raintree explains that "she was not happy with her life. Once she lost you girls and Anna died, she knew she would never get you girls back again" (199). Henry then went "up north" (199).
100 Mosionier, *In Search of April Raintree*, 91.
101 Ibid., 143.
102 Ibid., 194.
103 Ibid., 207.
104 Zwicker, "The Limits of Sisterhood," 326.
105 Ibid., 327.
106 Hanson, "Through White Man's Eyes," 27.
107 Mosionier, *In Search of April Raintree*, 207.
108 Hoy, "Nothing but the Truth," 286.
109 Mosionier, *In Search of April Raintree*, 207.
110 Ibid., 155.
111 Margery Fee, "Upsetting Fake Ideas: Jeannette Armstrong's 'Slash' and Beatrice Culleton's 'April Raintree,'" *Canadian Literature* 124–5 (1990), 176.
112 Mosionier, *In Search of April Raintree*, 101.
113 Ibid., 81.
114 Ibid., 91.
115 Ibid., 92.
116 Ibid., 114.
117 Ibid., 126.

118 Robinson, *Monkey Beach*, 296.
119 Ibid., 367.
120 Marx, *Manuscripts*, 112.
121 Daniel Heath Justice, "'*Go Away, Water!*' Kinship Criticism and the Decolonization Imperative," in *Reasoning Together: The Native Critics Collective*, eds. Craig S. Womack, Daniel Heath Justice, and Christopher B. Teuton (Norman: University of Oklahoma Press, 2008), 151.
122 Jennifer Andrews, "Rethinking the Canadian Gothic: Reading Eden Robinson's *Monkey Beach*," in *Unsettled Remains: Canadian Literature and the Postcolonial Gothic*, 205–27, ed. Cynthia Sugars and Gerry Turcotte (Waterloo, ON: Wilfred Laurier University Press, 2009), 206.
123 Ibid., 224.
124 Jodey Castricano, "Learning to Talk with Ghosts: Canadian Gothic and the Poetics of Haunting in Eden Robinson's *Monkey Beach*," *University of Toronto Quarterly: A Canadian Journal of the Humanities* 75, no. 2 (2006), 808.
125 Richard Lane, "Performing Gender: First Nations, Feminism, and Trickster Writing in Eden Robinson's *Monkey Beach*," *Canadian Literature* 184 (2005), 164.
126 Ibid., 170.
127 Kit Dobson, "Indigeneity and Diversity in Eden Robinson's Work," *Canadian Literature* 201 (2009): 54–67, 200. *Academic OneFile*. Accessed 19 February 2016. http://ezproxy.uwindsor.ca/login?url=http://go.galegroup.com.ezproxy.uwindsor.ca/ps/i.do?id=GALE%7CA234570503&v=2.1&u=wind05901&it=r&p=AONE&sw=w&asid=9f13b4844a7e107f77627a1417a5b5d9.
128 Fagan, "Tewatatha:wi," 12.
129 Ibid., 12–13.
130 Coulthard, *Red Skin, White Masks*, 7.
131 Kitimaat village and Kitimat are geographically discrete, connected by "an eleven-kilometre strip of concrete" (Robinson, *Monkey Beach*, 27). Lisamarie and her family live in Kitamaat Village. Kitimat is the town in which Alcan was built. While they are different towns, Robinson emphasizes the direct influence of Kitimat's economy on Kitamaat Village throughout.
132 Robinson, *Monkey Beach*, 5 (emphasis added).
133 "A History of Kitimat-Kemano Project," *Alcan BC Operations*, 21 June 2013, accessed 27 October 2014, http://www.ieee.ca/millennium/kitimat/kitimat_history.html.
134 I draw on Sarah De Leeuw's argument that an ideology underlying residential schooling conflated "the transformation of place with

the transformation of First Nations children." See De Leeuw's PhD dissertation, "Artful Places: Creativity and Colonialism in British Columbia's Indian Residential Schools," (Queen's University, 2007), 185.

135 "British Columbia Travel and Discovery," *OurBC.com*, accessed 28 May 2013, but the website has since been removed.

136 Robinson, *Monkey Beach*, 59–60.

137 Crosby, "Construction of the Imaginary Indian," 279.

138 Initiated in November 2012, Idle No More's convergence of mobilizations against Canadian colonial policies and tactics is described as follows by Sheelah McLean, co-founder of the movement: "The struggle is not just about what 'resource sharing' should and shouldn't look like. This is Indigenous land, and these are Indigenous resources. True sovereignty necessitates redistribution: the land, resources, and decision-making power has to go back to Indigenous people. Many communities have already decided on that route through land protection struggles. Grassy Narrows is an example of a long-standing barricade defending and protecting the lands." See PJ Lilley and Jeff Shantz, "From Idle No More to Indigenous Nationhood," *Upping the Anti* 15 (2013), 118. See also an interview with Freda Huson and Toghestiy, Wet'suwet'en land defenders and representatives of the Unist'ot'en Camp: "They enforce a Consent Protocol that determines who is allowed access to the area, and have evicted pipeline crews found working on Wet'suwet'en territory several times. Pipelines being blockaded include Enbridge's Northern Gateway, Chevron's Pacific Trails, and TransCanada's Coastal GasLink and Prince Rupert projects." *Upping the Anti* 17 (2015): 46.

139 *The Inconvenient Indian: A Curious Account of Native People in North America*, (Toronto: Random House, 2012), 218.

140 Ibid.

141 Ella Soper-Jones, "The Fate of the Oolichan: Prospects of Eco-Cultural Restoration in Eden Robinson's *Monkey Beach*," *Journal of Commonwealth Literature* 44, no. 2 (2009), 27.

142 Ibid., 24.

143 Ibid.

144 Ibid., 153.

145 Marx, *Manuscripts*, 112–13.

146 Robinson, *Monkey Beach*, 153.

147 Ibid., 154.

148 Ibid., 3.

149 Ibid., 277.

150 Ibid., 278.

151 Ibid., 279.
152 The school (or schools) to which they were sent is never specified, though there was a residential school in Kitimaat.
153 Ibid., 365.
154 Ibid., 319.
155 Chrisjohn et al., *The Circle Game*, 129.
156 McKegney's analysis is built on Robinson's description of the deadheads in *Monkey Beach*. See *Magic Weapons: Aboriginal Writers Remaking Community After Residential Schools* (Winnipeg: University of Manitoba Press, 2007), 12.
157 Ibid.
158 Robinson, *Monkey Beach*, 277.
159 Ibid., 279.
160 Ibid., 81.
161 Ibid., 199.
162 Ibid.
163 Judith Butler, "Imitation and Gender Subordination," in *The Judith Butler Reader*, ed. Sara Salih with Judith Butler (Malden, MA: Blackwell Publishing, 2004), 129.
164 Lane, "Performing Gender," 167.
165 "The 1950 agreement with the province provided Alcan with water rights to the Nechaka and Nanika rivers in perpetuity. It also allowed Alcan to … propose a second hydro project in 1984, which would bore new holes in the mountain and use up to 88 per cent of the Nechako River … called Kemano II or the Kemano Completion Project." See Robert Sheppard, "Power Play," *CBC News*, 21 August 2006.
166 Butler, "Performing Gender," 168.
167 Ibid., 166–7.
168 Robinson, *Monkey Beach*, 153.
169 Ibid. Lisamarie describes "the pattern of the little man's visits" (27) as seemingly random: "A variation of the monster under the bed … he liked to sit on the top of [her] dresser … and he had a shock of bright red hair which stood up in messy, tangled puffs that he sometimes hid under a black top hat" (27). Michèle Lacombe explains that, "like B'gwus, the red-haired, green-garbed little man … is so easily mistaken for an evil leprauchaun by readers and critics alike … [but] is a spirit associated with the cedar tree, [who] must be approached with caution … He appears to be a harbinger of death. However, he also represents the gift of vision that Lisamarie inherited from her mother, which is the gift of her Haisla ancestry and bloodline – her history, culture, and identity."

See "On Critical Frameworks for Analyzing Indigenous Literature," *International Journal of Canadian Studies* 41 (2010), 271, accessed 30 October 2014, doi: 10.7202/044170ar.

170 Robinson, *Monkey Beach*, 266.
171 Ibid., 275.
172 Ibid.
173 Castricano, "Learning to Talk with Ghosts," 805.
174 Ibid., 808.
175 Ibid., 805.
176 Robinson, *Monkey Beach*, 272.
177 Ibid., 274.
178 Ibid., 279.
179 Ibid., 294.
180 Ibid., 296.
181 Ibid., 313.
182 Ibid., 326.
183 Ibid., 327.
184 Ibid., 296.
185 McKegney, *Magic Weapons*, 12.
186 Justice, *"Go Away, Water!,"* 151.
187 Robinson, *Monkey Beach*, 372.
188 Ibid., 316.
189 Ibid., 69.
190 Ibid., 371.
191 Justice, *"Go Away, Water!,"* 151.
192 Robinson, *Monkey Beach*, 265.
193 "The term b'gwus, common to the Nisga'a, Gitskan, Tsimshian, Kwakw'ala, and Haisla languages, has evolved from an older root word pa'gwus or pi'kis, defined … in at least four different ways: 'monkey,' 'monkey woman,' 'wealth woman,' and 'land otter woman'" (Halpin quoted in Lacombe, "On Critical Frameworks," 261).
194 Robinson, *Monkey Beach*, 374.
195 Ibid., 316.
196 Episkenew, *Taking Back our Spirits*, 9.
197 Fagan, "Tewatatha:wi," 14.
198 Robinson, *Monkey Beach*, 310.
199 This phrase is taken from Carol Shields' novel, *Unless*. Reta refuses to accept that her daughter's seeming self-harming behaviour is solely explained by psychological factors. Instead, she develops a hypothesis that finds its most striking expression through a contemptuous letter to

the author of a study about philosophy's contributions to solving moral problems. After noting that "all the problem solvers in [his] examples are men, all fourteen" (219), Reta asserts, "it is my belief that there is a circuitry linking your philosophical approach and my daughter's resignation from life, her consignment to dysfunction" (220–1).

200 Daniel Heath Justice, "Conjuring Marks: On Indigenous Nationhood, Literature, and the Paracolonial Perils of the Nation-State," *The Kenyon Review* 32, no. 1 (2010), 5.

201 Butler, *Undoing Gender*, 1.

202 Justice, "Rhetorics of Recognition," 240.

203 Martin J. Cannon, "Changing the Subject in Teacher Education: Centering Indigenous, Diasporic, and Settler Colonial Relations," *Cultural and Pedagogical Inquiry* 4.2 (2012), 24.

204 Rob Schmidt, "The Harm of Native Stereotyping: Facts and Evidence," *Blue Corn Comics*, accessed 19 February 2016, http://www.bluecorncomics.com/stharm.htm.

205 Andrea Smith in "Building Unlikely Alliances: An Interview with Andrea Smith," interview with Sharmeen Khan, David Hugill, and Tyler McCreary, *Upping the Anti: A Journal of Theory and Action*, no. 10, accessed 19 February 2016, http://uppingtheanti.org/journal/article/10-building-unlikely-alliances-an-interview-with-andrea-smith/.

206 Razack, *Looking White People in the Eye*, 17.

207 Ibid., 14.

208 Cannon, "Changing the Subject in teacher education," 22.

209 Ibid.

210 Ibid., 29.

211 Ibid., 25.

212 Ibid., 26–7.

213 Razack, *Looking White People in the Eye*, 21.

214 Ibid.

215 Ibid.

216 Ibid.

217 Smith, "Building Unlikely Alliances."

218 Episkenew, *Taking Back our Spirits*, 8.

219 Ibid., 11.

220 Ibid.

221 Lee Maracle, "This is a Vision: A Conversation with Lee Maracle," in *Masculindians: Conversations about Indigenous Manhood*, by Sam McKegney (Winnipeg: University of Manitoba, 2014), 36.

222 Ibid.

223 Ibid.
224 Ibid., 32.
225 Ibid., 33.
226 "Addictive Behaviours among Aboriginal People in Canada," *The Aboriginal Healing Foundation Research Series* (Ottawa: Aboriginal Healing Foundation, 2007), 5.
227 Ibid., 16.
228 Ibid., iii.
229 The Aboriginal Healing Foundation was left out of the federal government's budget in March 2010, compelling the AHF to withdraw support from 134 healing initiatives across Canada.
230 Taiaike Alfred, *Peace, Power, Righteousness: An Indigenous Manifesto* (Oxford: Oxford University Press, 2009), 37.
231 "Decolonizing Together: Moving beyond a politics of solidarity toward a practice of decolonization," *Briarpatch*, 21 January 2012, accessed 19 February 2016, http://briarpatchmagazine.com/articles/view/decolonizing-together.

Conclusion

1 "The Imagination's Subsidies: Whiners, Elites, Ordinary People, and the Economy," *ESC: English Studies in Canada* 33, no. 3 (September 2007): 18.
2 Razack, *Looking White People in the Eye*, 22.
3 "Literature and Social Change: Writing, Criticism and Teaching in Neoliberal Canada," PhD Dissertation, University of Guelph, 2015, 2.
4 "Afterword: Sentiment or Action," *Transnationalism, Activism, Art*, Eds. Kit Dobson and Áine McGlynn (Toronto: University of Toronto Press, 2013), 229.
5 "Literature and Social Change," 71.
6 "'*Go Away, Water!*' Kinship Criticism and the Decolonization Imperative," in *Reasoning Together: The Native Critics Collective*, eds. Craig S. Womack, Daniel Heath Justice, and Christopher B. Teuton (Norman: University of Oklahoma Press, 2008), 159.
7 Keane, *What's Wrong with Addiction?*, 9.
8 Quoted in Anthony Weston's "Toward A Social Critique of Bioethics," *Journal of Social Philosophy*, 22, no. 2 (1991), 109.
9 Email message to the author, 1 May 2011.

Bibliography

"A History of Kitimat-Kemano Project." *Alcan BC Operations*. Accessed 19 February 2016. http://www.ieee.ca/millennium/kitimat/kitimat_history.html.

"A.A. Fact File." *Alcoholics Anonymous*. Accessed 19 February 2016. http://www.aa.org/assets/en_US/m-24_aafactfile.pdf.

Acker, Caroline J. "Stigma or Legitimation? A Historical Examination of the Social Potentials of Addiction Disease Models." *Journal of Psychoactive Drugs* 25, no. 3 (1993): 193–205.

"Addictive Behaviours among Aboriginal People in Canada." *The Aboriginal Healing Foundation Research Series*. Ottawa: Aboriginal Healing Foundation, 2007. Accessed 19 February 2016. http://www.ahf.ca/downloads/addictive-behaviours.pdf.

Alcoholics Anonymous: The Story of How Many Thousands of Men and Women Have Recovered from Alcoholism. 4th ed. New York: Anonymous World Services, 2001.

Alexander, Anna, and Mark S. Roberts, eds. *High Culture: Reflections on Addiction and Modernity*. Albany: State University of New York Press, 2003.

Alfred, Taiaiake. *Peace, Power, Righteousness: An Indigenous Manifesto*. Oxford: Oxford University Press, 2009.

Althusser, Louis. "Ideology and Ideological State Apparatus." In *Mapping Ideology*, ed. Slavoj Žižek, 100–40. New York: Verso, 1994.

Althusser, Louis, and Étienne Balibar. *Reading Capital*. Trans. Ben Brewster. London: Verso, 1997. Accessed 19 February 2016. https://www.marxists.org/reference/archive/althusser/1968/reading-capital/ch02.htm/.

Andrews, Jennifer. "Rethinking the Canadian Gothic: Reading Eden Robinson's *Monkey Beach*." In *Unsettled Remains: Canadian Literature and the Postcolonial Gothic*, eds. Cynthia Sugars and Gerry Turcotte, 205–27. Waterloo, ON: Wilfred Laurier University Press, 2009.

Angus, Charlie. "Taking on the Trolls: Why the Online Race-Hatred Against First Nations?" *The Huffington Post*, 16 July 2013, accessed 19 February 2016. http://www.huffingtonpost.ca/charlie-angus/aboriginal-online-commenters-_b_3600686.html.

"anorexia, n." OED Online. Oxford University Press, December 2015, accessed 15 February 2016. http://www.oed.com/view/Entry/8080?redirectedFrom=anorexia.

Applebaum, Barbara. *Being White, Being Good: White Complicity, White Moral Responsibility, and Social Justice Pedagogy*. Maryland: Lexington Books, 2010.

Appleford, Rob. "'Close, Very Close, a B'gwus Howls': The Contingency of Execution in Eden Robinson's *Monkey Beach*." *Canadian Literature* 184 (2005): 85–101.

Armstrong, Jeannette C. *Slash*. Penticton, BC: Theytus, 1985.

Atkins, Dawn, ed. *Looking Queer: Body Image and Identity in Lesbian, Bisexual, Gay, and Transgender Communities*. New York: Harrington Park Press, 1998.

Atwood, Margaret. *The Edible Woman*. London: A. Deutsch, 1969.

– *Payback: Debt and the Shadow Side of Wealth*. Toronto: Anansi, 2008.

Baker, G., and P.M.S. Hacker. "The Grammar of Psychology: Wittgenstein's Bemerkungen über die Philosophie der Psychologie." *Language and Communication* 2 (1982): 227–44.

Baldev, Satyen, Timothy Choi, Bushra Mahmood, Richelle Oslinker, Faten Sumrein, Aminah Waqar, and Carolyne J. White. "Being Leaders for Socially Just Education: Engaging New Politics of Possibility." *Cultural Studies ↔ Critical Methodologies* 13, no. 6 (2013): 489–96.

Banco, Lindsey Michael. *Travel and Drugs in Twentieth-Century Literature*. New York: Routledge, 2010.

Bar-Shalom, Jade. "Multicultural Critics-at-Large: Dis-Identification in Beatrice Culleton's *In Search of April Raintree*." In *Identity, Community, Nation: Essays on Canadian Writing*, eds. Danielle Schaub and Christl Verduyn, 113–25. Jerusalem, Israel: Magnes, 2002.

"Barriere Lake Legal Defense Fund." *Barriere Lake Solidarity*, 19 February 2016. Accessed 30 October 2014. http://www.barrierelakesolidarity.org/2011_08_01_archive.html.

Beck, Ulrich, and Elisabeth Beck-Gernsheim. *Individualization: Institutionalized Individualism and its Social and Political Consequences*. London: SAGE Publications Ltd., 2002.

Bell, Mebbie. "Re/Forming the Anorexic 'Prisoner': Inpatient Medical Treatment as the Return to Panoptic Femininity." *Cultural Studies ↔ Critical Methodologies* 6, no. 2 (2006): 282–307.

Beneventi, Domenic A. "Montreal Underground." *Journal of Canadian Studies/ Revue D'études Canadiennes* 46, no. 3 (Fall 2012): 263–86.

Bezanson, Kate, and Meg Luxton, eds. *Social Reproduction: Feminist Political Economy Challenges Neo-Liberalism*. Montreal, QC: McGill-Queen's University Press, 2006.

Bhargava, Rajeev. *Individualism in Social Science: Forms and Limits of a Methodology*. Oxford: Clarendon Press, 1992.

Bourdieu, Pierre. *Distinction: A Social Critique of the Judgment of Taste*. Trans. Richard Nice. Cambridge, MA: Harvard University Press, 1984.

Bordo, Susan. "Anorexia Nervosa: Psychopathology as the Crystallization of Culture." In *Food and Culture: A Reader*, 2nd edition, eds. Carole Counihan and Penny Van Esterik, 162–86. New York: Routledge, 2008.

– *Bodies*. New York: Picador, 2009.

– "Not Just 'A White Girl's Thing': The Changing Face of Food and Body Image Problems." In *Critical Feminist Approaches to Eating Dis/Orders*, eds. Helen Malson and Maree Burns, 46–59.. London: Routledge, 2009.

– *Unbearable Weight: Feminism, Western Culture, and the Body*. Berkeley: University of California Press, 1993.

Bornstein, Kate. *My Gender Workbook*. New York: Routledge, 1998.

Borst, Allan G. "Towards National Identity: Addiction, Subjectivity, and American Literary Culture." PhD diss., University of Illinois, 2009.

Bowker, Gordon. *Pursued by Furies: A Life of Malcolm Lowry*. Toronto: Random House of Canada, 1993.

Boyden, Joseph. *Three Day Road*. Toronto: Penguin, 2006.

Brand, Dionne. *Land to Light On*. Toronto: McClelland & Stewart Inc., 1997.

Bray, Abigail, and Claire Colbrook. "The Haunted Flesh: Corporeal Feminism and the Politics of (Dis)Embodiment." *Signs* 24, no. 1 (1998): 35–67.

Braziel, Jana Evans, and Kathleen LeBesco, eds. *Bodies Out of Bounds: Fatness and Transgression*. Berkeley: University of California Press, 2001.

"British Columbia Travel and Discovery." *OurBC.com*. Accessed 28 May 2013.

Brodie, Janet Farrell, and Marc Redfield, eds. *High Anxieties: Cultural Studies in Addiction*. Berkeley: University of California Press, 2002.

Brody, Hugh. *Indians on Skid Row*. Ottawa: Information Canada, 1971.

Brook, Barbara. *Feminist Perspectives on the Body*. London: Longman, 1999.

Brooke, Frances. *The History of Emily Montague*. Toronto: McClelland & Stewart, 2005.

Brown, Catrina, and Karin Jasper, eds. *Consuming Passions: Feminist Approaches to Weight Preoccupation and Eating Disorders*. Toronto: Second Story Press, 1993.

Brumberg, Joan Jacobs. *Fasting Girls: The Emergence of Anorexia Nervosa as a Modern Disease*. Cambridge, MA: Harvard University Press, 1988.

Burroughs, William S. *Naked Lunch: The Restored Text*. Eds. James Grauerholz and Barry Miles. New York: Grove Press, 2001.

Butler, Judith. *Bodies that Matter: On the Discursive Limits of "Sex."* New York: Routledge, 1993.

– "Imitation and Gender Subordination." In *The Judith Butler Reader*, eds. Sara Salih with Judith Butler, 119–37. Malden, MA: Blackwell Publishing, 2004.

– *Undoing Gender*. New York: Routledge, 2004.

Cain, Carole. "Personal Stories: Identity Acquisition and Self-Understanding in Alcoholics Anonymous." *Ethos* 19, no. 2 (1991): 210–53.

Calder, Alison. "How To Be Good." *Canadian Literature* 185 (2005): 165–7.

Campbell, Nancy. *Using Women: Gender, Drug Policy, and Social Justice*. New York: Routledge, 2000.

Campbell, Robin. Introduction to *Letters from a Stoic: Epistulae Morales Ad Lucilium*, by Lucius Annaeus Seneca, 7–29. Trans. Robin Campbell. Middlesex: Penguin Books, 1969.

Canadian Tuberculosis Committee. "Housing Conditions that Serve as Risk Factors for Tuberculosis Infection and Disease." *Canadian Communicable Disease Report* 33 (2007). Accessed 19 February 2016. http://www.phac-aspc.gc.ca/publicat/ccdr-rmtc/07pdf/acs33-09.pdfQ2.

Canadian Centre on Substance Abuse. "Substance Abuse in Corrections: FAQs." Ottawa: CCSA, 2004. Accessed 19 February 2016. www.ccsa.ca/Resource%20Library/ccsa-011058-2004.pdf.

Cannon, Martin J. "Changing the Subject in Teacher Education: Centering Indigenous, Diasporic, and Settler Colonial Relations." *Cultural and Pedagogical Inquiry* 4, no. 2 (2012): 21–37.

Case, Kim A., ed. *Deconstructing Privilege: Teaching and Learning as Allies in the Classroom*. New York: Routledge, 2013.

Case, Kim A., and Elizabeth R. Cole. "Deconstructing Privilege When Students Resist." In *Deconstructing Privilege: Teaching and Learning as Allies in the Classroom*, ed. Kim A. Case, 34–48. New York: Routledge, 2013.

Castricano, Jodey. "Learning to Talk with Ghosts: Canadian Gothic and the Poetics of Haunting in Eden Robinson's *Monkey Beach*." *University of Toronto Quarterly: A Canadian Journal of the Humanities* 75, no. 2 (2006): 801–13.

CBC Canada Reads 2014. Accessed 19 February 2016. http://www.cbc.ca/player/Shows/Shows/Canada+Reads/ID/2440911767/.

CBC News. "Brian Sinclair Inquest Wraps with Lawyer Calling ER Death a Homicide." 12 June 2014. Accessed 19 February 2016. http://www.cbc.ca/news/canada/manitoba/brian-sinclair-inquest-wraps-with-lawyer-calling-er-death-a-homicide-1.2672810.

– "PM Wants Mandatory Sentences for 'Serious' Drug Crimes." 4 October 2007. Accessed 19 February 2016. http://www.cbc.ca/news/canada/pm-wants-mandatory-sentences-for-serious-drug-crimes-1.647115.

– "Vancouver's Insite Drug Injection Clinic Will Stay Open." 30 September 2011. Accessed 19 February 2016. http://www.cbc.ca/news/canada/british-columbia/vancouver-s-insite-drug-injection-clinic-will-stay-open-1.1005044.

"Charlie Sheen's Bizarre New Interview: Slams Alcoholics Anonymous, Says His Rate for Beating Addiction is 100%." *Radar Online.com*. February 2011. Accessed 19 February 2016. http://radaronline.com/exclusives/2011/02/charlie-sheens-bizarre-new-interview-slams-alcoholic-anonymous-says-his-rate/.

Chernin, Kim. *The Obsession: Reflections on the Tyranny of Slenderness*. New York: Harper & Row, 1981.

Chrisjohn, Roland, Sherri Young, and Michael Maraun. *The Circle Game: Shadows and Substance in the Indian Residential School Experience in Canada*. Penticton, BC: Theytus, 1997.

Clarke, David B., Marcus A. Doel, and Kate M.L. Housiaux, eds. *The Consumption Reader*. London, New York: Routledge, 2003.

Coady, Lynn. "Wireless." In *Hellgoing*, 1–27. Toronto: House of Anansi Press, 2013.

– *Strange Heaven*. Fredericton: Goose Lane, 1998.

Cohen, Leonard. *Beautiful Losers*. Toronto: McClelland & Stewart, 1966.

Coleman, Daniel, and Smaro Kamboureli, eds. *Retooling the Humanities: The Culture of Research in Canadian Universities*. Edmonton: University of Alberta Press, 2011.

Collins, Susan E., Seema L. Clifasefi, Diane E. Logan, Laura S. Samples, Julian M. Somers, and G. Alan Marlatt. "Current Status, Historical Highlights, and Basic Principles." In *Harm Reduction: Pragmatic Strategies for Managing Risk Behaviors*, 2nd ed. G. Alan Marlatt, Mary E. Larimer, & Katie Witkiewitz, eds. New York: The Guilford Press, 2012. 3–35.

Collins, Wilkie. *Moonstone*. Ed. Steve Farmer. Peterborough: Broadview Press, 1999.

Conlin, Christy Ann. *Heave*. Toronto: Doubleday, 2002.

– "The System Sucks: A Discussion of Homeless Youth in Halifax." Nova Scotia Public Research Group, 1993.

Coté, Mark, Richard J.F. Day, and Greig de Peuter, eds. *Utopian Pedagogy: Radical Experiments Against Neoliberal Globalization*. Toronto: University of Toronto Press, 2007.

Cote-Meet, Sheila. *Colonized Classrooms: Racism, Trauma and Resistance in Post-Secondary Education*. Halifax & Winnipeg: Fernwood, 2014.

Coulthard, Glen Sean. *Red Skin, White Masks: Rejecting the Colonial Politics of Recognition*. Minneapolis: University of Minnesota Press, 2014.

Creal, Michael. "'What Constitutes a Meaningful Life?': Identity Quest(ion) s in *In Search of April Raintree*." In *In Search of April Raintree*, by Beatrice Culleton Mosionier, ed. Cheryl Suzack, 251–60. Winnipeg: Portage & Main Press, 1999.

Creelman, David. *Setting in the East: Maritime Realist Fiction*. Montreal & Kingston: McGill-Queen's University Press, 2003.

Crenshaw, Kimberlé. "Mapping the Margins: Intersectionality, Identity Politics, and Violence Against Women of Color." Stanford Law Review 43, no. 6 (1991): 1241–99.

Crosby, Marcia. "Construction of the Imaginary Indian." In Vancouver Anthology, *ed.* Stan Douglas, 267–91. Vancouver: Talonbooks, 1991.

Crozier, Lorna, and Patrick Lane, eds. *Addicted: Notes from the Belly of the Beast*. Vancouver: Greystone Books, 2001.

Cumyn, Alan. "Praise." In *The Empty Room*, by Lauren B. Davis, 237. Toronto: HarperCollins, 2013. Kindle edition.

Damm, Kateri. "Dispelling and Telling: Speaking Native Realities in Maria Campbell's *Halfbreed* and Beatrice Culleton's *In Search of April Raintree*." In *Looking at the Words of Our People: First Nations Analysis of Literature*, ed. Jeannette Armstrong, 93–114. Penticton, BC: Theytus Books, 1993.

Davis, Angela. *Are Prisons Obsolete?* New York: Seven Stories Press, 2003.

Davis, Lauren B. *The Empty Room*. Toronto: HarperCollins, 2013. Kindle edition.

de Leeuw, Sarah. "Artful Places: Creativity and Colonialism in British Columbia's Indian Residential Schools." PhD diss., Queen's University, 2007.

De Quincey, Thomas. *Confessions of an English Opium-Eater, and Other Writings*. Ed. Robert Morrison. Oxford: Oxford University Press, 2013.

Derrida, Jacques. "The Rhetoric of Drugs." In *High Culture: Reflections on Addiction and Modernity*, ed. Anna Alexander and Mark S. Roberts, 19–44. Albany, NY: SUNY University Press, 2003.

Diagnostic and Statistical Manual of Mental Disorders: DSM-5. 5th ed. Arlington, VA: American Psychiatric Association, 2013.

Diversi, Marcelo, and Claudio Moreira. "Real World: Classrooms as Decolonizing Sites Against Neoliberal Narratives of the Other." *Cultural Studies Critical Methodologies* 13, no. 6 (2013): 469–73.

Dixon, Chris. *Another Politics: Talking Across Today's Transformative Movements*. Foreword by Angela Davis. Oakland: University of California Press, 2014.

Dobson, Kathy. *With a Closed Fist*. Montreal: Véhicule Press, 2011.

Dobson, Kit. "Indigeneity and Diversity in Eden Robinson's Work." *Canadian Literature* 201 (2009): 54. *Academic OneFile*. Accessed 19 February 2016. http://ezproxy.uwindsor.ca/login?url=http://go.galegroup.com.ezproxy.uwindsor.ca/ps/i.do?id=GALE%7CA234570503&v=2.1&u=wind05901&it=r&p=AONE&sw=w&asid=9f13b4844a7e107f77627a1417a5b5d9.

Dunn, Robert G. *Identifying Consumption: Subjects and Objects in Consumer Society*. Philadelphia: Temple University Press, 2008.

Duran, Bonnie. "Indigenous versus Colonial Discourse: Alcohol and American Indian Identity." In *Dressing in Feathers: The Construction of the American Popular Culture*, ed. Elizabeth S. Bird, 111–28. Boulder, CO: Westview, 1996.

During, Simon. "Introduction." In *The Cultural Studies Reader*, 2nd edition, ed. Simon During, 1–28. London: Routledge, 1999.

Dworkin, Shari L. and Faye Linda Wachs. *Body Panic: Gender, Health, and the Selling of Fitness*. New York: New York University Press, 2009.

Episkenew, Jo-Ann. *Taking Back our Spirits: Indigenous Literature, Public Policy, and Healing*. Winnipeg: University of Manitoba Press, 2009.

Fabello, Melissa A. "Let's Talk about Thin Privilege." *Everyday Feminism*, 25 October 2013. Accessed 19 February 2016. http://everydayfeminism.com/2013/10/lets-talk-about-thin-privilege/.

Fagan, Kristina. "Tewatatha:wi: Aboriginal Nationalism in Taiaike Alfred's 'Peace, Power, Righteousness: An Indigenous Manifesto.'" *American Indian Quarterly* 28, no. 1/2 (2004): 12–29.

Fallon, Patricia, Melanie A. Katzman, and Susan C. Wooley, eds. *Feminist Perspectives on Eating Disorders*. New York: Guilford Press, 1994.

Fee, Margery. "Deploying Identity in the Face of Racism." *In Search of April Raintree*, by Beatrice Culleton Mosionier, ed. Cheryl Suzack, 211–26. Winnipeg: Portage and Main Press, 1999.

– "Upsetting Fake Ideas: Jeannette Armstrong's 'Slash' and Beatrice Culleton's 'April Raintree.'" *Canadian Literature* 124–125 (1990): 168–80.

"Feeding and Eating Disorders." *American Psychiatric Publishing*. Accessed 19 February 2016. http://www.dsm5.org/documents/eating%20disorders%20fact%20sheet.pdf.

Ferentzy, Peter. "Foucault and Addiction." *Telos* 125 (2002): 167–91.

First, Michael B., ed. *Diagnostic and Statistical Manual of Mental Disorders. (DSM-IV-TR™)*. 4th ed. Washington, DC: American Psychiatric Association, 2000. Accessed 30 October 2014. *STATRef Online Electronic Medical Library*.

Fithian, Lisa. "Anti-Oppression Principles and Practices." *Organizing for Power, Organizing for Change*. Accessed 19 February 2016. https://docs.google.com/document/d/1TnaLJXy6WSkJ-MQv4BlMhRXM1cc-4wBqNcgrD4W-VZQ/edit.

Fitzgerald, F. Scott. *The Great Gatsby*. Ed. Michael Nowlin. Peterborough: Broadview Editions, 2007.

Foucault, Michel. *Discipline and Punish: The Birth of the Prison*. Trans. Alan Sheridan. New York: Vintage Books, 1995.

– *History of Madness*. Trans. Jonathan Murphy and Jean Khalfa. Ed. Jean Khalfa. London: Routledge, 2009.

– *Technologies of the Self: A Seminar with Michel Foucault*. Eds. Luther H. Martin, Huck Gutman, and Patrick H. Hutton. Amherst: University of Massachusetts Press, 1988.

– *The Birth of the Clinic: An Archeology of Medical Perception*. Trans. A.M. Sheridan. London: Routledge, 2003.

– *The History of Sexuality: An Introduction*. Vol 1. Trans. Robert Hurley. New York: Vintage, 1990.

Francis, Daniel. *The Imaginary Indian: The Image of the Indian in Canadian Culture*. Vancouver: Arsenal Pulp Press, 1992.

Freeman, Elizabeth, Brian Herrera, Nat Hurley, Homay King, Dana Luciano, Dana Seitler, and Patricia White. "Trigger Warnings Are Flawed." *Inside Higher Education*. 29 May 2014. Accessed 19 February 2016. https://www.insidehighered.com/views/2014/05/29/essay-faculty-members-about-why-they-will-not-use-trigger-warnings.

Freire, Paulo. *Pedagogy of the Oppressed*. Trans. Myra Bergman Ramos. New York: Continuum, 2007.

Garfinkel, P.E., D.M. Garner. *Anorexia Nervosa: A Multidimensional Perspective*. New York: Brunner-Mazel, 1982.

Garner, D.M., P.E. Garfinkel, D. Schwartz, M. Thompson. "Cultural Expectations of Thinness in Women." *Psychological Reports* 47 (1980): 483–91.

Giardina, Michael D. and Norman K. Denzin. "Confronting Neoliberalism: Toward a Militant Pedagogy of Empowered Citizenship." *Cultural Studies ↔ Critical Methodologies* 13, no. 6 (2013): 443–51.

Gibb, Camilla. *Mouthing the Words*. Toronto: Pedlar Press, 1999.

Giroux, Henry. *On Critical Pedagogy*. New York: Continuum, 2011.

– *Neoliberalism's War on Higher Education*. Toronto: Between the Lines, 2014.

Godfrey, Rebecca. *The Torn Skirt*. Toronto: HarperFlamingoCanada, 2001.

Goldie, Terry. *Fear and Temptation: The Image of the Indigene in Canadian, Australian, and New Zealand Literatures*. Kingston, ON: McGill-Queen's University Press, 1989.

Goldman, Marlene, and Joanne Saul. "Talking with Ghosts: Haunting in Canadian Cultural Production." *University of Toronto Quarterly* 75, no. 2 (2006): 645– 55.

Goldsmith, Meredith. "Cigarettes, Tea, Cards, and Chloral: Addictive Habits and Consumer Culture in *The House of Mirth*." *American Literary Realism* 43, no. 3 (2011): 242–58.

Grace, Sherrill E. *Canada and the Idea of North*. Montreal: McGill-Queen's University Press, 2001.

Graff, Gerald. "Other Voices, Other Rooms: Organizing and Teaching the Humanities Conflict." *New Literary History* 21, no. 4 (1990): 817–39.

Gramsci, Antonio. *Selections from the Prison Notebooks*. Eds. and trans. Quintin Hoare and Geoffrey Nowell Smith. New York: International Publishers, 1971.

Grande, Sandy. *Red Pedagogy: Native American Social and Political Thought*. Lanham, Maryland: Rowman & Littlefield, 2004.

Grant, Agnes. "Abuse and Violence: April Raintree's Human Rights (If She Had Any)." *In Search of April Raintree*, by Beatrice Culleton Mosionier, ed. Cheryl Suzack, 237–46. Winnipeg: Portage & Main Press, 1999.

Groenke, Susan L., and J. Amos Hatch, eds. *Critical Pedagogy and Teacher Education in the Neoliberal Era: Small Openings*. New York: Springer, 2009.

Guattari, Felix. "Socially Significant Drugs." In *High Culture: Reflections on Addiction and Modernity*, 199–208. Eds. Anna Alexander and Mark S. Roberts. Albany, NY: SUNY University Press, 2003.

Haden, Mark. "The Evolution of the Four Pillars: Acknowledging the Harms of Drug Prohibition." *International Journal of Drug Policy* 17 (2006): 124–6.

Hamer, John, and Jack Steinburg. *Alcohol and Native Peoples of the North*. Washington: University Press of America, 1980.

Hannah, Don. *Wise and Foolish Virgins*. Toronto: Alfred A. Knopf Canada, 1998.

Hanson, Aubrey Jean. "'Through White Man's Eyes': Beatrice Culleton Mosionier's *In Search of April Raintree* and Reading for Decolonization." *Studies in American Literatures* 24, no. 1 (Spring 2012): 15–30.

Hardt, Michael, and Antonio Negri. *Empire*. Cambridge: Harvard University Press, 2000.

hooks, bell. *Teaching to Transgress: Education as the Practice of Freedom*. New York: Routledge, 1994.

"How it Works," *The Big Book*, 4th ed. Accessed 19 February 2016. http://www.aa.org/pages/en_US/alcoholics-anonymous.

Horne, Dee. *Contemporary American Indian Writing: Unsettling Literature*. New York: Peter Lang, 1999.

Hoy, Helen. *How Should I Read These?: Native Women Writers in Canada*. Toronto: University of Toronto Press, 2001.

– "'Nothing But the Truth': Discursive Transparency in Beatrice Culleton." In *In Search of April Raintree*, by Beatrice Culleton Mosionier, ed. Cheryl Suzack, 273–93. Winnipeg: Portage & Main Press, 1999.

Hunt, Alan. *Governing Morals: A Social History of Moral Regulation*. Cambridge: Cambridge University Press, 1999.

– "Moral Regulation and Making-up the New Person: Putting Gramsci to Work." *Theoretical Criminology* 1, no. 3 (1997): 275–301.

Huson, Freda, and Toghestiy. "Indigenous Sovereignty Fuels Pipeline Resistance." *Upping the Anti* 17 (2015): 46–59.

Imarisha, Walidah. Introduction in *Octavia's Brood: Science Fiction Stories from Social Justice Movements*, eds. adrienne maree brown and Walidah Imarisha, 3–5. Oakland: AK Press, 2015.

Infantino, Stephen C. "Female Addiction and Sacrifice: Literary Tradition or User's Manual?" In *The Languages of Addiction*, eds. Jane Lilienfeld and Jeffrey Oxford, 91–102. New York: St. Martin's Press, 1999.

Irlbacher-Fox, Stephanie. *Finding Dahshaa: Self-Government, Social Suffering, and Aboriginal Policy in Canada*. Vancouver: UBC Press, 2009.

Jackson, Richard D. "The Devil, The Doppelgänger, and the Confessions of James Hogg and Thomas De Quincey." *Studies in Hogg and His World* 12 (2001): 90–103.

Jameson, Frederic. *Postmodernism, or, the Cultural Logic of Late Capitalism*. Durham: Duke University Press, 1991.

– *The Political Unconscious: Narrative as a Socially Symbolic Act*. Ithaca: Cornell University Press, 1981.

Johnston, Allan. "Consumption, Addiction, Vision, Energy: Political Economies and Utopian Visions in the Writings of the Beat Generation." *College Literature* 32, no. 2 (2005): 103–26.

Justice, Daniel Heath. "'*Go Away, Water!*' Kinship Criticism and the Decolonization Imperative." In *Reasoning Together: The Native Critics Collective*, eds. Craig S. Womack, Daniel Heath Justice, and Christopher B. Teuton, 147–68. Norman: University of Oklahoma Press, 2008.

– "Rhetorics of Recognition: On Indigenous Nationhood, Literature, and the Paracolonial Perils of the Nation-State." *The Kenyon Review* 32, no. 1 (2010): 236–61.

Kaslik, Ibi. *Skinny*. Toronto: HarperCollins, 2005.

Keane, Helen. *What's Wrong with Addiction?* Carlton South: Melbourne University Press, 2002.

Khalfa, Jean. Introduction in *History of Madness*, by Michel Foucault. Ed. Jean Khalfa, trans. Jonathan Murphy and Jean Khalfa, xiii–xxv. London: Routledge, 2009.

Killing Us Softly: Advertising's Image of Women. DVD. Directed by Jean Kilbourne. United States: Cambridge Documentaries, 1979.

– *Still Killing Us Softly: Advertising's Image of Women*. Directed by Margaret Lazarus and Renner Wunderlich. United States: Cambridge Documentaries, 1987.
– *Killing Us Softly 3*. Directed by Sut Jhally. United States: Media Education Foundation, 1999.
– *Killing Us Softly 4: Advertising's Image of Women*. Directed by Sut Jhally. United States: Media Education Foundation, 2010.
Kinew, Wab. "Strombo: Soap Box: Wab Kinew." 10 January 2012. *YouTube*. Accessed 19 February 2016, https://www.youtube.com/watch?v=GlkuRCXdu5A.
King, Thomas. Introduction in *The Native in Literature*, eds. Thomas King, Cheryl Calver, and Helen Hoy, 7–14. Winnipeg: ECW Press, 1987.
– *The Inconvenient Indian: A Curious Account of Native People in North America*. Toronto: Random House, 2012.
Kinsella, W.P. "First Novels." *Books in Canada* 31, no. 4 (2002): 38–40.
Kitzinger, Celia, and Rachel Perkins. *Changing our Minds: Lesbian Feminism and Psychology*. New York: New York University Press, 1993.
Kleinman, Arthur, Veena Das, and Margaret Lock, eds. *Social Suffering*. Berkeley: University of California Press, 1997.
Koepke, Melora. "Ibi Kaslik's *Skinny*: Spilling Some Pink." *Hour Community*, 27 May 2004. Accessed 27 October 2014. http://hour.ca/2004/05/27/spilling-some-pink/.
Kopelson, Karen L. "Radical Indulgence: Excess, Addiction, and Female Desire." *Postmodern Culture: An Electronic Journal of Interdisciplinary Criticism* 17, no. 1 (2006). Accessed 30 October 2014. doi: 10.1353/pmc.2007.0006.
Kosovski, Jason R., and Douglas C. Smith. "Everybody Hurts: Addiction, Drama, and the Family in the Reality Television Show *Intervention*." *Substance Use & Misuse* 46 (2011): 852–8.
Kouimtsidis, Christos, Paul Davis, Martine Reynolds, Colin Drummond, and Nicholas Tarrier. *Cognitive-Behavioural Therapy in the Treatment of Addiction: A Treatment Planner for Clinicians*. West Sussex: John Wiley & Sons, 2007.
Lane, Richard. "Performing Gender: First Nations, Feminism, and Trickster Writing in Eden Robinson's *Monkey Beach*." *Canadian Literature* 184 (2005): 161–71.
Lacombe, Michèle. "On Critical Frameworks for Analyzing Indigenous Literature: The Case of *Monkey Beach*." *International Journal of Canadian Studies* 41 (2010), 253–76. Accessed 30 October 2014. doi: 10.7202/044170ar.
Lai, Larissa. "The Imagination's Subsidies: Whiners, Elites, Ordinary People, and the Economy." *ESC: English Studies in Canada* 33, no. 3 (September 2007): 16–19.

Lau, Evelyn. *Inside Out*. Toronto: Doubleday Canada, 2001.

Levy, Jerrold E. *Indian Drinking: Navajo Practices and Anglo-American Theories*. New York: Wiley, 1974.

Lilienfeld, Jane. Introduction in *The Languages of Addiction*, eds. Jane Lilienfeld and Jeffrey Oxford, xiii–xxvii. New York: St. Martin's Press, 1999.

Lowry, Christine T. "Rejection and Belonging in Addiction and Recovery: Four Urban Indian Men in Milwaukee." In *American Indians and the Urban Experience*, eds. Susan Lobo and Kurt Peters, 277–90. New York: Altamira Press, 2001.

Lowry, Malcolm. *Under the Volcano*. New York: New American Library, 1966.

Lundgren, Jodi. "'Being a Half-breed': Discourses of Race and Cultural Syncreticity in the Works of Three Métis Women Writers." *Canadian Literature* 144 (Spring 1995): 62–77.

Macdonald, Mark. *Flat*. Vancouver: Arsenal Pulp Press, 2000.

MacDonald, Mary Lu. "Red & White Men; Black, White, & Grey Hats: Literary Attitudes to the Interaction Between European and Native Canadian in the First Half of the Nineteenth Century." In *Native Writers and Canadian Writing*, ed. W.H. New, 92–111. Vancouver: UBC Press, 1990.

Malson, Helen. *The Thin Woman: Feminism, Post-Structuralism and the Social Psychology of Anorexia Nervosa*. New York: Routledge, 1998.

Malson, Helen, and Maree Burns, eds. *Critical Feminist Approaches to Eating Dis/Orders*. New York: Routledge, 2009.

Maracle, Brian. *Crazywater: Native Voices on Addiction and Recovery*. Toronto: Penguin, 1993.

Maracle, Lee. *Daughters Are Forever*. Vancouver: Polestar, 2002.

– "This is a Vision: A Conversation with Lee Maracle." In *Masculindians: Conversations about Indigenous Manhood*, by Sam McKegney, 30–40. Winnipeg: University of Manitoba Press, 2014.

Maraun, Michael D. "What Does It Mean That an Issue is Conceptual in Nature?" *Journal of Personality Assessment* 85, no. 2 (2005): 128–33.

Marlowe, Ann. *How to Stop Time: Heroin from A to Z*. New York: Anchor Books, 1999.

Martin, Courtney E. *Perfect Girls, Starving Daughters: The Frightening New Normalcy of Hating Your Body*. New York: Free Press, 2007.

Martin, Keavy. *Stories in a New Skin: Approaches to Inuit Literature*. Winnipeg: University of Manitoba Press, 2012.

Marx, Karl. *Economic and Philosophic Manuscripts of 1844*. New York: International Publishers, 1964.

– *The Marx-Engels Reader*. 2nd ed. Ed. Robert C. Tucker. New York: Norton, 1978.

Maté, Gabor. *In the Realm of Hungry Ghosts: Close Encounters with Addiction.* Toronto: Knopf, 2008.

McClintock, Anne. "The Angel of Progress: Pitfalls of the Term 'Post-Colonialism.'" *Social Text* 31/32 (1992): 84–98.

McClure, Andrew S. "The Word, Image, and Addiction: Language and the Junk Equation in William S. Burroughs' *Naked Lunch.*" *Dionysos: The Literature and Addiction TriQuarterly* 6, no. 2 (1996): 6–19.

McIntosh, Peggy. "White Privilege: Unpacking the Invisible Knapsack." *Independent School* 49 (1990): 31–5.

McIntyre, Richard. "Consumption in Contemporary Capitalism: Beyond Marx and Veblen." *Review of Social Economy* 50, no. 1 (1992): 40–57.

McKegney, Sam. *Magic Weapons: Aboriginal Writers Remaking Community after Residential School.* Winnipeg: University of Manitoba Press, 2007.

Meltzer, Marisa. "Are Fat Suits the New Blackface?" In *BITCHFest: Ten Years of Cultural Criticism from the pages of Bitch Magazine,* eds. Lisa Jervis and Andi Zeisler, 267–70. New York: Farrar, Straus, and Giroux, 2006.

Meuret, Isabelle. *Writing Size Zero: Figuring Anorexia in Contemporary World Literatures.* Brussels: P.I.E. Peter Lang, 2007.

Mohanty, Chandra Talpade. "On Race and Voice: Challenges for Neoliberal Education in the 1990s. *Cultural Critique* 14 (1989–90): 179–208.

Monkman, Leslie. A *Native Heritage: Images of the Indian in English-Canadian Literature.* Toronto: University of Toronto Press, 1981.

Moodie, Susanna. *Roughing It in the Bush.* Toronto: McClelland & Stewart, 1989.

Morrison, Robert. *The English Opium Eater: A Biography of Thomas De Quincey.* London: Weidenfeld & Nicholson, 2010.

Mosionier, Beatrice Culleton. *In Search of April Raintree.* Ed. Cheryl Suzack. Winnipeg: Portage & Main Press, 1999.

Mullens, Anne. "Addicted or Afflicted?: Should Your Tax Dollars Buy Drugs for Abusers?" *Reader's Digest,* August 2008.

Nance, Kimberly A. *Can Literature Promote Justice? Trauma Narrative and Social Action in Latin American Testimonio.* Nashville: Vanderbilt University Press, 2006.

National Treatment Strategy Working Group. "A Systems Approach to Substance Use in Canada: Recommendations for a National Treatment Strategy." Ottawa: National Framework for Action to Reduce the Harms Associated with Alcohol and Other Drugs and Substances in Canada, 2008.

O'Keefe, Derrick. "Harper in denial at G20: Canada has 'no history of colonialism.'" *rabble,* 28 September 2009. Accessed 19 February 2016. http://rabble.ca/blogs/bloggers/derrick/2009/09/harper-denial-g20-canada-has-no-history-colonialism.

O'Neill, Heather. *lullabies for little criminals*. Toronto: Harper, 2006.

"Official Records for 4 November 2008." Legislative Assembly of Ontario. Accessed 19 February 2016. http://www.ontla.on.ca/web/house-proceedings/house_detail.do?Date=2008-11-04.

"Origins." *Alcoholics Anonymous*. Accessed 19 February 2016. http://www.aa.org/pages/en_US/aa-timeline.

Olsen, Greta. *Reading Eating Disorders: Writings on Bulimia and Anorexia as Confessions of American Culture*. Frankfurt am Main: Peter Lang, 2000.

Orbach, Susie. *Bodies*. New York: Picador, 2009.

– *Fat is a Feminist Issue: The Anti-diet Guide to Permanent Weight Loss*. New York: Berkley Books,1978.

"Origins: 1935." *Alcoholics Anonymous*. Accessed 19 February 2016. http://www.aa.org/pages/en_US/aa-timeline.

Oxford Dictionaries. "'He or She' Versus 'They.'" Accessed 19 February 2016. http://www.oxforddictionaries.com/words/he-or-she-versus-they.

Palahniuk, Chuck. *Fight Club*. Ed. Thomas E. Wartenberg. New York: Routledge, 2012.

Patterson, Kevin. *Consumption*. Toronto: Vintage Canada, 2007.

Peart, Neil, Alex Lifeson, and Geddy Lee. "Subdivisions." *Signals* by Rush. Mercury Records, 1982.

Peele, Stanton. "War over Addiction: Evaluating the DSM-V." *The Huffington Post*, 11 February 2010. Accessed 19 February 2016. http://www.huffingtonpost.com/stanton-peele/war-over-addiction-evalua_b_456321.html.

PJ Lilley and Jeff Shantz. "From Idle No More to Indigenous Nationhood." *Upping the Anti* no. 15 (2013): 113–127.

Poe, Edgar Allan. *The Complete Tales and Poems of Edgar Allan Poe*. New York: The Modern Library, 1938.

Probyn, Elspeth. "The Anorexic Body." In *Body Invaders: Panic Sex in America*, eds. Arthur and Marilouise Kroker, 201–12. Don Mills, ON: Oxford University Pres, 1987.

Radway, Janice. "Reading is Not Eating: Mass-Produced Literature and Theoretical, Methodological, and Political Consequences of Metaphor." *Book Research Quarterly* 2, no. 3 (1986): 7–29.

Ratcliffe, Krista. "A Rhetoric of Classroom Denial: Resisting Resistance to Alcohol Questions While Teaching Louise Erdrich' *Love Medicine*." In *The Languages of Addiction*, Ed. Jane Lilienfeld and Jeffrey Oxford, 105–21. New York: St. Martin's Press, 1999.

Razack, Sherene. *Looking White People in the Eye: Race, Gender, and Culture in Courtrooms and Classrooms*. Toronto: University of Toronto Press, 1998.

Regan, Paulette. *Unsettling the Settler Within: Indian Residential Schools, Truth Telling, and Reconciliation in Canada*. Vancouver: UBC Press, 2010.

Richards, David Adams. *Nights Below Station Street*. Toronto: McClelland & Stewart, 1988.

Ridgeway, Shannon. "20+ Examples of Thin Privilege." *Everyday Feminism*, 30 November 2012. Accessed 19 February 2016. http://everydayfeminism.com/2012/11/20-examples-of-thin-privilege/.

Rimstead, Roxanne. *Remnants of Nation: On Poverty Narratives by Women*. Toronto: University of Toronto Press, 2001.

Robinson, Eden. *Blood Sports*. Toronto: McClelland & Stewart, 2006.

– *Monkey Beach*. Toronto: Alfred A. Knopf, 2000.

Ronell, Avital. *Crack Wars: Literature Addiction Mania*. Urbana & Chicago: University of Illinois Press, 2004.

Rothman, Claire. "Readers Will Root for This Heroine." *The Montreal Gazette*, 9 February 2002. K4.

Saltmarsh, Sue. "Becoming Economic Subjects: Agency, Consumption and Popular Culture in Early Childhood." *Discourse: Studies in the Cultural Politics of Education* 30, no. 1 (2009): 47–59.

Samuels, Andrew. *The Political Psyche*. New York: Routledge, 1993.

Sanders, Jolene M. "Women and the Twelve Steps of Alcoholics Anonymous: A Gendered Narrative." *Alcoholism Treatment Quarterly* 24, no. 3 (2006): 3–29.

Sangster, Joan. *Girl Trouble: Female Delinquency in English Canada*. Toronto: Between the Lines, 2002.

Saukko, Paula. "A Critical Discussion of Normativity in Discourses on Eating Disorders." In *Critical Feminist Approaches to Eating Disorders*, eds. Helen Malson and Maree Burns, 65–73. London: Routledge, 2009.

Schmidt, Robert. "The Harm of Native Stereotyping: Facts and Evidence." *Blue Corn Comics*. 2007. Accessed 19 February 2016. http://www.bluecorncomics.com/stharm.htm.

Sedgwick, Eve Kosofsky. "Epidemics of the Will." In *Tendencies*, 142–153. London: Taylor & Francis e-library, 2004. Accessed 30 October 2014. http://www.myilibrary.com?ID=6801.

Shantz, Jeff. *Against All Authority: Anarchism and the Literary Imagination*. Charlottesville, VA: Imprint Academic, 2011.

Shaughnessy, Bishop-Stall. *Down to This: Squalor and Splendour in a Big-City Shantytown*. Toronto: Random House, 2004.

Sheppard, Robert. "Power Play." *CBC News*. 21 August 2006. Accessed 28 May 2013.

Shields, Carol. *Unless*. Toronto: Vintage Canada, 2003.

Shupak, Greg. "Literature and Social Change: Writing, Criticism and Teaching in Neoliberal Canada." PhD diss., University of Guelph, 2015.

Siddiqui, Shereen. "Teaching to Transform: Toward an Action-Oriented Feminist Pedagogy in Women's Studies." PhD diss., Florida Atlantic University, 2015.

Smith, Andrea. "Beyond the Pros and Cons of Trigger Warnings: Collectivizing Healing." *Andrea366*, 13 July 2014. Accessed 19 February 2016. http://andrea366.wordpress.com/2014/07/13/beyond-the-pros-and-cons-of-trigger-warnings-collectivizing-healing/.

– "Building Unlikely Alliances." *Upping the Anti: A Journal of Theory and Action* no. 10 (2010): 41–52.

– "Heteropatriarchy and the Three Pillars of White Supremacy: Rethinking Women of Color Organizing." In *Color of Violence: The INCITE! Anthology*, Eds. Andrea Smith, Beth E. Richie, and Julia Sudbury, 66–73. Cambridge, MA: South End Press, 2006.

Smith, Christopher B.R. "Harm Reduction as Anarchist Practice: A User's Guide to Capitalism and Addiction in North America." *Critical Public Health* 22, no. 2 (2012): 209–21.

Smith, Ruth L. "Order and Disorder: The Naturalization of Poverty." *Cultural Critique* 14 (1989–90): 209–29.

Smulders, Sharon. "'A Double Assault': The Victimization of Aboriginal Women and Children in In Search of April Raintree." *Mosaic: A Journal for the Interdisciplinary Study of Literature* 39, no. 2 (2006): 37–55.

– "'What is the Proper Word for People Like You?': The Question of Métis Identity in *In Search of April Raintree*." *English Studies in Canada* 32, no. 4 (2006): 75–100.

Soper-Jones, Ella. "The Fate of the Oolichan: Prospects of Eco-Cultural Restoration in Eden Robinson's *Monkey Beach*." *Journal of Commonwealth Literature* 44, no. 2 (2009): 15–33.

Sorensen, Sue. "Seclusion and Compulsion." *Canadian Literature* no. 186 (Autumn, 2005): 160–1. Accessed 19 February 2016. http://ezproxy.uwindsor.ca/login?url=http://search.proquest.com/docview/218781383?accountid=14789.

Stalcup, Scott. "Trainspotting, High Fidelity, and the Diction of Addiction." *Studies in Popular Culture* 30, no. 2 (2008): 119–36.

"stigma, *n*." *OED Online*. Oxford University Press. Accessed 30 October 2014.

Judy Stoffman. "Lyrical Lullabies: Heather O'Neill's First Novel, Inspired by her Hardscrabble Childhood, Draws Raves." *Toronto Star*, 13 December 2006. D4.

"Substance-Related and Addictive Disorders." *American Psychiatric Association: DSM-5 Development*. American Psychiatric Publishing, 2013. Accessed 19 February 2016. http://www.dsm5.org/Documents/Substance%20Use%20Disorder%20Fact%20Sheet.pdf.

Szabados, Bela and Kenneth G. Probert, eds. *Writing Addiction: Towards a Poetics of Desire and Its Other*. Regina: Canadian Plains Research Center, 2004.

Tarlau, Rebecca. "From a Language to a Theory of Resistance: Critical Pedagogy, the Limits of 'Framing,' and Social Change." *Educational Theory* 64, no. 4 (2014): 369–92.

Tesh, Sylvia. *Hidden Arguments: Political Ideology and Disease Prevention Policy.* New Brunswick, NJ: Rutgers University Press, 1988.

"The North West Store: History." *The North West Company*. Accessed 16 June 2013.

Thompson, Becky W. *A Hunger So Wide and So Deep: American Women Speak Out on Eating Disorders*. Minneapolis: University of Minnesota Press, 1994.

– "Food, Bodies, and Growing Up Female: Childhood Lessons about Culture, Race, and Class." In *Feminist Perspectives on Eating Disorders*, eds. Patricia Fallon, Melanie A. Katzman, and Susan C. Wooley, 355–78. New York: Guilford Press, 1994.

Thompson, Hunter S. *Fear and Loathing in Las Vegas*. New York: Popular Library, 1971.

Thompson, Judith. *The Crackwalker*. Toronto: Playwrights Canada Press, 1980.

Thrasher, Anthony Apakark. *Thrasher ... Skid Row Eskimo*. Toronto: Giffen House, 1976.

Tolman, Deborah L., and Elizabeth Debold. "Conflicts of Body and Image: Female Adolescents, Desire, and the No-body Body." In *Feminist Perspectives on Eating Disorders*, eds. Patricia Fallon, Melanie A. Katzman, and Susan C. Wooley, 301–17. New York: Guilford Press, 1994.

"Tories Sorry for Comments to Native Protester." *Caledonia Wake Up Call.* 18 September 2008. Accessed 19 February 2016. http://www.caledoniawakeupcall.com/updates/080918ctv.html.

Valverde, Mariana. *Diseases of the Will: Alcohol and the Dilemmas of Freedom.* Cambridge: Cambridge University Press, 1998.

Van Amsterdam, Noortje. "Big Fat Inequalities, Thin Privilege: An Intersectional Perspective on 'Body Size.'" *European Journal of Women's Studies* 20, no. 2 (2013), 1–15. Accessed 24 October 2014. doi: 10.1177/1350506812456461.

Van Camp, Richard. *The Lesser Blessed*. Vancouver: Douglas & McIntyre, 1996.

Van Den Bergh, Nan, ed. *Feminist Perspectives on Addictions*. New York: Springer Publishing, 1991.

Wagamese, Richard. *Keeper'n Me*. Toronto: Doubleday, 1994.

Walcott, Rinaldo. "Afterword: Sentiment or Action." In *Transnationalism, Activism, Art*. Eds. Kit Dobson and Áine McGlynn, 227–38. Toronto: University of Toronto Press, 2013.

Waldram, James B. *Revenge of the Wendigo: The Construction of the Mind and Mental Health of North American Aboriginal Peoples*. Toronto: University of Toronto Press, 2004.

Walia, Harsha. "Decolonizing Together: Moving beyond a Politics of Solidarity toward a Practice of Decolonization." *Briarpatch*, 21 January 2012. Accessed 19 February 2016. http://briarpatchmagazine.com/articles/view/decolonizing-together.

Wallen, Jeffrey. *Close Encounters: Literary Politics and Public Culture*, Minneapolis: University of Minnesota Press, 1998.

Wallimann, Isidor. *Estrangement: Marx's Conception of Human Nature and the Division of Labor*. Westport, CT: Greenwood Press, 1981.

Waxman, Chaim I. *The Stigma of Poverty: A Critique of Poverty Theories and Policies*. New York: Pergamon Press, 1977.

Weiner, Eric J. *Private Learning, Public Needs: The Neoliberal Assault on Democratic Education*. New York: Peter Lang Publishing, 2004.

Weinstone, Ann. "Welcome to the Pharmacy: Addiction, Transcendence, and Virtual Reality." In *High Anxieties: Cultural Studies in Addiction*. Eds. Janet Farrell Brodie and Marc Redfield, 161–74. Berkeley: University of California Press, 2002.

West, Kanye, Shawn Carter, K. Dean, Larry Griffin, Jr., Scott Mescudi, Quincy Jones, Harvey Mason, Jr., Joel Rosenbaum, Caiphus Semenya, Bill Summers, Mihaela Modorcea, Gabriella Modorcea."Murder to Excellence." *Watch the Throne*. Kanye West and Jay-Z. Roc-A-Fella, Roc Nation, Def Jam, 2011.

Weston, Anthony. "Toward a Social Critique of Bioethics." *Journal of Social Philosophy* 22, no. 2 (1991): 109–18.

Whitehead, Paul C., and Michael J. Hayes. *The Insanity of Alcohol: Social Problems in Canadian First Nations Communities*. Toronto: Canadian Scholars' Press, 1998.

Wiebe, Rudy, and Yvonne Johnson. *Stolen Life: The Journey of a Cree Woman*. Toronto: Alfred A. Knopf, 1998.

Wilson, Scott. "Dying for a Smoke: Freudian Addiction and the Joy of Consumption." *Angelaki* 7, no. 2 (2002): 161–73.

Winehouse, Amy. "Rehab." *Back to Black*. Amy Winehouse. Island Records, 2006.

Wittgenstein, Ludwig. *Philosophical Investigations*. Ed. P.M.S. Hacker. West Sussex: Wiley-Blackwell, 2009.

White, Nancy J. "Alcoholics Anonymous Has a Terrible Success Rate, Addiction Expert Finds." *The Toronto Star*, 28 March 2014. Accessed 19 February 2016. http://www.thestar.com/life/2014/03/28/alcoholics_anonymous_has_a_terrible_success_rate_addiction_expert_finds.html.

Wolf, Naomi. *The Beauty Myth*. Toronto: Vintage, 1990.
"Years of Service." *Nurse Jackie: Season Two*. Written by Liz Brixius and Linda Wallem. Directed by Paul Feig. Alliance Films, 2011. DVD.
Zwicker, Heather. "The Limits of Sisterhood." In *In Search of April Raintree*, by Beatrice Culleton Mosionier, ed. Cheryl Suzack, 323–37. Winnipeg: Portage & Main Press, 1999.

Index

www.ingramcontent.com/pod-product-compliance
Lightning Source LLC
LaVergne TN
LVHW040150080826
844660LV00014B/911/J

* 9 7 8 1 4 4 2 6 3 1 9 6 0 *